Implementation Monitoring & Process Evaluation

I dedicate this book to students who have generously shared
their professional experiences and perspectives related to implementing and
monitoring interventions that take place in "real-world" settings. I am deeply grateful
for their support and encouragement throughout my discovery process.

⊗SAGE | **50** YEARS

SAGE was founded in 1965 by Sara Miller McCune to support the dissemination of usable knowledge by publishing innovative and high-quality research and teaching content. Today, we publish more than 750 journals, including those of more than 300 learned societies, more than 800 new books per year, and a growing range of library products including archives, data, case studies, reports, conference highlights, and video. SAGE remains majority-owned by our founder, and after Sara's lifetime will become owned by a charitable trust that secures our continued independence.

Los Angeles | London | Washington DC | New Delhi | Singapore | Boston

Implementation Monitoring & Process Evaluation

Ruth P. Saunders
University of South Carolina

Los Angeles | London | New Delhi
Singapore | Washington DC | Boston

Los Angeles | London | New Delhi
Singapore | Washington DC | Boston

FOR INFORMATION:

SAGE Publications, Inc.
2455 Teller Road
Thousand Oaks, California 91320
E-mail: order@sagepub.com

SAGE Publications Ltd.
1 Oliver's Yard
55 City Road
London EC1Y 1SP
United Kingdom

SAGE Publications India Pvt. Ltd.
B 1/I 1 Mohan Cooperative Industrial Area
Mathura Road, New Delhi 110 044
India

SAGE Publications Asia-Pacific Pte. Ltd.
3 Church Street
#10-04 Samsung Hub
Singapore 048763

Acquisitions Editor: Helen Salmon
Editorial Assistant: Anna Villarruel
Production Editor: Jane Haenel
Copy Editor: Lana Todorovic-Arndt
Typesetter: C&M Digitals (P) Ltd.
Proofreader: Jennifer Grubba
Indexer: Terri Corry
Cover Designer: Anupama Krishnan
Marketing Manager: Nicole Elliott

Printed in the United States of America

Library of Congress Cataloging-in-Publication Data

Saunders, Ruth P., author.

Implementation monitoring and process evaluation / Ruth P. Saunders.

p. cm.
Includes bibliographical references and index.

ISBN 978-1-4833-0809-8 (pbk. : alk. paper)

I. Title. [DNLM: 1. Health Plan Implementation—methods. 2. Data Collection—methods. 3. Program Evaluation—methods. WA 525]

RA408.5
362.1072'3—dc23   2014045442

This book is printed on acid-free paper.

15 16 17 18 19 10 9 8 7 6 5 4 3 2 1

Brief Contents

Detailed Contents

Step 4. Establish Complete and Acceptable Delivery/Installation of the Program, Policy, or Practice 77

PHASE IV. IMPLEMENTATION 189

Step 9. Implement the Program, Policy, or Practice and Use Implementation Data for Formative Purposes 191

Step 10. Collect and Manage Implementation Data 213

PHASE V. ANALYSIS/SYNTHESIS, REPORTING, AND USE 239

Step 11. Analyze and Synthesize Implementation Monitoring Data 241

Step 12. Report and Use Implementation Data 261

Future Directions 299

Preface

The primary purpose of this book is to provide a practical guide that describes and illustrates the steps a program planner and/or program evaluator would take to plan and carry out a comprehensive approach to implementing and monitoring the implementation of a new program, policy, or practice in an organizational setting.

This textbook is the product of a discovery process that began some years ago when I ventured outside of the classroom into the "real world" to carry out practice and research interventions in public health settings. The challenge of translating idealized, context-independent program plans into a meaningful process that actual people with varied motivations and skills could carry out in complex, real-world settings with the aim of producing certain desired outcomes was and continues to be a transformative experience. Equally challenging was maintaining oversight during the implementation process, summarizing and analyzing volumes of data, and using the information to keep projects on track and to better understand outcomes. Having gained so much from these experiences, I have had the pleasure of teaching a course about the implementation and implementation monitoring processes and sharing these lessons with course participants. This textbook is the culmination of these experiences to date.

This book can serve as a primary text for a process evaluation, implementation monitoring, or implementation science course or as a supplemental text in a broader evaluation or program planning course. The primary audiences for the textbook include practitioners, researchers, students preparing to be program planners, program implementers, and program evaluators in public health, nonprofit, and educational settings. It is applicable to social and educational programs in a variety of organizational settings including recreational facilities, senior centers, group homes, faith-based organizations, hospitals, clinics, and other community-based organizations.

The entire focus of this text is a comprehensive overview of program implementation and implementation monitoring/process evaluation. Specifically, this textbook describes *the process of planning, conducting, analyzing, and using data obtained from monitoring program, policy, and practice implementation in organizational settings*. There are few textbooks devoted exclusively to process evaluation and implementation monitoring. Instead, process evaluation content and methods are typically covered as a section or a chapter within evaluation textbooks that have a broader scope. With few exceptions, scarce detail on a systematic approach to implementation planning, formulating implementation monitoring methods, carrying out the implementation monitoring, and analyzing process data is provided. This textbook aims to bridge this gap by providing a practical and flexible tool that guides the reader through the process.

Another unique feature of this book is its emphasis on program, policy, and practice change in contrast to an emphasis on individual behavior change. Behavior change in populations of individuals who spend time in a targeted organizational setting is frequently an intervention focus within public health, nonprofit, and educational fields. The majority of the literature, however, focuses on individual behavior change; this textbook provides a model for environmental and population change.

Implementation Monitoring and Process Evaluation emphasizes practical application methods presented as a sequence of steps within phases and incorporates the use of examples, an ongoing case study, "Your Turn" and resource boxes, and a set of worksheets that are also available online. The steps are not intended to be followed as a rigid "cookbook," but rather in a more flexible fashion. Examples are used throughout the textbook to illustrate key concepts and points. The case study provides a detailed illustration of all core concepts and steps and is developed sequentially throughout each chapter of the textbook. The worksheets provide tools for the reader to apply the concepts and steps to her or his own projects. The reader can select the worksheets that are applicable for the specific setting and project.

The "Your Turn" boxes stimulate critical thinking and discussion, and the resource boxes provide access to the many additional resources available to the reader. Each chapter begins with a quotation and is guided by a set of learning objectives. There is also a list of boldfaced terms defined in the glossary at the end of the book. For students, researchers, and practitioners, the textbook emphasizes a balance between the ideal/conceptual, which is often emphasized in abstract planning, and the practical/applied use of these concepts in real-world settings.

This book does not address methods and issues commonly associated with summative evaluation, such as impact or outcome evaluation, nor does it address evaluation of the collaborative or participatory process that may be engaged to achieve program, policy, or practice change. These are quite important but are simply beyond the scope of this book.

Acknowledgments

I express my deep gratitude and appreciation to Ann Blair Kennedy for her able assistance throughout all phases of the textbook development process. Her contributions, enthusiastic support, and skillful assistance made this project a supremely enjoyable experience!

I value and appreciate the opportunities and support from the research teams including Lifestyle Education for Activity Program (LEAP) (Russ Pate, Principal Investigator), Study of Health and Activity in Preschool Environments (SHAPES) (Russ Pate, Principal Investigator), Faith, Activity, and Nutrition (FAN) (Sara Wilcox, Principal Investigator), and Environmental Interventions in Children's Homes (ENRICH) that enabled me to focus on process evaluation and implementation monitoring.

I provide a special thanks to Kerry McIver, Glenn Weaver, Michael Beets, Sara Wilcox, Kelli Kenison, Carley Prynn, Lauren Workman, and Sarah Griffin for their contributions to selected sections of the textbook, as noted within the body of the book.

I gratefully acknowledge Rona Bernstein's valuable and timely editorial assistance in the final drafts of the manuscript. I appreciate your attention to detail and gentle suggestions for clearer articulation of the information presented.

Thanks to the many students, staff, and researchers who attended my implementation monitoring seminars and provided feedback on early versions of the book manuscript. I truly value their encouragement and input, which has greatly strengthened the final product: Kassy Alia, Stephanie Child, Kimberly Comer, Amy Mattison Faye, Nicole Gribben, Emily Heberlein, Kelli Kenison, Deborah Kinnard, Katherine Leith, Justin Moore, Theresa Oniffry, Sharon Ross, Danielle Schoffman, Chiwoneso Tinago, Kristen van De Griend, Christine Veschusio, Megan Weiss, Lisa Wigfall, Cassandra Wineglass, Lauren Workman, and Marissa Yingling.

I would also like to thank the following SAGE reviewers for their valuable feedback: Joanne G. Carman, University of North Carolina–Charlotte; Tracey L. O. Sullivan, University of Ottawa; Anirudh V. S. Ruhil, Ohio University; Iris E. Smith, Emory University; and Florence Tarrant, Dalhousie University.

About the Author

Ruth P. Saunders, Ph.D., is a distinguished professor emeritus in the Department of Health Promotion, Education, and Behavior in the Arnold School of Public Health at the University of South Carolina. Dr. Saunders has 25 years of research and practice experience in conducting program, policy, and practice change in organizational settings, including preschools, schools, afterschool settings, children's group homes, and faith-based settings. Her roles in these projects, which include eight large-scale interventions, have encompassed using multilevel conceptual models to develop a comprehensive model of organizational environments; constructing scales and indexes to assess contextual factors and implementation processes; addressing challenges involved in intervention design and implementation in field-based settings; and designing and carrying comprehensive intervention implementation monitoring. She has authored or coauthored numerous publications based on her research. Dr. Saunders also has 28 years of teaching experience with master's and doctoral level courses in program planning, program evaluation, process evaluation and implementation monitoring, and interventions targeting physical and social environments.

Not everything that can be counted counts, and not everything that counts can be counted.

—William Bruce Cameron

Introduction, Overview, and Perspectives

The Lifestyle Education for Activity Program (LEAP), a multicomponent physical activity intervention for girls in 12 high schools, focused on changing the schools' instructional and physical environments to promote physical activity. The LEAP intervention was successful, as evidenced by more girls being vigorously physically active in the intervention compared to the control group (Pate et al., 2007). Furthermore, these effects were sustained through 12th grade in the four schools that maintained LEAP instructional and environmental elements for 3 years following the formal instructional intervention that took place in ninth grade (Ward, Saunders, & Pate, 2007). This outcome-only evaluation of LEAP leaves many questions unanswered. What exactly was the LEAP intervention? Were some components carried out better than others? What were the LEAP schools like, and did their characteristics matter? Did all 12 schools carry out LEAP the same way? Did some schools do a better job with implementation than other schools? Did differing levels of implementation affect the outcomes? Would schools beyond the LEAP study be able to achieve the same results achieved by the 12 LEAP schools?

As illustrated in the above scenario, we need to know more than whether or not an intervention "worked" for it to have application beyond the initial evaluation study. We need to understand what was supposed to happen, what actually happened, and the context in which it happened. Implementation monitoring and process evaluation helps us answer questions like these. This textbook provides an introduction to the implementation monitoring processes and methods needed to address these questions and issues. LEAP will be used as a case example to illustrate planning, implementation, and evaluation processes.

Program Evaluation and the Contribution of This Textbook

For simplicity, I will divide the many approaches to and purposes for program evaluation into two categories: (1) summative or effectiveness evaluation and (2) process evaluation. In a **summative** or an **effectiveness evaluation,** the evaluation members of the planning team assess the extent to which the project achieved its objectives or attained desired outcomes or impacts; in essence, did the program work? In this type of evaluation, data are often collected at the beginning and end of the project to determine what effect, if any, the program had on key indicators. Data analysis typically occurs after the project has been completed, to determine whether it achieved its objectives.

In contrast, in a **process evaluation,** the evaluation members of the planning team examine what happens during program **implementation**. Implementation is the process through which an innovation is assimilated into an organization (Damschroder et al., 2009) or the "act of converting program objectives into actions, policy changes, regulation, and organization" (Green & Kreuter, 2005, p. G-5). Additional terms used interchangeably with implementation in this book are *program delivery* and *policy and/or practice installation*. Process evaluation is a broad term that encompasses methods employed: (1) *prior to* implementation, to assess quality of the program plan and materials, and technical and cultural competence of the program providers (Baranowski & Stables, 2000; Steckler & Linnan, 2002); (2) *during* implementation, to monitor and assess the implementation process and context *in real time*; and (3) *following* implementation, to describe the program, implementation process, and/or context with regard to the methods used to conduct assessment *after-the-fact*.

Prior to the 1980s, process evaluation was used primarily during planning, prior to program implementation, to examine program quality. Process evaluation has become increasingly sophisticated over time, reflecting the increasing size and complexity of interventions (Steckler & Linnan, 2002). Well-funded public health intervention trials in community and school settings in the 1980s and 1990s, including the Stanford Five-City Program, Pawtuckett Heart Health Program, Minnesota Heart Health Program, Community Intervention Trial for Smoking Cessation (COMMIT), Child and Adolescent Trial for Cardiovascular Health (CATCH), and Working Well helped expand the scope of process evaluation to include additional elements (Baranowski & Stables, 2000; Bartholomew, Parcel, Kok, & Gottlieb, 2006; Steckler & Linnan, 2002) that apply to implementation monitoring, including completeness, fidelity, and reach.

A comprehensive approach to program evaluation includes both effectiveness evaluation and process evaluation to examine, respectively, *what effects* the program had and *what actually took place* during the program. The focus of this textbook is **implementation monitoring,** which is a component of process evaluation that emphasizes understanding what actually takes place during active program implementation and the context in which it takes place. Implementation monitoring can serve a number of useful purposes in program evaluation:

- Fine-tuning or keeping a program on track during active implementation

- Determining whether or not the program took place at all; if it did take place, determining the extent to which it did so as planned and was operationalized in a manner consistent with underlying theory and philosophy

- Examining what happened in the program to better understand and interpret study outcomes using qualitative and/or quantitative statistical methods

- Measuring inevitable variability in implementation across settings, examining factors related to variability in implementation, and examining effects of variable implementation on outcomes

- Testing the mechanisms through which the program is hypothesized to work by testing the program theory

- Creating a detailed and rich program description, including what actually happened in the program, who participated, what staff did and how participants reacted, and documenting unintended and unexpected effects of an intervention

- Distinguishing between theory failure (i.e., idea didn't work) and implementation failure (i.e., program was not carried out) in outcome evaluation

- Providing information to inform future planning (Baranowski & Stables, 2000; Devaney & Rossi, 1997; Helitzer, Yoon, Wallerstein, & Dow y Garcia-Velarde, 2000; Scheirer, Shediac, & Cassady, 1995; Steckler & Linnan, 2002; Viadro, Earp, & Altpeter, 1997)

Organizational Settings

The implementation monitoring approach described in this textbook applies most directly to interventions that take place in **organizational settings**, where people gather to live, to work, to learn and/or to play and that are directed by rules and norms specific to that organization or setting (Green & Kreuter, 2005). These may include educational, government, business, nonprofit, health care, faith-based, and other community-based organizations. Interventions are designed for and delivered in organizational settings, in part because these settings are convenient locations to reach defined groups of people. Each organization type has unique characteristics; for example, preschool, health care clinic, and worksite settings have different missions, serve different populations, and operate differently. Variability may occur within a given type; for example, not all schools, even within the same district, have the same practices and structures in place. However, some commonalities exist among all types of organizations, which must be considered when planning and evaluating programs. For example, all organizational settings have influential leadership, a hierarchy of roles and tasks, and a communication infrastructure.

Program, Policy, and Practice Change

The intervention approach emphasized within this textbook is program, policy, and/or practice change. This emphasis is in contrast to change efforts that emphasize individual behavior change. **Programs** are considered to be a set of external activities, curricula, or other stand-alone entities that will be introduced into an organizational setting. **Policies and organizational practices** (also denoted as policies and practices) refer to existing procedures, policies, bylaws, practices, or routines within an organization. **Program, policy, and practice interventions** refer specifically to a process of intended, introduced, and planned social and/or physical changes in an organizational setting to achieve certain objectives or obtain certain benefits within that setting (Chen, 2015; McDavid, Huse, & Hawthorn, 2013). These can include adding new policies or practices or making adjustments to preexisting policies or practices. Depending on the professional field and the setting, the *program, policy, practice change being implemented* may be called by a variety of terms including program, policy, organizational practices, treatment, project, and **innovation**. The actions being taken to facilitate implementation of the change or the change effort is an **intervention**. The terminology used throughout this textbook maintains the distinction between what is being implemented (an innovation or a program, policy, or practice) and the process of facilitating its implementation (an intervention).

Perspectives on Program, Policy, and Practice Change Within Organizational Settings

Comprehensive implementation monitoring is based on an understanding of the program, policy, and practice uptake as well as an understanding of the organizational context in which uptake takes place. Each program, policy, and practice innovation and setting has unique features that must be considered; however, certain principles are common to all. Two of these principles inform the approach described in this textbook:

- Uptake of program policy and practice change within organizational settings takes place in iterative phases over time, with different influences at differing phases.

- The change process is "messy" due to the inherent complexity within organizational systems.

Principle 1: Uptake of program, policy, and practice change within organizational settings takes place in iterative phases over time, with different influences at differing phases.

Program, policy, or practice change in an organizational setting is best understood through a **program life cycle** perspective (Scheirer, 2005), in which program, policy, or practice uptake happens through a series of nonlinear steps. The iterative and overlapping phases of the program life cycle from a research perspective are development, adoption, implementation, sustainability or termination, and dissemination and/or diffusion (Bopp, Saunders, & Lattimore, 2013; Scheirer, 2005), although not all interventions progress through all phases. This process is iterative rather than linear, in that the planning team will revisit decisions multiple times throughout the life of the program.

The first step in program, policy, or practice change is *program, policy, or practice* **innovation development**, which—under ideal circumstances—is conducted by a **planning team** made up of planners and evaluators using a systematic planning process. **Adoption** by a potential implementing organization follows and is typically a decision made by an administrator, decision maker, board of directors, or some other authority. Adoption may take place at multiple levels depending on the organizational structure. *Implementation* may follow adoption and is action oriented, signaling a series of moves designed to put the program, policy, or practice into place in the setting. Implementation typically requires working with different stakeholders than those involved in adoption, often including front line workers. **Sustainability** refers to the continuation or integration of a program, policy, or practice within an organizational setting, whereas *termination* refers to noncontinuation. Finally, **dissemination and diffusion** refer to planned and unplanned spread, respectively, of the program, policy, or practice beyond the initial implementing organization. The cycle is then repeated in new organizations (see Figure 1) (Bopp et al., 2013).

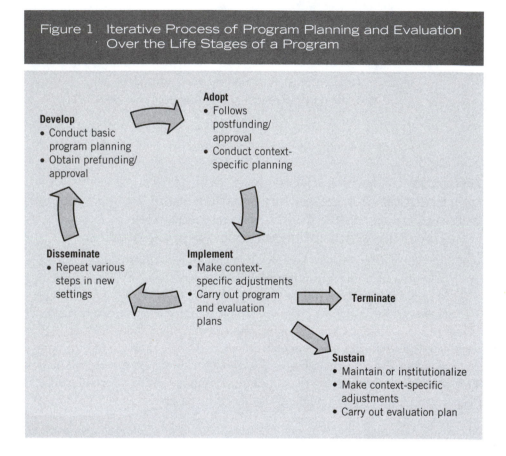

Figure 1   Iterative Process of Program Planning and Evaluation Over the Life Stages of a Program

To illustrate this process simplistically, suppose that a planning team, such as a team of university researchers, *develops* a smoking cessation program for clients with chronic mental illness. The researchers submit a proposal to test this program to a federal funding agency, and the agency approves it for funding. The intervention members of the planning team then recruit community mental health centers, and the agency heads agree to *adopt* the program for use in their centers. Next, center staff who will implement the program are identified and trained. Staff carry out the program, which is evaluated by evaluation members of the planning team (or by external evaluators not on the planning team). If the program proves to be ineffective, it may be *terminated*. If the program is effective and a good fit with the organizational setting, it may be *sustained* over time. Furthermore, it may be *disseminated* to additional mental health clinics and centers as an evidence-based program. Then, the program life cycle is repeated in new settings.

The ultimate goal is for a new program to be adopted, implemented, and assuming the program is effective, sustained. This is best accomplished by actively addressing the factors that influence this process. An overview of these influences is presented below and in Figure 2. Most frameworks that address factors influencing this process focus on a single phase such as implementation only or sustainability only; the information presented here draws from multiple frameworks and incorporates all phases. Different experts categorize the influences in slightly different ways. However, labels on categories per se are not as important for the planning team as is consideration of the range of factors that will influence adoption, implementation, and sustainability of the program, policy, or organizational practice. (See Resource Box 1.)

Resource Box 1
Adoption, Implementation, and Sustainability Processes

To facilitate the adoption, implementation, and sustainability processes, it is important to understand influences on them. Several useful review articles and frameworks help guide understanding of influences on the adoption, implementation, and sustainability process for program, policy, and practice (see Damschroder et al., 2009; Durlak & DuPre, 2008; Fixsen, Naoom, Blase, Friedman, & Wallace, 2005; Greenhalgh, Robert, Macfarlane, Bate, & Kyriakidou, 2004; Johnson, Hays, Center, & Daley, 2004; Pluye, Potvin, & Denis, 2004; Pluye, Potvin, Denis, Pelletier, & Mannoni, 2005; Rogers, 2003; Scheirer, 2005; Shediac-Rizkallah & Bone, 1998).

Seven categories of influences are shown in Figure 2 and are grouped into three broad areas: (1) factors over which implementers have the most control (implementation approach/processes and innovation characteristics); (2) factors that can be influenced or "nudged" (organizational leadership and support, adopter/implementer characteristics, and resources); and (3) factors that are

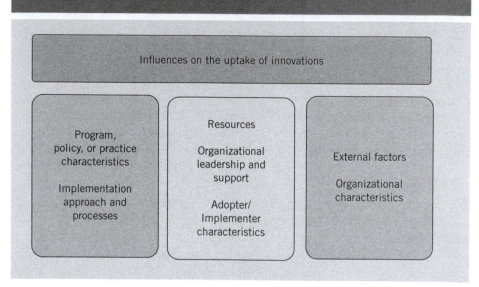

Figure 2   Categories of Influence on Adoption, Implementation, and Sustainability

important to know but less amenable to influence: organizational characteristics and external factors. The first category pertains to how the innovation is developed and how intervention members of planning teams work with implementing settings to carry out the intervention. The second category includes factors that intervention members of planning teams can address to some extent by capacity development activities. For example, the planning team can work with leadership to cultivate and maintain support and provide staff development to implementers to enhance motivation and skills. The third category includes factors that are inherent in the organization and therefore not as feasible to change. These include the size and location of the organization and the services that it provides, as well as outside events over which it has little or no control, such as professional association requirements, federal mandates, or disaster events. Not all constructs within each domain will be equally applicable to all settings, so the planning team should select those that are most applicable.

Different types of evaluation approaches are optimal at different phases of the program life cycle. For example, formative evaluation or a developmental evaluation approach (Patton, 2008) may be useful for developing innovations; process evaluation may be useful for monitoring adoption, implementation, and sustainability; and impact/outcome or summative evaluation is most useful in a mature program that has been well implemented. An evaluability assessment

(Wholey, Hatry, & Newcomer, 2010) may be appropriate prior to investing considerable resources into outcome/impact evaluation. Similarly, some experts recommend a phased approach to the development, implementation, and evaluation of interventions (Campbell et al., 2000).

Understanding the program life cycle phase will enhance the evaluator's ability to monitor uptake of the program, policy, and/or practice by informing the selection of appropriate data sources. Furthermore, in a comprehensive approach to implementation monitoring, the planning team may also assess influences on the adoption, implementation, and sustainability processes.

Principle 2: The change process is "messy" due to the inherent complexity within organizational systems.

The approach to program, policy, and practice implementation in organizational settings that is taken in this textbook assumes a **systems perspective** that includes an appreciation for the role of local context. A systems perspective includes the premises that the whole is greater than the sum of the parts, parts are interdependent, focus is on interconnected relationships, systems are made up of subsystems that function within larger systems, and systems boundaries are both necessary and arbitrary (Patton, 2008, pp. 365–367). An organizational setting exemplifies a complex system, embedded in and influenced by social, political, and cultural factors (MacDonald & Green, 2001) that come from within and outside of the organization. It is not the passive, convenient location that outside planning teams often assume when they approach implementing a program, policy, or practice change.

The complex nature of settings means that the people working within them may consciously or unconsciously resist change (Sterman, 2006) because they feel overwhelmed, have "concerns" (Hall & Hord, 2015) about the implications of the changes for their job, or any number of other reasons. They may wish to change but tend to fall back on rote procedures, habits, and "rules of thumb" when they are unsure (Sterman, 2006). The organization may also lack the capacity to enable and maintain the change that is needed (Potter & Brough, 2004). In other words, introducing a new program, policy, or practice can cause a response by people within the organization—and the organization as a system—that can result in minimal intervention effects, and may even exacerbate the problem the intervention was meant to address (Hawe, Shiell, & Riley, 2009; Sterman, 2006). For example, policies requiring automobile makers to include safety features have resulted in more aggressive driving (Sterman, 2006). This dynamic complexity has important implications for how an innovation is conceptualized and how the intervention members of the planning team facilitate program, policy, or practice change. It also indicates the need to identify unanticipated effects of interventions in addition to evaluating the anticipated results. And it shows the importance of identifying and using multiple sources of data in implementation monitoring to develop a fuller "picture" of what is happening.

Social interactions play a crucial role at all levels of a system (Alliance for Health Policy and Systems Research, & World Health Organization, 2009) and social structures and relationships within systems are likely to be important influences on intervention effectiveness (Marks, Barnett, Foulkes, Hawe, & Allender, 2013). An understanding of the organizational context will enable the intervention members of planning teams to conceptualize innovations and intervention delivery purposely and to anticipate the corresponding implementation and evaluation challenges of programs that emphasize program, policy, and practice change. Figure 3 contrasts a simplistic view of how we expect innovations to work with a more realistic portrayal of how they actually work. The top part of the figure portrays the linear, simplistic way we often view introducing an innovation into an organizational setting. In this view, introducing a policy into an organization without considering context is straightforward and results in the anticipated outcomes. The more realistic view, provided in the bottom part of the figure, recognizes that the program, policy, or practice is being introduced into a setting in which many factors are at play. Everyone in that setting has established roles and ways of operating, which may or may not be consistent with how the innovation is designed to operate. In practical terms, the planning team must consider the setting itself a key player that responds to and acts on/with the program, policy, or practice, not simply as a good place to find participants.

Introducing an innovation into an organization affects many existing activities, requires many adjustments, and as an unintended side effect, may replace previous activities. Outcomes produced from the intervention are likely attenuated in this more realistic view. For example, new health screening procedures introduced into a work site will "compete" with existing procedures and activities, may add additional burdens to already overburdened staff, and may result in staff dropping prior health activities or events to accommodate the changes. The net effect of disruption in routines and elimination of previous, effective activities may adversely affect the outcomes/impacts of interest. A simple summative outcome-only evaluation would miss much of what is happening as a result of the program, whereas a comprehensive approach to evaluation that includes implementation monitoring would provide a more complete understanding of the program, its context, and how it produces (or doesn't produce) program effects.

Figure 3 How Interventions "Work": Expectations Versus Reality

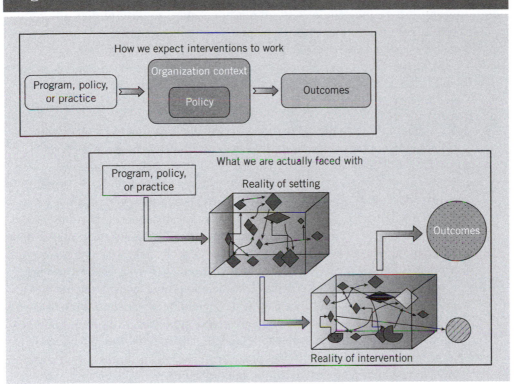

Source: Adapted from Foster-Fishman, P. G., Nowell, B., & Yang, H. (2007). Putting the system back into systems change: A framework for understanding and changing organizational and community systems. *Am J Community Psychol., 39*(3/4), 197–215. doi:10.1007/s10464-007-9109-0. With kind permission from Springer Science and Business Media.

Systems approaches include systems dynamics, soft systems methodology, complex adaptive systems, and cultural historical activity (Behrens & Foster-Fishman, 2007), and each has a particular emphasis that may be applicable to program, policy, and practice change. For example, systems dynamics is useful for showing how changes in one part of a system may have a delayed impact on other parts; soft systems methodology helps identify and examine different purposes of a system; and cultural historical activity theory emphasizes how people understand and think about the world (Behrens & Foster-Fishman, 2007). From a practical point of view, however, having an understanding of some basics of systems theories enables the planning team to avoid overly simplistic thinking about intervening and evaluating change efforts in organizational systems.

A systems view recognizes the interdependence among different levels of the system and acknowledges that changes at any level affect all parts. This means that the program, policy, and practice changes to be implemented have larger ramifications than the planning team likely can visualize and that changes at different levels of the system may have very strong influences on the implementation process. Also, an organization is not a closed system, but rather is embedded in and linked to many other systems. Therefore, the organization may be influenced by changes originating outside of the implementing organization.

Returning to the example of the smoking cessation program in mental health centers, none of the organizations that agree to adopt the program are "blank slates" waiting for programs to be carried out. Rather, staff members, who work in a hectic and crisis-oriented environment, are typically already at or beyond their work capacity when they are approached about this new program. The new program will require adjustments in work load, organizational procedure, and possibly organizational policy. Not all supervisors and administrators may support the program initially. Adjustments in work and case load may depend on scarce or nonexistent resources. Implications for organizational accreditation also need to be considered. These are complex considerations and changes that will take time, even after staff members are trained. Depending on personal attitudes and behavior, the working environment, and level of supervisory support, staff may embrace the program or may resist it. Similarly, clients may respond favorably or negatively, depending on a number of factors including readiness to quit smoking, and as a result, some clients may drop out of the program. The new program may displace another health-related program, creating negative effects within and outside of the mental health center. For example, a board member may object to her favorite program being "squeezed" to accommodate the new program. Furthermore, the approach taken by the intervention members of the planning team for working with the mental health centers to install the new program will influence the implementation process positively or negatively. Clearly, under these circumstances, achieving positive outcomes for quitting smoking is more challenging than the simplistic view of the life cycle would suggest.

Introducing Lifestyle Education for Activity Program (LEAP)

The LEAP will be used throughout this textbook to illustrate planning, implementation, and evaluation processes. LEAP was a multicomponent physical activity intervention for high school girls that focused on changing school instruction and environments to promote physical activity. LEAP took place in

12 high schools (with an additional 12 high schools composing a control group) in South Carolina. LEAP began when an interdisciplinary team of researchers had an idea about improving the physical activity experiences of high school girls as a way to reduce the decline in physical activity in this age group.

LEAP was guided by a social ecological framework informed by social cognitive theory (Pate et al., 2007). The model indicated that intervention activities would positively influence girls' enjoyment of physical activity, self-efficacy, and social support, which would in turn positively impact the amount of physical activity they engaged in. The conceptual model was used to develop intervention methods and strategies (e.g., facilitation of enjoyment, self-efficacy, and a socially supportive school environment) as well as to guide selection of constructs and corresponding measures that should be assessed in impact/outcome evaluation (e.g., physical activity, enjoyment, self-efficacy, and social support).

LEAP was a multicomponent innovation that included a gender-sensitive physical education (PE) program with activities designed to be fun and age appropriate for high school girls. LEAP also emphasized developing physical activity self-efficacy and self-management skills in a school environment that promoted and supported physical activity for young women. LEAP included six components of a Coordinated School Health Program organized into two domains: instructional practices and healthy school environment. Instructional practices included (1) LEAP PE and (2) health education. The goal of LEAP PE was to provide girls with the physical and behavioral skills needed to adopt a physically active lifestyle during their teenage years and to maintain that active lifestyle into adulthood. The goal of health education was to reinforce messages delivered in PE classes concerning the benefits of physical activity and to provide training in behavioral skills that would enable students to initiate and maintain a physically active lifestyle.

Healthy school environment included (3) policies and practices related to physical activity, (4) school health services, (5) faculty and staff health promotion, and (6) family and community involvement. The goal of instituting schoolwide policies and practices was to promote the physical activity within and outside of the school. The goal of school health services was to increase the involvement of the school nurse in creating a school environment that supports and reinforces physical activity among students. The goal of faculty and staff health promotion was to create a supportive school environment that included physically active adult role models. The goal of family and community involvement was to assist students in being physically active outside of school by enhancing parental support and by linking students to physical activity opportunities outside of school (Ward et al., 2006).

LEAP involved the research team working with school teachers and staff in a flexible, adaptive approach to facilitate the installation of the LEAP guiding principles, known as the LEAP Essential Elements (presented in detail in Step 4). The flexible, adaptable approach encouraged each school to adapt LEAP guided by the Essential Elements to better fit local contexts. There was no LEAP curriculum, for example; rather, each school adapted the LEAP Essential Elements to best fit its needs and resources. The LEAP project team developed the LEAP Essential Elements prior to approaching the schools, and worked with schools very closely in partnership during the implementation process. LEAP was implemented by teachers and staff with training, guidance, and support from the LEAP intervention staff.

LEAP PE was integrated into ninth-grade PE; health education was implemented based on each individual school's approach to offering health education; and the school environment components were implemented via the LEAP team, which consisted of some combination of PE teacher, health or other classroom teacher, school nurse, wellness coordinator, and media specialist.

LEAP intervention staff developed a variety of training and support materials. They conducted 10 workshops in Year 1 and six workshops in Year 2 that focused on behavioral skills, sport education model, PE resistance training, aerobics instruction, and kickboxing. LEAP programs developed by intervention staff included Communities-in-Motion and Active Teacher of the Month. Staff also developed a variety of supportive materials such as PA (physical activity) Prescription Pads, How Do I Know It's LEAP (assessment tool), LEAP Lookout Newsletters, and the school librarian LEAP Resource Kit (Ward et al., 2006).

Implementation Monitoring Process Presented in This Textbook

Planning and carrying out comprehensive implementation monitoring for a program, policy, and/or practice intervention in an organizational setting is accomplished through five phases, depicted in Figure 4 and described below.

Phase I, Basic Program Planning, describes the initial planning process for an innovation. This phase presents a brief review of Basic Program Planning because many resources exist on basic program and evaluation planning. Basic program planning is a multistep, iterative process that typically entails assessment and plan development. Depending on the setting and context, the final program plan may take the form of a simple document that outlines an approach or a complex program proposal submitted to an agency to obtain funding.

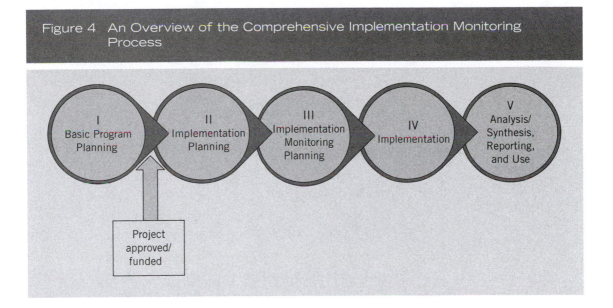

Figure 4 An Overview of the Comprehensive Implementation Monitoring Process

I Basic Program Planning

II Implementation Planning

III Implementation Monitoring Planning

IV Implementation

V Analysis/ Synthesis, Reporting, and Use

Project approved/ funded

Phase II, Implementation Planning, begins when a project has been approved and/or funded. This is where the primary focus of this textbook begins. The initial, basic level of planning rarely has sufficient detail for implementation. Furthermore, subsequent phases in the implementation monitoring process are guided by decisions made during implementation planning. Therefore, implementation planning, which may typically be considered a part of program planning, is a necessary step for evaluation planning. It is very challenging to monitor implementation in real time, as the program is happening, without knowing what is supposed *to* happen and understanding the context in which it will take place.

Phase III, Implementation Monitoring Planning, entails developing the detailed evaluation methods to monitor program implementation as the program is taking place. Ideally, it is based on complete recognition of what is supposed to happen in the program as well as a comprehensive understanding of the contexts in which the program is to take place.

Phase IV, Implementation, refers to the period during which the intervention is implemented and the implementation monitoring plan is carried out. Data collection and management and formative use of implementation monitoring data are primary tasks for implementation monitoring in this phase.

Phase V, Analysis/Synthesis, Reporting, and Use, entails analyzing and synthesizing the data collected, using it in a suitable manner, and reporting results in an appropriate fashion to stakeholders.

Organization of the Textbook

Accordingly, this textbook is organized into six sections, listed below. The five phases are divided into a total of 12 steps:

Phase I: Basic Program Planning

Step 1. Conduct Preimplementation Planning

Phase II: Implementation Planning

Step 2. Describe the Program, Policy, or Practice, Organizational Setting, and Broader Context

Step 3. Determine Strategies for Facilitating Adoption of the Program, Policy, or Practice at the Organizational Level

Step 4. Establish Complete and Acceptable Delivery/Installation of the Program, Policy, or Practice

Step 5. Develop Strategies for Facilitating Program, Policy, or Practice Implementation and Sustainability

Step 6. Develop or Update the Action Model, Action Plan, and Logic Model to Integrate Planning

Phase III: Implementation Monitoring Planning

Step 7. Develop Initial Implementation Monitoring Questions

Step 8. Choose Implementation Monitoring Methods and Compile the Comprehensive Implementation Monitoring Plan

Phase IV: Implementation

Step 9. Implement the Program, Policy, or Practice and Use Implementation Data for Formative Purposes

Step 10. Collect and Manage Implementation Data

Phase V: Analysis/Synthesis, Reporting, and Use

Step 11. Analyze and Synthesize Implementation Monitoring Data

Step 12. Report and Use Implementation Data

Future Directions

KEY POINTS FOR INTRODUCTION, OVERVIEW, AND PERSPECTIVES

- Effectiveness or summative evaluation alone constitutes outcome evaluation, whereas process evaluation examines processes during the implementation process.

- Implementation monitoring is a subset of process evaluation that monitors intervention activities, including context, during active program, policy, or practice implementation.

- The focus of this textbook is program, policy, and practice change that takes place in organizational settings, where people gather to live, to work, to learn, and/or to play.

- Program, policy, or practice change in an organizational setting is best understood through a program lifecycle perspective in which intervention uptake happens through a series of nonlinear steps.

- Successful change in organizational settings requires attention to influences on adoption, implementation, and sustainability.

- Conducting and evaluating programs in organizational settings is "messy" due to the real-world context.

- It is essential to understand the specific context or setting into which the program, policy, or practice will be introduced.

- The implementation monitoring process presented in this textbook has 12 steps within five phases.

Basic Program Planning

Phase I involves basic program planning for the intervention and the evaluation that precedes project funding or approval. Basic program planning is a multistep, iterative planning process to develop or design an intervention, and address a particular problem or issue in a defined population and/or setting. This process is represented in this textbook by one step: preimplementation planning.

Figure I.1   The Implementation Planning and Monitoring Process, With Phase I, Basic Program Planning, Highlighted

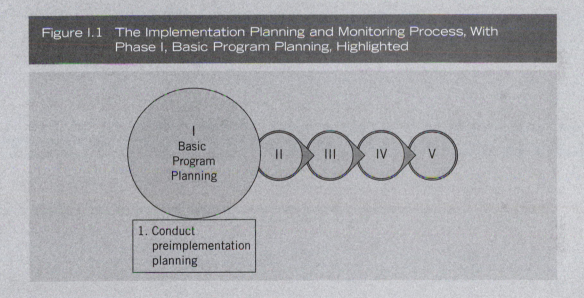

Plans are nothing; planning
is everything.
                    -Dwight D. Eisenhower

STEP 1

Conduct Preimplementation Planning

The planning team, which consists of program planners and evaluation planners, must develop the new program, policy, or practice before it can be adopted, implemented, and evaluated in the organizational setting. This optimally happens through a multistep, systematic planning process in which the planning team develops a written plan, prospectus, or proposal that is then submitted for approval or funding. Many resources describe and prescribe the basic program planning and evaluation planning processes for program development in detail (see Resource Box 1.1), so this chapter provides an overview of this process.

Ideally, the program and evaluation plans are developed together in a process best described as iterative, building, and evolving over time, and both are completed prior to program, policy, or practice implementation. This is the ideal scenario, however; reality is far messier. For example, sometimes detailed planning has not been conducted prior to initiating implementation, or no program plan exists prior to developing an evaluation plan. In these cases, the evaluation members of the planning team must work with the implementers to understand the key elements and objectives of the program before developing an evaluation plan. Even though this situation is common, it is not optimal, particularly for implementation monitoring planning that relies on knowledge of many of the details about the program, policy, or practice. Therefore, if preimplementation planning has not been conducted or has only been partially conducted, it will be important for the planning team to conduct this basic planning step before proceeding.

Learning Objectives

By the end of the chapter you will be familiar with

1. The basic program planning and evaluation planning process

2. Important considerations for enhancing the effectiveness of the program planning and evaluation planning process

Resource Box 1.1
Program Planning and Evaluation Planning

Program Planning

Bartholomew, L. K., Parcel, G. S., Kok, G., & Gottlieb, N. H. (2006). *Planning health promotion programs: An intervention mapping approach* (2nd ed.). San Francisco, CA: Jossey-Bass.

Green, L. W., & Kreuter, M. W. (2005). *Health program planning: An educational and ecological approach* (4th ed.). New York, NY: McGraw-Hill Publishing.

Issel, L. M. (2008). *Health promotion program planning and evaluation: A practical, systematic approach for community health* (2nd ed.). Sudbury, MA: Jones & Bartlett Publishers.

RE-AIM program planning model. Retrieved from http://www.re-aim.org/

Evaluation Planning

Grembowski, D. (2001). *The practice of health program evaluation.* Thousand Oaks, CA: Sage.

King, J. A., Morris, L. L., & Fitz-Gibbon, C. T. (1987). *How to assess program implementation.* Thousand Oaks, CA: Sage.

McDavid, J. C., Huse, I., & Hawthorne, L. R. L. (2013). *Program evaluation and performance measurement: An introduction to practice* (2nd ed.). Thousand Oaks, CA: Sage.

Patton, M. Q. (2008). *Utilization-focused evaluation* (4th ed.). Thousand Oaks, CA: Sage.

Patton, M. Q. (2011). *Essentials of utilization-focused evaluation.* Thousand Oaks, CA: Sage.

Pawson, R. (2013). *The science of evaluation.* Thousand Oaks, CA: Sage.

Rossi, P. H., Lipsey, M. W., & Freeman, H. E. (2004). *Evaluation: A systematic approach* (7th ed). Thousand Oaks, CA: Sage.

Ryan, K. E., & Cousins, J. B. (Eds.). (2009). *The SAGE international handbook of educational evaluation.* Thousand Oaks, CA: Sage.

Participatory and Stakeholder Approaches to Program and Evaluation Planning

Centers for Disease Control and Prevention. (2012, September). A framework for program evaluation. Retrieved from http://www.cdc.gov/eval/framework/index.htm

Chen, H.-T. (2015). *Practical program evaluation: Theory-driven evaluation and the integrated evaluation perspective* (2nd ed.). Thousand Oaks, CA: Sage.

Chinman, M., Imm, P., & Wandersman, A. (2004). *Getting To Outcomes™ 2004. Promoting accountability through methods and tools for planning, implementation, and evaluation.* Rand Technical Report. Retrieved from http://130.154.3.8/pubs/technical_reports/TR101.html

Fetterman, D. M., & Wandersman, A. (2005). *Empowerment evaluation principles in practice.* New York, NY: The Guilford Press.

Minkler, M., & Wallerstein, N. (Eds.). (2008). *Community-based participatory research for health: From process to outcomes.* San Francisco: CA. Wiley.

Effective program, policy, or practice innovation plans include an assessment of **priority audience** needs and interests, preferably using an established framework. The priority audience is the intended program, policy, or practice beneficiaries. This systematic assessment may be oriented toward "objective" needs of the priority audience, such as needs identified through state or national data or a population-specific assessment or survey. Conversely, it may be oriented toward "perceived" needs of the priority audience that are identified through a participatory process or a survey with the population of interest. The former tend to be more expert driven in practice and minimally involve stakeholders, whereas the latter tend to be more facilitative, participatory processes with greater stakeholder involvement. Many methods combine elements from both of these approaches. The material presented in this textbook applies to both expert-driven and stakeholder-driven approaches in all organizational settings, and also pertains to evaluation research and evaluation practice approaches.

An Overview of the Basic Program Planning and Evaluation Planning Process

Overview of Program Planning Process

As depicted by the vertical arrows in Figure 1.1, basic program planning is a series of assessment activities occurring at multiple levels accompanied by planning activities appropriate to that level and culminating in the development of an objective. Planning typically begins with the activities shown at the top of Figure 1.1, in which the planning team assesses needs and establishes outcome objectives. Outcomes may be related to distal or proximal conditions or factors. For example, health outcomes may include distal changes in conditions such as diabetes or heart disease or risk factors such as total serum cholesterol or high blood pressure. Alternatively, health outcomes may include proximal behaviors such as physical activity or diet that contribute to outcomes. Similarly, in education settings, distal outcomes may include graduation rates or employment, whereas proximal outcomes may include academic performance or skills. Depending on the population, scope, and time frame of the program, policy, or practice change, project outcomes may focus on the behavior, performance, and/or skill levels or on more distal conditions and outcomes. For example, in the Lifestyle Education for Activity Program (LEAP) the primary outcome was proximal: physical activity behavior in adolescent girls. The distal health condition, a cardiovascular disease, does not manifest until many years beyond adolescence and was therefore outside the scope of LEAP. See Green and Kreuter (2005) for more detailed guidance on planning health-related programs.

The next level of assessment and planning addresses factors that influence the selected outcome of interest. In LEAP, this entailed identifying influences on physical activity in adolescent girls, which was accomplished primarily through examining evidence in published literature. It revealed the importance of targeting factors such as perceived self-efficacy and social support for physical activity, as research shows these factors are consistently associated with physical activity in youth. That is, youth who have confidence in their ability to overcome common barriers to physical activity and who have social support and encouragement for being physically active are more likely to be physically active.

Following the selection of important factors that influence the outcome of interest, the next step in planning is to identify intervention strategies that are designed to impact these factors. This level of assessment includes examining evidence in both published literature and theory to identify appropriate methods and strategies. The LEAP team selected confidence-building and fun approaches that enabled girls to socialize during physical education class in order to develop physical activity self-efficacy and social support (Ward et al., 2006). Bartholomew and colleagues provide a detailed planning process for identifying theory- and evidence-based program methods and strategies (Bartholomew et al., 2006).

The final level of assessment and planning, depicted in the bottom arrow in Figure 1.1, pertains to project or program structure and processes that must be in place to get the work done in the setting. In organizational settings, this refers to organizational resources and materials, including staff members who are needed for program implementation. In LEAP, this level included the two full-time LEAP intervention staff who worked with schools, as well as school resources such as space, scheduling, and appropriate equipment. That is, the school provided physical education within an appropriately equipped gymnasium, and qualified personnel such as physical education teachers and other school staff who were trained to carry out LEAP conduct the activities with the high school girls.

Overview of Evaluation Planning Process

Each level of assessment and planning, as shown in Figure 1.1, has a corresponding evaluation approach, depicted in the boxes to the right of the arrows. The **outcome evaluation** (top box in Figure 1.1) addresses questions, objectives, or aims about the extent to which the intervention impacts the primary outcome. The **impact evaluation** (second box from the top in Figure 1.1) addresses questions, objectives, or aims about the extent to which the intervention has a positive impact on factors that influence outcomes. Assessing the effects of the intervention on the outcome and influence variables is also considered a **summative evaluation.** Outcome and impact evaluation—both of which are examples of effectiveness evaluation and are beyond the focus of this textbook— deserve additional comment here. Various evaluation frameworks define these two terms differently. In the PRECEDE/PROCEED (Green & Kreuter, 2005) framework, distal effects are considered to be *outcomes*; that is, they take long periods of time to be realized, as in chronic diseases that take nearly a lifetime to develop. In contrast, the CDC evaluation framework (Centers for Disease Control and Prevention, 1999) labels distal effects as *impacts*. In this textbook, both words are used together (outcome/impact) to refer to the proposed indicator for program effectiveness at distal and proximal levels.

Implementation monitoring (third box from the top in Figure 1.1) refers to methods used during active program implementation to monitor the ongoing implementation process and context. Plan quality and resource assessment (bottom box in Figure 1.1) encompass methods employed during preimplementation to assess the quality of the program plan and materials as well as the technical and cultural competence of program providers. Implementation monitoring and process evaluation methods may be used in a **formative evaluation** to further develop a program and/or to keep a developed program on track, although it is possible to use implementation monitoring and process data in a summative manner, as well.

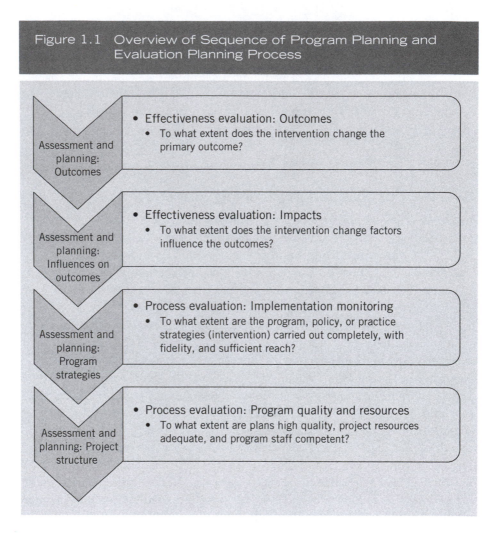

Figure 1.1 Overview of Sequence of Program Planning and Evaluation Planning Process

Assessment and planning: Outcomes

- Effectiveness evaluation: Outcomes
  - To what extent does the intervention change the primary outcome?

Assessment and planning: Influences on outcomes

- Effectiveness evaluation: Impacts
  - To what extent does the intervention change factors influence the outcomes?

Assessment and planning: Program strategies

- Process evaluation: Implementation monitoring
  - To what extent are the program, policy, or practice strategies (intervention) carried out completely, with fidelity, and sufficient reach?

Assessment and planning: Project structure

- Process evaluation: Program quality and resources
  - To what extent are plans high quality, project resources adequate, and program staff competent?

Important Considerations for Enhancing the Effectiveness of the Program Planning and Evaluation Planning Process

Three important considerations for improving the quality of the program, the evaluation planning processes, and the planning products of these processes are as follows:

- Effective program, policy, or practice change entails extensive collaboration with people from the implementing settings.

- Intervention planning is optimally guided by a conceptual framework that includes an understanding of the causal mechanisms that will enable the program, policy, or practice to produce expected outcomes/impacts.

- Program planning, implementation, and evaluation are best conducted within collaborative interdisciplinary teams.

Effective program, policy, or practice change entails extensive collaboration with people from the implementing settings.

Research from diverse fields provides consistent evidence for the importance of collaborating with setting stakeholders to facilitate program, policy, or practice change in those settings (Foster-Fishman, Nowell, & Yang, 2007; Hawe, Shiell, & Riley, 2009; Plsek & Greenhalgh, 2001; Shiell, Hawe, & Gold, 2008; Sterman, 2006). Meaningful involvement with and input from stakeholders and change agents early in the process is considered beneficial and is associated with better implementation and sustainability in real-world settings (Durlak & DuPre, 2008; Scheirer, 2005). The tradeoff is an increase in the amount of time needed for collaborative planning. Because intervention and evaluation activities can be disruptive, the ability to successfully implement and evaluate program, policy, or practice change in real-world contexts depends in part on identifying and working with appropriate people affiliated with setting and establishing effective **working relationships,** characterized by positive interactions and harmony among people working together to achieve a common goal.

There are two broad categories of setting collaborators: **stakeholders,** who have an investment, interest, or stake in the outcome of a program and/or are affected by the program, (Green & Kreuter, 2005; "Stakeholder," 2013), and **change agents—** individuals, groups, or other units that work as catalysts for change within an organization (Rogers, 2003). Change agents can create environmental change through program, policy, or practice implementation (Commers, Gottlieb, & Kok, 2007). According to the diffusion of innovations theory, change agents are often external to the implementing organization; however, in this textbook, the change agent is considered internal to the implementing organization, an approach that is consistent with environmental (Commers et al., 2007) and sustainable change.

Change agents provide a link between the implementing organization and the planning team (Rogers, 2003). It is important that the appropriate individuals or teams are identified. The change agent approach also has potential for organizational capacity development; this does not occur automatically, but rather depends largely on the approach to implementation. Optimally, stakeholders and change agents will understand how intervention activities can contribute to the organizational mission and to accomplishing their primary job. They should also know what to expect in terms of evaluation data collection including how it will influence operations and why data collection is important. Establishing and maintaining effective two-way communication is essential as part of this process. This requires a reliable communication infrastructure, which must be established if it does not already exist in the setting or settings.

Identifying Stakeholders

Identifying and beginning to establish working relationships with change agents and other stakeholders from early in the process will enable planning teams to obtain vitally important setting- and population-specific perspectives and information (Poland, Krupa, & McCall, 2009). Working with stakeholders effectively has the potential to increase "buy-in" for the program, enhance implementation and sustainability, expand contacts and potential resources, and share the workload. However, planning teams must identify stakeholders prior to enlisting their support. Stakeholders are setting- and context-specific and may include, but are not limited to, individuals and representatives of groups listed below (Rossi, 2004):

- Funders (federal, state, or private), sponsors, and community partners who provide financial and in-kind support, as well as other resources that support the program including volunteers and donated equipment and services.

- Representatives from regulatory agencies, professional associations, coalitions, or other professional networks who may be in a position to influence adoption, implementation, and/or sustainability of the program, policy, or practice.

- Decision makers from within the organization or at higher levels of a multilevel organization who are often in a position to act on or make decisions about the program, especially in the early phases; examples include agency heads, middle management, and coordinators.

- Planning team members including intervention members who are involved in determining the direction and details for the program as well as supporting the implementation process, as well as evaluation members who will evaluate the implementation and outcome/impact processes.

- Program implementers or those involved in carrying out the program in the setting, who are often personnel from within the organization; examples include front-line staff, service providers, and change agents.

- Program participants (both primary and secondary) or members of the priority population who will receive or benefit from the program, policy, or practice change. These individuals are directly served by the program or are affected by it in some way; examples include children and their parents/caretakers/guardians.

This is intended as an initial list for the planning team. For example, in addition to working with school personnel to arrange meetings, establish communication, provide training, and provide ongoing technical assistance, the planning team will need to work with parents/guardians and school teachers and staff to obtain informed consent, to schedule recruitment and training activities, and to schedule data collection prior to beginning implementation activities.

Working Relationships

The innovation is only one of the many components that change agents and other stakeholders are dealing with in the setting(s) of interest, and prior to the establishment of working relationships, the program, policy, or practice change is not likely to be a high priority for them. It is, therefore, essential that the planning team begin the process of establishing effective working relationships, preferably prior to beginning the implementation process. As with any relationship, working relationships with stakeholders must be maintained over time. The process of developing new stakeholder relationships will likely continue through much of the project as the planning team learns more about the setting and makes connections with key people in the setting.

The literature on principles of effective community-based partnerships (Green, Daniel, & Novick, 2001) is informative for establishing working relationships. It is essential that both parties understand the other's organizational mission and develop a shared understanding of intervention goals and outcomes (Green et al., 2001). This process requires multiple interactions over time. Other aspects of productive working relationships include clear, two-way communication among the partners and transparency concerning how decisions are made (Green et al., 2001). Interactions should convey respect for the other and his or her position and role (Green et al., 2001). Unfortunately, a planning team contact who is very focused on getting a specific task accomplished may come across as disrespectful or unconcerned about how the innovation influences the particulars of the change agent's job or the organization's mission. Over time, mutual trust and commitment must develop for the working relationship to be an effective one (Green et al., 2001).

Developing an effective working relationship is more easily accomplished if there is a mutual understanding of the purpose and scope of the innovation (e.g., changing an existing system or creating something new), and if the innovation is conceptualized as systems change from the very beginning (Foster-Fishman & Behrens, 2007). Of course, the planning team must first have a very well-developed understanding of the desired program, policy, or practice and the system into which it is to be introduced.

McDonough and Doucette (2001) discussed effective working relationships based on literature on interpersonal relationships, business relationships, and collaborative care within health care settings. A collaborative working relationship is developed over time through a series of stages that progress from basic awareness through professional recognition, exploring and developing a professional relationship and, finally, commitment to the collaborative working relationship (McDonough & Doucette, 2001). Progression through these stages is influenced by characteristics of the individuals involved, such as knowledge, attitudes, beliefs, and past professional experiences; characteristics of the context, such as proximity of individuals, which influences the amount of interaction they have and the extent to which the respective organizations support collaboration; and characteristics of their interaction, such as bidirectionality of communication, handling of power and fairness, development of norms and expectations, and manner in which conflict is resolved (McDonough & Doucette, 2001).

In the early stages of working relationship development, interactions tend to center around requests and responses to specific, discrete tasks that need to be accomplished. However, these types of limited, task-oriented requests are not sufficient to develop effective working relationships. To advance relationship development, the planning team contact person, who is generally the initiator of interactions, should communicate an interest in working together, describe services that he or she can provide, and schedule or arrange future interactions (McDonough & Doucette, 2001). The goal is to develop a relationship characterized by respect, trust, and bilateral communication (McDonough & Doucette, 2001).

In other words, providing effective staff development, technical assistance, and support to facilitate implementation is the tip of the iceberg; it is equally important to work on the ongoing process of establishing and maintaining effective working relationships with implementers and other stakeholders (see Figure 1.2). The optimal approach is characterized by the Learning Collaborative, originally developed for health care settings and applied to children in the Connecticut child welfare system who suffered from undiagnosed or untreated stress due to experiencing trauma (Lang, Franks, & Bory, 2011). In contrast to traditional training approaches that provide time-limited training for specific individuals, the Learning Collaborative methodology featured extended and interactive contact with teams of change agents.

The questions provided in Table 1.1, largely adapted from Poland and colleagues (Poland et al., 2009), provide useful guidance for identifying key stakeholders and understanding their perspectives and roles, which can facilitate development of effective working relationships. A template to summarize some of the key elements of working with change agents and other stakeholders can be found in Worksheet 1.1.

Figure 1.2 Working With Setting Stakeholders for Program, Policy, or Practice Implementation

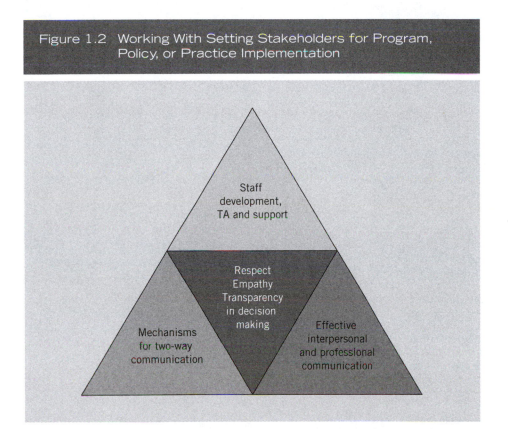

Table 1.1 Questions to Understand the Perspectives of Organizational Stakeholders Including Change Agents

Who are important stakeholders within and outside the organization?

What are their agendas, their stake in change or the status quo, access to resources?

What are the functions of this setting for different stakeholders (e.g., hospital functions as site of healing for patients, home for long-term or palliative care patients, workplace for staff, site of professional and class conflict)?

Who is absent from this setting? Why?

What is the meaning of [focus of program, policy, or practice to be introduced] from different stakeholder perspectives and its salience to them?

How do power relations come into play in this setting?

What is the relative power of stakeholders? How is power exerted?

Who controls access to this setting?

Who sets the agenda in this setting?

What stakeholders or stakeholder groups are influential on the organizational decision-making process?

Who participates in decision making? On what basis? On whose conditions?

Who has voice? What is the relative role and power of experts and of the lay public in agenda setting, problem definition, intervention planning, implementation, and evaluation?

What—or who—drives (or blocks) change in this setting?

What are the best strategies for working with the various stakeholders to assess their needs and interests?

What is the most effective approach for ongoing, two-way communication between planning team and stakeholders?

What roles are appropriate for various stakeholders in this setting during the implementation and sustainability processes? What specific roles will each stakeholder play (e.g., advisor, consultant, member of planning team, implementer, volunteer in program, etc.)?

How will the planning team ensure that stakeholder roles and expectations for stakeholder participation are clarified initially and over time?

How will the planning team appropriately incorporate stakeholder resources (funds, in-kind, volunteer, etc.)?

For change agents: How will we ensure the implementers have the skills, technical support, and organizational support to support the intervention? What are likely barriers and how can these be addressed?

Source: Adapted from Poland et al. (2009)

Worksheet 1.1   Summary of Key Considerations for Working With Change Agents and Other Stakeholders in Organizational Settings

Category	Description
Identify key stakeholders.	
Identify change agents.	
Describe approach to ongoing communication with stakeholders in change agents.	
Describe the primary roles that stakeholders, including change agents, will play throughout the intervention process.	
Describe other relevant information for working with stakeholders and change agents within this setting or settings (from Table 1.1).	

LEAP Case Illustration

LEAP intervention staff developed relationships and ongoing contact with teachers and staff in the schools; the research team and LEAP schools worked together as partners (Saunders, Ward, Felton, Dowda, & Pate, 2006). An illustration of the use of Worksheet 1.1 with a LEAP high school is provided in Table 1.2. As shown in the table, LEAP identified the key contact person, a LEAP champion, and other school teachers and staff with whom they were going to work as change agents throughout the project. Each of these people had important LEAP roles within their school and each received training and ongoing support from the LEAP interventionists. LEAP developed several mechanisms for ongoing communication that included newsletters, an electronic listserv, phone contact, and face-to-face contact through planned training events as well as site visits. The change agents implemented all of the LEAP components within the schools with guidance from the LEAP intervention staff. LEAP also maintained contact with school administrators as key supporters.

Intervention planning is optimally guided by a conceptual framework.

Program planning and evaluation planning are ideally guided by a **change** or **conceptual model** (Chen, 2015) that is based on theory and/or evidence (Bartholomew et al., 2006). This conceptual model should specify the causal mechanisms that will enable the program, policy, or practice to produce expected outcomes/impacts. A change or conceptual model shows relationships among key constructs (i.e., influences on the outcome of interest) and outcomes, and

Table 1.2   Summary of Key Considerations for Working With Change Agents and Other Stakeholders in LEAP High Schools

Organization: LEAP high schools

Category	Description
Identify key stakeholders.	After school district approval, initial contact was made with the principal, who identified an ongoing contact person in the school. The ongoing contact usually became the LEAP champion; however, in some cases, this was not the person initially identified as the best "champion" by the principal. The LEAP champion provided the linkage to LEAP intervention staff and facilitated communication and local school planning. Local planning within the school was done by the school-based LEAP team. LEAP staff also worked closely with all teachers and staff involved in LEAP in each school.
Identify change agents.	PE and health education (or other designated) teachers, school nurse (as available at the schools), school wellness coordinator (as available), school media staff/librarian, and any others interested in promoting physical activity in girls by serving on school LEAP team.
Describe approach to ongoing communication with stakeholders and change agents.	There were several types of ongoing communication including the LEAP Lookout (newsletter) and an electronic listserv. In addition, there were regularly scheduled central and school workshops and planning meetings with the LEAP teams. There was also regular communication with administrators as well as one planned central administrator meeting.
Describe the primary roles that stakeholders, including change agents, will play throughout the intervention process.	The change agents implemented all components of LEAP in the schools with the guidance of the LEAP interventionists. Teachers and staff in the local schools identified local resources, for example guest instructors in PE, as well as additional local stakeholders. Each LEAP team conducted assessment, planning, and implementation based on local school needs and resources. LEAP staff provided training, consultation, information, and connections to resources to facilitate the local schools' processes (see Worksheet 4.1 for specific roles).

conveys assumptions about the causal processes through which an intervention is supposed to work (Chen, 2015). Change models should guide both intervention strategies and impact/outcome measurement. Otherwise, a planning team may carry out a great intervention, but the evaluation may be for a different program than the one that took place.

A poor understanding of how the program, policy, or practice innovation is expected to produce desired results can lead to great disappointment and tensions among stakeholders. It also makes it very difficult to create appropriate adaptations during implementation, as there is no shared understanding of what is important. Having a clear and detailed understanding of the program, policy, or practice—including how it should result in expected changes and how to effectively communicate this to all stakeholders—also facilitates collaboration. It takes time to work out these details, but it is time well spent.

The example of a conceptual model presented in Figure 1.3 draws from program theory in evaluation (Chen, 2015), approaches to changing environments (Commers et al., 2007), and conceptualization of mechanisms through which environments influence behavior (Kremers et al., 2010). The environment can influence the outcomes/impacts through four possible pathways: (1) environmental conditions affect outcomes/impacts directly; for example, air pollution affects health; (2) environmental conditions affect outcomes/impacts via behavior; for example, being outdoors cues physical activity in children, which improves health; (3) environmental conditions affect outcomes/impacts via mediating factors; for example, cognitively mediated stress affects health; and (4) environmental conditions influence outcomes/impacts via perception-mediated influence on health behavior; for example, social norms for physical activity increase physical activity, which enhances health (Commers et al., 2007).

The conceptual model for each project will likely be unique to that project, reflecting a theory- and evidence-based understanding of the problem and mechanisms through which the problem influences behavior and/or outcomes/impacts of interest. Furthermore, conceptual/change models are intended to be helpful, flexible guides that the planning team can use to navigate intervention implementation and evaluation in complex, real-world settings. It is not useful to "force" reality to fit the model; rather, the model should help the planning team better understand and approximate reality. This, in turn, should result in a better intervention plan as well as a better evaluation plan.

LEAP Case Illustration

LEAP was guided by a social ecological framework informed by social cognitive theory (Pate et al., 2007). The model, developed as part of the planning process, indicated that intervention activities would positively influence girls' enjoyment of physical activity, self-efficacy, and social support, which would in turn positively impact physical activity, reflected as Pathways 3 and 4 in Figure 1.3. The conceptual model was used to develop intervention methods and strategies that facilitate enjoyment, self-efficacy,

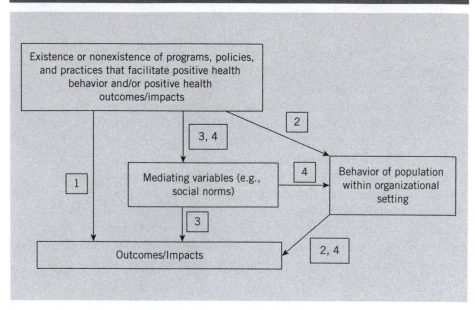

Figure 1.3 Conceptual Model for Environmental Influences on Outcomes/Impacts With Numbered Pathways Showing Mechanisms of Influence

Sources: Adapted from Chen (2015), Commers et al. (2007), and Kremers et al. (2010).

and a socially supportive school environment, as well as to guide selection of constructs that should be measured in the impact/outcome evaluation. Analyses conducted subsequent to the LEAP intervention showed that increases in enjoyment partially mediated the positive effects of the LEAP intervention (Dishman et al., 2004) and that self-efficacy moderated the relations between changes in physical activity and perceived social support (Dishman, Saunders, Motl, Dowda, & Pate, 2009), supporting the inclusion of these constructs in causal models.

Program planning, implementation, and evaluation are best conducted within collaborative interdisciplinary teams.

Working within a collaborative team process has the potential to greatly enhance the quality of program planning, implementation, and evaluation (Bartholomew et al., 2006). An interdisciplinary team is more likely to have the broad perspective and variety of skills needed to carry out the steps in this process effectively. The planning team, such as a research or project team, may have membership that is internal, such as a curriculum committee within a school; external, such as a health department project team working with a school on an afterschool program; or blended (internal and external), such as staff and volunteers in a nonprofit organization.

Many of the principles for effective working relationships also apply to relationships within the planning team (McDonough & Doucette, 2001). Team member roles including intervention and evaluation roles should be clearly defined, communication should be clear, and decision-making processes should be transparent. In the early stages of program planning and evaluation planning (Phases I through III) for a program, policy, or practice innovation that has not been carried out, it is ideal for intervention and evaluation team members to work together to ensure that they have the same detailed understanding of the program, policy, or practice and its conceptual basis. This will enable them to develop plans that are congruent. Intervention staff will need to operationalize the program plan into appropriate intervention strategies whereas evaluation staff will need to base the implementation monitoring plan on the detailed understanding of the innovation.

Throughout the planning process the roles of the intervention team members should remain distinct from the roles of the evaluation team members because evaluators are ultimately concerned with assessing implementation and outcomes/impacts and are not involved in the intervention process. This role division becomes very clear in Phases IV through V, in which interventionists facilitate program, policy, or practice change whereas evaluators carry out evaluation activities.

Due to the importance and ubiquity of team approaches to conducting program and evaluation planning and the necessity of application of concepts for learning, this textbook takes the perspective that you will develop an implementation monitoring plan for a specific program, policy, or practice change in a defined setting as a member of a planning team as you move through the steps. Accordingly, you will derive the most benefit from this textbook if you actively apply each step in the implementation monitoring process to a specific project in a specific setting, ideally as a member of a small team; the project may be real or hypothetical. The worksheets presented in subsequent chapters are designed to facilitate both the planning and learning process.

KEY POINTS FOR PREIMPLEMENTATION PLANNING

- Effective plans are developed through a systematic process that includes an assessment of needs and interests of the priority audience.

- Program planning and evaluation planning are concurrent and linked processes.

- Successful implementation and evaluation entails identifying and working with stakeholders and change agents within the implementing setting.

- The evaluation plan and intervention strategies, materials, and media messages should be guided by a conceptual or change model.

- The quality of the program planning, implementation, and evaluation process is enhanced by working within a collaborative, interdisciplinary team with clearly defined roles for team members.

Implementation Planning

Implementation planning takes place after a specific project has been funded and/or approved. Basic planning has been completed, the approach approved, and now the team is preparing to put the program, policy, and/or organizational practices into place within a specific setting or settings. Implementation planning consists of five steps to describe the intervention and context in more detail and to prepare for detailed planning for implementation monitoring.

Figure II.1   The Implementation Planning and Monitoring Process, With Phase II, Implementation Planning, Highlighted

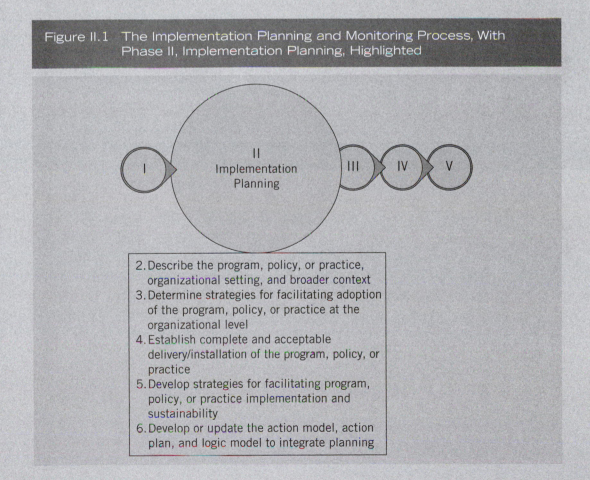

2. Describe the program, policy, or practice, organizational setting, and broader context
3. Determine strategies for facilitating adoption of the program, policy, or practice at the organizational level
4. Establish complete and acceptable delivery/installation of the program, policy, or practice
5. Develop strategies for facilitating program, policy, or practice implementation and sustainability
6. Develop or update the action model, action plan, and logic model to integrate planning

All things appear and disappear because
of the concurrence of causes and
conditions. Nothing ever exists entirely
alone; everything is in relation to
everything else.

-Buddha

Describe the Program, Policy, or Practice, Organizational Setting, and Broader Context

In Step 1, you developed a program proposal or plan to carry out a program or create a policy or practice change in a setting. This proposal or plan has subsequently been approved or funded; it is now time for the more detailed implementation planning process to begin, with Step 2. Successful implementation monitoring and process evaluation are based on a comprehensive understanding of the intended program, policy, or practice change and the setting into which they will be introduced. Therefore in Step 2, ideally as a member of a planning team, you will begin implementation planning processes that will position you to develop and carry out a comprehensive implementation monitoring plan as your progress through the steps in this textbook.

Describe the program, policy, or practice that is to be implemented.

The program, policy, or practice description should include the components, activities, media products, conceptual guide, and other elements as appropriate, as well as a description of the overall intervention approach. After a project is funded or approved, you revisit the original plan or proposal to describe it in detail. In this step, you should describe the innovation's purpose, change or conceptual model, objectives, strategies, expected outcomes/impacts, and other details as previously planned (Saunders, Evans, & Joshi, 2005). Some of these elements may need to be spelled out in more detail, as they may have been in abbreviated form in the proposal that was funded or approved. The level of detail should be sufficient so that someone not on the

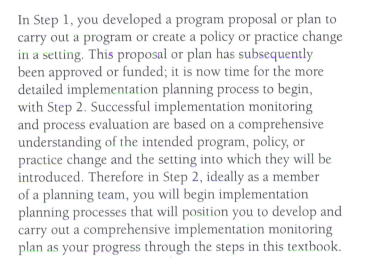

Learning Objectives

By the end of the chapter, you will be able to

1. Describe the program, policy, or practice that is to be implemented

2. Portray the organization in which the program, policy, or practice will be implemented

3. Define the broader context of the organization in which the program, policy, or practice will be implemented

planning team would have a thorough understanding of the program, policy, or practice change. Below are elements that should be included in the description.

Setting/Scope of Study

Describe the organizational setting or settings for which the innovation was designed, for example, nonprofit, school, faith-based, etc. Also indicate the number of sites, the geographic spread, and the number of partners and/or collaborators involved.

Purpose

Describe the study and innovation purposes. The purpose of the program, policy, or practice change is project specific and usually refers to its primary focus or what the project implementers hope to achieve. The purpose may also be reflected through primary and secondary objectives, aims, and/or hypotheses, as applicable.

Change Model

Describe the change or conceptual model that guides the planning process for the program, policy, or practice change. Articulate in detail how the program, policy, or practice is supposed to have the desired effects on outcomes/impacts of interest. It should be clear how the conceptual model elements inform intervention activities, strategies, and events. The conceptual model should also clearly link to the measured impacts and outcomes of the study.

Program, Policy, or Practice Description

Describe the components or elements of the desired program, policy, or practice and levels of change attempted (e.g., individual, interpersonal, policy, physical environment) as well as the methods, strategies, materials, and media messages that will be used to facilitate uptake of the innovation at each level. The length and duration of intervention activities and frequency of sessions, if applicable, should also be described. A detailed timeline should sequence all activities and events that are part of the intervention process.

It is also important to describe program coverage in terms of numbers of sites and geographic spread. For example, are changes made in a single or multiple settings? Is it situated locally or across one state, multiple states, one country, or multiple countries? Increasing the number of sites and the geographic spread increases the complexity and amount of resources it will take both to implement and to monitor implementation.

Intervention Implementation Approach

The approach to implementation originates from the planning team's philosophical stance and past experiences concerning how best to work with stakeholders to install a particular program, policy, or practice within a given setting. This philosophy or general approach may operationalize into very different forms of working with stakeholders to facilitate uptake of programs, policies, and practices.

Describe the general approach to implementation, including conceptualization of the innovation as a product versus a process, the timing and level of stakeholder involvement from late to early engagement and little to extensive involvement, and the role of the planning team in delivery or installation of the program, policy, or practice with direct versus indirect delivery.

Conceptualization of the Innovation

Innovations may be conceptualized on a continuum with endpoints that range from "product" to "process." Conventionally, an innovation is often conceptualized as a product that is viewed as an enduring "package" to be delivered into a setting. It is standardized and expected to have a similar form in all settings. The innovation is seen as a stable entity that does not interact with the setting and therefore has little variability from site to site. **Adaptation** or **reinvention** (Rogers, 2003), changes or modifications to the innovation by the user (Rogers, 2003, p. 476), are typically discouraged. For example, a product-oriented innovation might specify a list of topics and activities with preestablished frequency and duration that must be carried out within a specific time frame. This view is derived from a biomedical model in which the "innovation" is analogous to a drug that tends to act similarly within similar physiological systems whether it is administered in a hospital, clinic, home, or school (Chen, 2015).

At the other end of the continuum is an alternative perspective of the innovation as a standardized process, defined in interaction within a given setting due to the dynamic complexity of the setting. In effect, the innovation cannot be fully realized until it interacts with that setting. This view is consistent with **mutual adaptation** (Berman & McLaughlin, 1975), in which the innovation and implementing setting are changed (Rogers, 2003, p. 425). The function is standardized across settings; however, the form may vary. Accordingly, appropriate adaptation is encouraged. For example, an innovation may specify guidelines or principles along with some examples that can be used to adapt current practices to meet a common standard. This view is consistent with that of Hawe and colleagues, who conceptualized an intervention as an event or series of events introduced into a dynamic and evolving setting over time (Hawe, Shiell, & Riley, 2009).

Experiences of researchers over many years and across multiple fields are consistent with the perspective that interventions in field-based settings are processes; for example, adaptation of innovations or mutual adaptation between the innovation and the setting during adoption and implementation are ubiquitous (Berman & McLaughlin, 1975; Dearing, 2008; Rogers, 2003). Fortunately, adaptations to improve "fit" are associated with both implementation and sustainability (Durlak & DuPre, 2008; Scheirer, 2005). In reality, many intervention approaches are hybrids of these extreme points on the product–process continuum, though a given planning team may have strong tendencies toward a particular view.

The Gatehouse Project illustrates an approach that is consistent with these principles (Patton, Bond, Butler, & Glover, 2003). This project aimed to enhance students' sense of school connection, reduce health risk behavior, and improve wellbeing. This was accomplished with a flexible, adaptive approach that addressed the school social context. Implementation was standardized around a survey of the school social environment, creation of a school-based action team, and use of strategies matched to a school's profile of need.

If the planning team conceptualizes innovations as context-independent products, it tends to develop "stable" products to be introduced into a variety of local contexts. The expectation is that the form will be similar from locale to locale. Alternatively, if the planning team conceptualizes innovations as a process, it will tend to develop approaches that allow for adaptation during the implementation process and that may be based on common goals, guidelines, and/or principles. The expectation is that the underlying principles or process is standardized across settings although the form may vary from site to site. We will discuss the implications of this continuum further as we define the concept of fidelity in the next chapter.

Timing and Degree of Change Agent and Stakeholder Involvement

The timing of stakeholder involvement can vary on a continuum of early to late engagement in the program life cycle, and the degree or extent of stakeholder involvement can range from minimal involvement to extensive participatory engagement. Level and timing of stakeholder engagement can also vary independently. For example, it is possible for the planning team to contact stakeholders early in the process, but without involving them very much, and conversely, to contact stakeholders late in the process with expectations of extensive engagement. Because engaging stakeholders entails relationship development, the process usually takes time, which makes it risky to engage stakeholders late in the process, when timelines are tight. In participatory processes such as Community Based Participatory Research, (Minkler & Wallerstein, 2008) insiders, who are stakeholders within the implementation setting, and outsiders, who are stakeholders outside the setting such as the planning team, work together from the beginning to identify needs and the focus of project, and then to develop and carry out an intervention.

Delivery/Installation of the Program, Policy, or Practice

The way the program, policy, or practice innovation is installed or delivered also has implications for both implementation and sustainability (Durlak & DuPre, 2008; Scheirer, 2005). Delivery/installation pertains largely to who carries out or facilitates the change process. If the planning team installs or delivers the program policy, or practice in the setting, it is termed **direct delivery/installation**. If setting change agents deliver or install the innovation with or without guidance from the planning team, it is termed **indirect delivery/installation**.

Traditionally, direct delivery or installation by an agent of the planning team that is external to an implementing setting is done in the context of an efficacy study and is not intended to simulate real-world conditions (Mercer, DeVinney, Fine, Green, & Dougherty, 2007). The planning team is likely to have more control over the implementation process, which may minimize contextual influences; however, this reduces the generalizability to real-world settings (Glasgow, Lichtenstein, & Marcus, 2003). Conversely, indirect delivery or installation as described here involves the planning team working with setting stakeholders by providing training and technical assistance to internal change agents, who in turn implement the program, policy, or practice; this approach is much less controlled and much messier, but is also more realistic and generalizable. Given systems dynamics in which the innovation is defined in interaction with the setting, the latter approach presents a better "test" of the program, policy, or practice in actual, real-world settings.

The three elements of the intervention implementation approach are summarized in Figure 2.1: stakeholder involvement, innovation concept, and innovation delivery/installation. Use Worksheet 2.1 to summarize the description of the program, policy, or practice and the intervention implementation approach. This worksheet is intended to be a summary of previous planning. However, if discussion has not taken place prior to this point, the planning team will need to come to consensus on these issues about the stakeholder involvement, innovation concept, and program, policy, or practice delivery/installation.

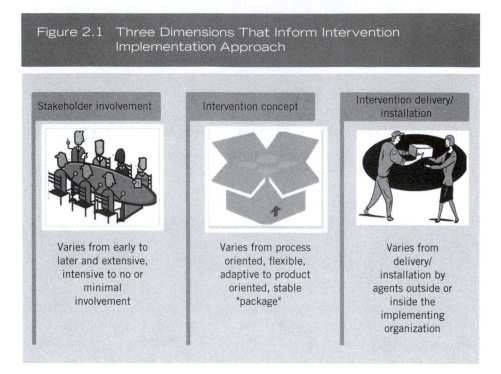

Figure 2.1   Three Dimensions That Inform Intervention Implementation Approach

Stakeholder involvement

Varies from early to later and extensive, intensive to no or minimal involvement

Intervention concept

Varies from process oriented, flexible, adaptive to product oriented, stable "package"

Intervention delivery/ installation

Varies from delivery/ installation by agents outside or inside the implementing organization

LEAP Case Illustration

An example of Worksheet 2.1 describing Lifestyle Education for Activity Program (LEAP) is presented in Table 2.1. LEAP took place in 12 intervention and 12 control high schools in South Carolina and entailed the research team partnering with school teachers and staff. LEAP promoted physical activity among high school girls using a unique school-based intervention designed to be adapted by teachers and staff at each school. It was based on a public health approach emphasizing school environment and instructional practices for promotion of physical activity in adolescent girls (Saunders, Ward, Felton, Dowda, & Pate, 2006). There was no LEAP curriculum; rather, each school participated in standardized training, received technical assistance based on need, and adapted instructional practices and the school environment to address the LEAP principles in a manner that best fit the school's needs and resources. See Table 2.1 for a detailed description of the LEAP study and intervention process.

Worksheet 2.1   Template for Summarizing Elements of the Innovation and
                Intervention Implementation Approach

Name of program, policy, or practice innovation: _____

Category	Description
Setting(s) for which innovation was designed (e.g., nonprofit, school, faith-based, etc.)	
Scope of study (e.g., number of settings and/or sites, geographic spread, number of partners or collaborators involved)	
Primary and secondary study outcomes (as reflected in the change model)	
Primary and secondary intervention objectives	
Primary and secondary populations (as applicable) for whom innovation was designed	
Change model (conceptual framework) guiding intervention planning	
Program, policy, or practice components and component descriptions	
Timing, duration, and frequency of intervention activities, sessions, and events (as applicable)	
Materials, media products, equipment, etc. (as applicable)	
Specific methods, strategies, activities, etc. and their conceptual basis	
Intervention implementation approach (process versus product conceptualization, timing and extent of stakeholder involvement, and insider versus outsider delivery)	

Portray the organization in which the program, policy, or practice will be implemented.

The description of the organization in which the program, policy, or practice will be implemented should include its mission, characteristics and structures, populations it serves, and those who will be intended beneficiaries of the innovation. In addition to describing the program, policy, or practice and

Table 2.1   Summary of LEAP Intervention Elements and Approach

Name of Program, Policy, or Practice: Lifestyle Education for Activity Program (LEAP)

Category	Description
Setting(s) for which innovation was designed	Public high schools
Scope of study	Twelve intervention and 12 control high schools (total number of schools = 24) within South Carolina; the intervention schools were the primary organizational partners.
Primary and secondary study outcomes	Primary study outcomes were percentage of girls engaging in physical activity (i.e., vigorous physical activity and moderate to vigorous physical activity); secondary study outcomes were scores on measures of determinants of physical activity in high school girls (i.e., perceived self-efficacy, social support, social norms, enjoyment).
Primary and secondary intervention objectives	The primary intervention objective was to change personal, social, and environmental factors related to physical activity for high school girls in the school setting by focusing on school instructional practices (primarily in physical education) and the school environment.
Primary and secondary populations for innovation	The primary population was high school girls; the secondary populations were teachers and school staff in the high school setting, who worked directly with the high school girls to promote physical activity.
Change model (conceptual framework) guiding intervention planning	A socio-ecological model drawn primarily from social cognitive theory informed an understanding of behavior change; the Coordinated School Health Program (CSHP) guided changes to instructional practices and school environment.
Program, policy, or practice components and component descriptions	LEAP was a multicomponent intervention that included a gender-sensitive physical education (PE) program with activities designed to be fun and age appropriate for high school girls. LEAP also emphasized developing physical activity self-efficacy and self-management skills in a school environment that promoted and supported physical activity for young women. LEAP included six components of a CSHP organized into two categories: *Instructional Practices* included LEAP PE and health education. The goal of LEAP PE was to provide girls with the physical and behavioral skills needed to adopt a physically active lifestyle during their teenage years and to maintain that active lifestyle into adulthood. The goal of health education was to reinforce messages delivered in PE concerning the benefits of physical activity and to provide training in behavioral skills that will enable students to initiate and maintain a physically active lifestyle. *Healthy school environment* included policies and practices related to physical activity (PA), school health services, faculty staff health promotion, and family and community involvement. The goal of *Healthy school environment* was to institute schoolwide policies and practices that promote the physical activity within and outside of the school. The goal of school health services was to increase the involvement of school health services (i.e., the school nurse) in the creation of a school environment that supports and reinforces physical activity

Category	Description
	among students. The goal of faculty and staff health promotion was to create a supportive school environment with physically active adult role models. The goal of family and community involvement was to assist students in being physically active outside of school by enhancing parental support and by linking students to physical activity opportunities outside of school (Ward et al., 2006).
Timing, duration, and frequency of intervention activities, sessions, and events, as applicable	LEAP PE was integrated into ninth-grade PE; health education was implemented based on the individual school's approach to offering health education; and the school environment components were implemented via the LEAP Team, which met and planned based on schedules of LEAP Team members within each school. LEAP Team membership and size varied by school but often included some combination of PE teacher, health (or other classroom) teacher, school nurse, wellness coordinator, and media specialist.
Materials, media products, equipment, etc., as applicable	LEAP intervention staff developed a variety of training and support materials for usage in 10 workshops in year one and 6 workshops in year two (e.g., behavioral skills, sport education model, PE resistance training, aerobics instruction, kickboxing); LEAP programs (Communities-in-motion, Active Teacher of the Month); a variety of instructional handouts (Female role models, How parents can encourage girls to be physically active, Promoting PA outside the gym, PA prescription pads, Fitness calendar); LEAP tools (How do I know it's LEAP? LEAP strategic plan, LEAP linkages); and media tools (LEAP Lookout newsletters, stall talkers, school librarian resource kit) (Ward et al., 2006).
Specific methods, strategies, activities, etc., and their conceptual basis	*Instructional practices* in LEAP were based largely on social cognitive theory and designed to develop physical activity self-efficacy, behavioral skills, and enhanced enjoyment of physical activity. Accordingly, LEAP PE incorporated "girl-friendly" practices to enhance social interaction and fun while learning skills and being physically active. Strategies to enhance skills and self-efficacy included demonstration, practice, goal setting, and feedback. LEAP PE used strategies to enhance social interaction, obtained input from girls about preferred physical activities, and organized the class into small, ongoing social groups. *Healthy school environment* practices were based on the CHSP components and were led by an internal LEAP Team that assessed the school environment, developed plans, and implemented them to promote and support physical activity among girls by creating opportunities for girls and promoting PA and PA opportunities. LEAP intervention staff provided training and ongoing support for all of these activities (Ward et al., 2006).
Intervention implementation approach: process versus product conceptualization, timing and extent of stakeholder involvement, and insider versus outsider delivery	LEAP was implemented by teachers and staff with training, guidance, and support from the LEAP intervention staff. LEAP was flexible/adaptable and process oriented, allowing each school to adapt the intervention guided by the LEAP "Essential Elements" (described in Worksheet 4.1) to better fit local contexts. There was no LEAP curriculum, for example; rather, each school participated in standardized training, received technical assistance based on need, and adapted instructional practices and the school environment to address the LEAP principles in a manner that best fit needs and resources. The LEAP project team developed LEAP principles prior to approaching the schools, and worked with them very closely in partnership during the implementation process.

Sources: Adapted from Felton et al. (2005), Pate et al. (2005, 2007), and Ward et al. (2006).

implementation approach in detail, it is essential to describe the organization(s) into which it will be implemented. This includes its mission, characteristics and structures, populations served, those who will be intended beneficiaries of the program, policy, or practice change, and the broader context of the organization.

This section is heavily informed by a settings perspective (Poland, Krupa, & McCall, 2009). Poland and colleagues' "settings approach" is particularly applicable to innovations involving program, policy, or practice changes within organizational settings due to their emphasis on contextual factors, stakeholder involvement, and social change.

There is a tendency to view the implementation setting or settings as a convenient site in which to carry out the innovation. As will become clear in this chapter, the setting has a much larger role in the change process than might be assumed traditionally. In fact, it would be difficult to overstate the importance of the implementation setting and its context, which includes the populations served as well as its internal (e.g., administrators, staff, and teachers) and external (e.g., parents and community agency collaborators) stakeholders.

Mission and Characteristics

Identify the mission of the implementing organization, which is generally straightforward and easy to determine, as it is usually publicly known. It is important to identify the mission at the outset of the implementation planning process, discuss it with setting stakeholders, and refer to it repeatedly throughout the entire project. In most cases, the goals of the planning team will not be completely congruent with the mission and goals of the implementing setting, at least initially. Therefore, it is very important to be mindful of the formal and informal priorities of the implementing setting and to work in such a way as not to challenge those priorities. A set of exploratory questions, adapted from Poland and colleagues (Poland et al., 2009) provides guidance for understanding the organizational setting (see Table 2.2). According to Poland and colleagues, these questions should be answered by multiple individuals and can be posed in a reworded format to stakeholders within the setting. Some of the questions may be answered by the implementation team through informal observation while spending time in the setting, but ultimately, it is best to obtain answers to these questions via conversations with people in the implementing setting.

Structures and Processes

Identify levels of the organization and the formal and informal structures and processes of each organization with which you are working. For structures, start

What makes this category of setting (e.g., hospitals) different from (or similar to) other categories of settings (e.g., schools, workplaces)?

What diversity can be expected within this category of setting? (e.g., inner city vs. suburban or rural schools; large, corporate vs. small, family-run workplaces, etc.)

What assumptions are usually made about this setting? Are these assumptions warranted in this case?

How has the conceptualization (as well as role and nature) of this setting evolved over time?

What elements of the [structural, social and/or physical aspects of the organization] influence [focus of program, policy, or practice] in this setting?

To what extent do the following aspects of the psychosocial environment have a bearing on [focus of program, policy, or practice] and the possibilities for intervention in this setting?

- Social composition with respect to age, gender, race, and class
- Stress, decision latitude, control over pace, and demands of work
- Status hierarchies
- Work–life balance
- Behavioral norms and expectations (social sanctions)
- Quality of human relations (trust, reciprocity, social capital and social cohesion, bullying)
- Lines of accountability and reporting structures
- Organizational culture and readiness for change
- Internal politics, recent history of accommodation, or prior conflict

Source: Adapted from Poland et al. (2009, p. 508).

with the formal organizational chart but don't stop there. What are the units and departments within the organization? In what ways are they connected? Learn about and document informal processes, including how formal and informal communication takes place, how things really operate, and what a typical day is like within the organization. This understanding will develop over time. For example, formal structure indicates that the principal is the head of the organization in the school setting and the physical education teacher is the official person who addresses physical activity in the school. However, in terms of informal processes, the assistant principal may have more day-to-day influence on school activities, and there may be a science teacher or receptionist who is enthusiastic about promoting physical activity. These informal contact persons can potentially be as important for implementation as the formally identified contact persons.

Resources and Resource Flexibility

Describe the availability of resources and economic indicators for the organization. Total budget and budget related to the area of interest is an economic indicator that speaks to total resources and organizational priorities relative to the area of interest. However, additional resource considerations include available staff in the areas of interest, and the ability of staff to take on new tasks or restructure daily practices. In many settings, including nonprofit and educational settings, overburdened staff may be the norm, resulting in low resource flexibility. For example, schools may have school nurses who are interested in health promotion, but these individuals may have so many existing responsibilities and requirements that it is not feasible to involve them in new intervention activities. Organizational staff may be available but require extensive training and/or extensive ongoing support to carry out a new set of activities within the setting. Frequency of staff turnover, which necessitates additional training, is also an important resource consideration.

Another potential resource in some organizations is the availability of volunteers at the individual level and organizational partners at the organizational level. As with paid staff, the resource assessment for working with volunteers and organizational partners entails considering their current roles and responsibilities, flexibility within these roles and responsibilities, expertise and needed training, and commitment to follow through on tasks.

Populations Served

In most organizational settings, the population(s) served will be clear as the planning team is often working with this particular implementing setting specifically to reach this population, also known as the priority audience or priority population. In many cases the planning team is intentionally focusing on a subset of the population(s) served; however, it is important to be mindful of the other populations in the setting and how carrying out the program, policy, or practice may affect them.

After clarifying the population(s) served, describe the priority audience for the program, policy, or practice change. This should go beyond basic demographic and epidemiologic descriptions to encompass needs and interests of potential participants, both broad as well as specific to the innovation focus.

Use Worksheet 2.2 to summarize the preliminary set of organizational characteristics.

Worksheet 2.2   Template for Summarizing Organizational Characteristics

(This information is needed for all organizations involved in the intervention.)

Characteristic	Description
Geographic location	
Size and age of organization	
Resource availability and economic indicators	
Mission/primary purpose	
Current organizational priorities	
Units and structures within an organization	
Primary mechanisms for/recipients of internal communication	
Primary mechanisms for/recipients of external communication	
Population(s) served by organization (detailed description)	
Service(s) provided (detailed descriptions)	
Priority population for program, policy, or practice and detailed, data-based characteristics (e.g., demographic, epidemiological, needs, interests)	
Relevant historical information	
Relevant psychosocial environment information	
Other relevant information	

LEAP Case Illustration

The summary of organizational characteristics for one LEAP school, illustrating use of Worksheet 2.2, is described in Table 2.3. The LEAP project team compiled a profile for each school by conducting a formative assessment of each school at the beginning of the project.

Define the broader context of the organization in which the program, policy, or practice will be implemented.

It is important to be aware of potentially influential factors in the external environment such as competing events, controversy about the innovation, external political factors, history, and events that happen concurrently with

Table 2.3 LEAP Organizational Characteristics for One Case Study School

Organization: LEAP case study school

Characteristic	Description
Geographic location	Suburban school district in the Midlands of South Carolina
Size and age of organization	Approximately 1700 students
Resource availability and economic indicators	Approximately 11% of students received reduced-price lunch
Mission/primary purpose	Educational institution
Current organizational priorities	Academic achievement and student wellbeing
Units and structures within an organization	Grades 9–12; formative assessment provided additional information about the academic schedule, instructional program, and other services. Students were required to complete one Carnegie unit of PE and most students met this requirement by taking one 90-minute class of PE for one semester in the ninth grade. Health education was delivered through a required, one-semester course in the ninth grade.
Primary mechanisms for/ recipients of internal communication	Primarily newsletters (at the time of the LEAP intervention)
Primary mechanisms for/ recipients of external communication	
Population(s) served by organization (detailed description)	Students in Grades 9–12; 48% female; 50% white, 45% African-American, and 5% Asian or Hispanic.
Service(s) provided (detailed descriptions)	In addition to educational services, the school employed a school nurse who provided student health services 2 to 3 days per week. All ninth and eleventh graders received health screenings, and the nurse coordinated on-site health screenings for teachers and staff. An environmental assessment showed that the school had seven playing fields, two gymnasiums, and eight showers. Physical activity and physical activity opportunities received minimal media attention in the school newspaper and bulletin boards. School policy permitted students, teachers, staff, and agencies to use the grounds and facilities before and after school and on weekends (if they wished to take advantage of this).
Priority population for program, policy, or practice and detailed, data-based characteristics (e.g., demographic, epidemiological, needs, interests)	Ninth-grade girls; average age 14.5 years; 46% white, 44% African-American, 10% other racial/ethnic groups

Characteristic	Description
Relevant historical and other information	The school has a history of supporting physical activity and wellness and had a supportive school administrator. There was more emphasis on major sports events and competitions, with less opportunity for other youth. The school was amenable to working within a committee framework for implementation (i.e., the LEAP Team). LEAP identified a strong champion as the primary liaison between the school and the research team.

Source: Adapted from Felton et al. (2005).

the program (Scheirer, Shediac, & Cassady, 1995; Viadro, Earp, & Altpeter, 1997). The organization influences and is influenced by its broader context, as the organization is not a closed or isolated system. The neighborhood, community, region, and state in which the organization is situated define its broader context.

Most organizations are part of a **multilevel organizational system**, and nearly all organizations have membership in **interorganizational networks.** A multilevel organizational system refers to the larger system of which the implementation setting is considered a part (e.g., classrooms within schools, schools within school districts). It is important to identify these larger systems, taking into account that there will likely be more than one. For example, schools are organized within school districts, which are regulated by a state-level agency, which are subject to state and federal regulations. There will be variation from site to site within organizations that are part of a larger system such as schools in a school district, so it will be important to characterize each site.

Interorganizational networks are multiple organizations participating in formal groups (e.g., professional associations) and informal groups (e.g., loosely organized coalitions) of organizations. The organization or people within it may also belong to influential community coalitions and professional groups at local, state, and national levels. For example, a nonprofit organization may also be a member of a professional association composed of organizational members. These interorganizational linkages can influence implementation positively by providing important resources or negatively through conflicting norms or guidelines. Laws, regulations, standards, and guidelines imposed by local, regional, state, or federal agencies; accrediting bodies; and/or professional associations are very important influences on implementation and sustainability.

It is very challenging to facilitate change in a setting that is strongly influenced by outside forces; in fact, you may need to intervene at higher levels of the system in these situations. For example, changes in nutrition policies and practices at youth-serving organizations, including schools, must consider federal funding requirements and state-level policies and guidelines. Changes to physical education in school settings must consider state and district curricula and/or standards. It will be very difficult and likely counterproductive to attempt changes that are not consistent with current federal, state, and accrediting body guidelines. If there are problems with these higher level guidelines, then advocacy for change in laws and regulations may be required. This is typically an entirely new and separate undertaking with a greater scope than most setting-specific innovations, and it often requires considerable resources including coalition development among individuals and organizations working together for a common cause. Therefore, it is important to find out about these requirements up front.

Poland (Poland et al., 2009, p. 508) recommends the following questions to explore the broader context:

- How does the setting interact with other related settings and systems as well as the local environment to accomplish its goals?

- What is the role of the broader sociopolitical context in supporting or limiting change efforts? Is there a need for higher level policy change and advocacy work across settings and locales?

Use Worksheet 2.3 to describe and summarize organizational characteristics related to multilevel systems, interorganizational networks, and other external factors.

LEAP Case Illustration

Table 2.4 illustrates Worksheet 2.3 using one LEAP intervention school. This worksheet describes how this school was part of multilevel systems as well as a participant in several interorganizational networks that were relevant to LEAP.

Where to Begin?

There are many sources of the needed information to begin to understand a setting including records, data that have been collected, and the original proposal, as applicable. The best approach, however, is to work with setting stakeholders to understand the setting, its history, the broader context, and the populations that it serves. This necessarily takes place in an ongoing process.

Worksheet 2.3   Template for Preliminary List of Organizational Characteristics Related to Multilevel Systems, Interorganizational Networks, and Other External Factors

Characteristic	Description
Description of neighborhood, community, region, and/or state including economic indicators	
History and role of organization within its broader context	
Membership as part of a multilevel system, including regulatory and funding agencies	
Relationship with "higher" levels in multilevel system	
Relevant laws, regulations, standards, guidelines, and policies	
Relationship with/potential influences from other members of multilevel system	
Influence from accrediting and other professional regulatory bodies	
Membership of organizational agents (individuals) in professional groups, coalitions, partnerships, or other interorganizational groups	
Potential influence of interorganizational groups	
Possible relevant national, state, and/or local media and events	
Other relevant information	

Table 2.4   One LEAP School's Organizational Characteristics Related to Multilevel Systems, Interorganizational Networks, and Other External Factors

Organization: LEAP case study school

Characteristic	Description
Description of neighborhood, community, region, and/or state including economic indicators	The school is in one of the most rapidly growing school districts in South Carolina and serves both suburban and rural communities. The school is less than 30 minutes from Columbia, where state government, the University of South Carolina, and Fort Jackson are located. Several industries are located in the school's attendance zone. The school district is recognized for academic excellence.
History and role of organization within its broader context	The school opened on a 60-acre campus in the fall of 1995 and was relatively new during the LEAP project. The class of 1998 was the first full class to graduate. The school is known for its athletic programs.

(Continued)

Table 2.4 (Continued)

Characteristic	Description
Membership as part of a multilevel system, including regulatory and funding agencies and potential influence from other members of multilevel system	Three middle schools feed into this high school, which is one of five high schools in this school district. All school districts and schools are regulated by the State Department of Education. The school district serves as a primary resource and supporter for physical education, physical activity promotion, and health education in the school. The State Department of Health regulates and supports school nurses.
Relevant laws, regulations, standards, guidelines, and policies	State PE standards apply to this and other LEAP high schools. LEAP was designed to be in compliance with state physical education standards.
Membership of organizational agents in professional groups, coalitions, partnerships, or other interorganizational groups and potential influence of interorganizational groups	Physical education teachers are active members of a statewide physical activity professional organization that is very influential in supporting and promoting physical education.
Possible relevant national, state, and/or local media and events	The school has been a recipient of "Healthy School Awards," coordinated through a school health coalition and the State Department of Education. This program is based on principles similar to those espoused in LEAP.

Source: Content from Felton et al. (2005).

In summary, it is important to describe, understand, and take into account the characteristics of the implementing organization, the populations served, and the priority population, as well as the organization's history, surrounding social systems including interorganizational linkages, and partnerships (Earp et al., 1997; Scheirer et al., 1995).

LEAP was a process-oriented intervention, but many school-based interventions are product oriented. Your task is to facilitate a discussion about the approach to implementing a new reading curriculum among middle school teachers and staff. They wish the program to be sustainable. The group has identified an evidence-based program that has been successful in controlled studies in other middle schools. What key points supporting a "product" orientation (i.e., implementing the evidence-based program with no adaptation) would you make? What key points supporting a "process" orientation (i.e., implementing the evidenced-based program with appropriate adaptation) would you make? What would be your final recommendation? Why?

KEY POINTS FOR DESCRIBING THE PROGRAM, POLICY, OR PRACTICE, ORGANIZATIONAL SETTING, AND THE BROADER CONTEXT

- The program, policy, or practice should be described completely including its purpose; change model; factors including components, methods, strategies, materials, media messages, duration, and frequency, as applicable; and intervention implementation approach.

- The intervention implementation approach is defined by conceptualization of the innovation on the product–process continuum, timing and degree of change agent and stakeholder involvement, and approach to delivery/installation of the innovation.

- An understanding of the organizational setting includes articulating its mission and characteristics; structures and processes; populations served; and broader professional, community, and larger contexts.

If you always do what you've always done, you'll always get what you've always got.

—Anonymous

Determine Strategies for Facilitating Adoption of the Program, Policy, or Practice at the Organizational Level

Before moving forward to the implementation phase, organizations potentially serving as the implementing settings must agree to participate in or adopt the program, policy, or practice. In this step, you, ideally as a member of the planning team, will describe the approach the intervention members of the team will take to facilitate organizational adoption of the innovation based on an understanding of the influences on the adoption process.

Adoption at the organizational level entails a decision to make full use of an innovation (Rogers, 2003, p. 473) and is typically a decision made by an administrator, decision maker, board of directors, or some other decision-making authority. Many adopters are individuals who can act somewhat independently of their organization, in addition to representing the organization. It is also possible for an adoption decision to be made sequentially or concurrently at multiple levels of responsibility within an organization. To facilitate adoption in a particular organizational setting or system, it is important to understand how adoption decisions are made. For example, in school settings, the planning team needs approval from the school district level prior to approaching the principal or school-level administrator, and approval is required at the school level prior to approaching classroom teachers or school staff about implementing a program, policy, or practice in that setting. Some principals may make decisions to adopt a program, policy, or practice change on their own, whereas others may do so after receiving input from school teachers and staff.

Learning Objectives

By the end of the chapter, you will be able to

1. Describe the steps needed to facilitate organizational adoption of a program, policy, or practice

2. Develop a plan detailing strategies for facilitating organizational adoption of a program, policy, or practice

It is important to note that adoption at the organizational level is necessary but not sufficient to facilitate implementation of new programs, policies, and practices. Formal adoption does not necessarily lead to implementation for any number of reasons. In some cases, adoption may be symbolic rather than substantive. For example, decision makers may want to appear cooperative but may lack organizational resources or commitment necessary for implementation. Implementation is typically accomplished by front line staff and must be facilitated at that level. However, the path to implementation must pass through organizational level adoption, so that is where we begin.

Describe the steps needed to facilitate organizational adoption of a program, policy, or practice.

Use the following steps to guide planning for facilitating an adoption decision for a program, policy, or practice change within an organizational setting:

1. Determine how adoption decisions are made within the organization.

2. Identify likely influences on the adoption decision-making process within the setting, and select appropriate strategies.

3. Develop appropriate strategies to facilitate the adoption decision based on factors that influence adoption in this setting.

These steps are discussed below.

Determine how adoption decisions are made within the organization.

Determining how adoption decisions are made within the organization includes identifying the decision-making time frame and who should be involved in the decision-making process within each organization involved. It is crucial to identify the decision-making entities and how decisions are made within the organization or organizations of interest. Even within a single system, there may be variation in how adoption decisions are made; for example, each division within a large corporation may have a different approach. Questions that the planning team can use to explore and understand the perspectives of organizational decision makers are provided in Table 3.1. This information

Table 3.1	Questions to Guide Understanding of the Perspectives of Organizational Decision Makers

Who are the decision-making entities within the organization?

What are their agendas, their stake in change or the status quo, and their access to resources?

What is the meaning of [focus of program, policy, or practice to be introduced] to decision makers?

How do power relations come into play in this setting?

What is the relative power among decision-making entities and stakeholders that influence them? How is power exerted?

Who controls access to this setting?

Who sets the agenda in this setting?

Who participates in decision making? On what basis? On whose conditions?

Who has voice? What is the relative role and power of experts and of the lay public in agenda setting, problem definition, intervention planning, implementation, and evaluation?

What—or who—drives (or blocks) change in this setting?

What is the best strategy or strategies for approaching facilitation of the adoption decision?

What is the most effective approach for ongoing, two-way communication between the planning team and decision makers?

What, if any, roles will decision makers play in program, policy, or practice uptake after the adoption decision is made? What role and roles would be appropriate for decision makers in this setting?

Source: Adapted from Poland, Krupa, and McCall (2009).

should help inform how the intervention members of the planning team approach decision makers within organizations to facilitate substantive adoption decisions.

Identify likely influences on the adoption decision-making process within the setting, and select appropriate strategies.

A list of factors associated with program, policy, and practice adoption is presented in Table 3.2 and summarized here (Bopp, Saunders, & Lattimore, 2013). This list of influence factors was derived from multiple sources including Roger (2003), Greenhalgh (2004), and Durlak and DuPre (2008). As noted in the Introduction, these factors are grouped into three categories: (1) factors that

Table 3.2 Adoption Process: Engaging Decision Makers in the Adoption Decision

Category (boldface) and Specific Influences (bulleted)	Questions to Facilitate Planning
Factors Over Which the Planning Team Has Control	
Characteristics of innovation • Nature of the program (complexity, relative advantage, trialability, observability, uncertainty) • Scope for reinvention (adaptability, flexibility) • Fit with organizational/stakeholder needs, goals, priorities, skills, work practices	- How will decision makers perceive the innovation, including its scope for reinvention? - How will decision makers view the innovation's fit with organizational goals, priorities, and work practices? - How can we best communicate about the features of the innovation?
Adoption approach/process • Timing and degree of adopter involvement • Nature of adoption decision	- What is the best approach and timing for working with decision makers? - How might the nature of the adoption decision (e.g., mandated, requested, voluntary) influence the process?
Factors That Can Be Influenced (to some extent)	
Leadership and support; resources • Establishing priorities, consensus • Investment of resources needed for activities (staff, funding, equipment) • Organizational slack (uncommitted resources available)	- How are decisions to adopt new programs, policies, and practices made in this setting? - What is the best way to work with leadership to establish the innovation as a priority? - What organizational resources can be committed toward the innovation? - What additional resources are needed?
Characteristics of adopters • Awareness/concern related to (specific area addressed by the program, policy, or practice) • Support for issue (e.g., prevention, treatment) • Perceived need	- What are the best strategies for communicating/working with decision makers to best instill awareness of, concern about, and an understanding of the need for the innovation?
Important Factors Less Amenable to Influence	
Characteristics of the organization • Features such as maturity (+), size (+), complexity (+), centralization (−), and formalization (−)	- What are the characteristics of this organization; how can descriptive information inform our approach to the organization?

Category (boldface) and Specific Influences (bulleted)	Questions to Facilitate Planning
• Norms, openness to change, risk taking, innovation • System openness, members linked to others outside organization • Expertise in assessment, planning and evaluation; use of evaluation data, feedback	- Do we need to plan additional organizational assessments to better understand the organization? - What are the implications for adoption?
External factors • Support from interorganizational networks • Features of networks (structure, homophily, boundary spanners) • Political support or opposition • Intentional spread (dissemination) • Connection to "research system," access to information on "what works"	- To what interorganizational networks does this organization belong? - How might networks and external partnerships be engaged to facilitate adoption? - What are likely sources of political support or opposition for the innovation? - Are additional strategies needed to facilitate a more supportive context?

Source: Content adapted from Bopp, Saunders, and Lattimore (2013).

implementers can control: implementation approach/processes and innovation characteristics; (2) factors that can be influenced or nudged: organizational leadership and support, adopter/implementer characteristics, resources; and (3) factors that are important to know but less amenable to influence: organizational characteristics and external factors.

Factors Over Which the Planning Team Has Control

Characteristics of the innovation (i.e., the program, policy, or practice) and the approach to facilitating adoption are within the control of the planning team. The planning team can develop the program, policy, or practice so that characteristics are favorable with regard to complexity, relative advantage compared to current practices, trialability, observability, and level of certainty about its use and effects. Similarly, the program, policy, or practice can be designed with reinvention in mind. The innovation should clearly align with the organizational mission, leadership priorities, and structures and procedures.

In some cases, the issue is how the characteristics or nature of the program, policy, or practice are communicated to the stakeholders, rather than its design per se. A good "fit" between the innovation and organization won't matter if the fit is not clear to organizational decision makers and other influential stakeholders. Meaningful engagement of adoption decision makers early in the process facilitates communication and adoption.

The nature of the adoption decision/process is also important; for example, innovations originating internally are more likely to be adopted than those coming from outside of the organization; this can produce challenges for planning teams that wish to facilitate adoption of externally mandated programs, policies, and practices. The planning team would likely approach facilitating adoption in different ways depending on the location and role of the planning team and the origin and nature of the innovation. For example, a planning team or committee internal to children's residential homes that is facilitating an internal organizational decision to adopt wellness policies would operate differently than an external planning team with the same goal. The dynamics would also be different if wellness policies were mandated from an external source, such as a requirement from the federal government to receive certain federal funds.

Factors That Can Be Influenced

Organizational characteristics that can be addressed through the intervention process include organizational leadership and support. Specifically, the member of the planning team involved with facilitating program, policy, or practice change can meet with decision makers and provide relevant information to increase decision makers' awareness of, concern about, and perception of need for the program, policy, or practice (McCormick, Steckler, & McLeroy, 1995) with the goal of making the innovation a priority for organizational leadership.

Additional resources may also be needed for the implementation process, especially if the organization does not have enough resources to cover it. The planning team can provide resources to "seed" implementation as part of a grant or the planning process and/or can work with community partners to address the need for resources.

Characteristics of the adopters may be influenced somewhat by providing them with information and/or materials to make a persuasive argument in favor of the new program, policy, and/or practice. Another strategy is to identify "natural" supporters and enlist their help.

Factors Less Amenable to Change

Characteristics of the organization that are positively associated with adoption are maturity, larger size, and complexity of the organization; openness to change and innovativeness; and expertise in/use of evaluation. Characteristics that are negatively associated with adoption are increasing levels of formalization and centralization. Many of these organizational characteristics are relatively stable or fixed and cannot easily be changed, but are useful to know, in the same way that understanding characteristics of individuals (e.g., age and gender) can't be changed, but can be useful to know. For example, you might use different strategies with small versus large or rural versus urban children's group homes to install wellness policies.

Some features, such as openness to change, innovativeness, and expertise in/use of evaluation, will be unknown unless the planning team conducts a formal assessment of organizational characteristics. Again, if the resources are available to assess these characteristics, the information could be useful in informing the approach. For example, the planning team would likely use a different approach with innovative organizations that are very open to change compared to those that are less open to change and less innovative. The latter may require more intensive work.

External factors including political support and the extent to which the organization is connected to outside organizations and networks, including access to research information about effective programs, policies, and practices, are positively associated with adoption. Again, it may be difficult to change some of these factors, but this information can be used in planning the appropriate strategies to build support for adoption among decision makers. For example, supportive external partners may be enlisted to encourage adoption. In some cases, actions at higher levels are needed prior to adoption by an individual organization. For example, adoption of a particular curriculum in a school setting may be dependent on statewide or district-level adoption.

Questions that the planning team can use to facilitate planning discussions related to influences on the adoption process are provided in Table 3.2. For each category of influence, a series of questions and considerations are provided to facilitate the planning process. Also note that not all categories and all specific influences within each category may be applicable in all organizational settings; therefore, this list is intended to be a general guidance for adoption plan development.

Suggestions and considerations for adoption of programs, policies, and practices are listed below based on influences at each phase of this process:

- Consider how the nature of the adoption decision (e.g., unfunded and mandated versus voluntary) and the timing and nature of involving stakeholders might influence the adoption process.

- Determine the extent to which decision makers in the implementing setting perceive the need for the program, policy, or practice, and the extent to which they are aware of and concerned about the issues in the program, policy, or practice.

- Understand the characteristics and features of the organization, and how these might influence the adoption process at the organizational level.

- Consider how the characteristics of the innovation might influence the implementation process and how best to communicate these characteristics to decision makers to facilitate organizational adoption.

- Do not assume that the organization has the resources needed to carry out the program, policy, or practice; it will likely be necessary to invest some initial resources to seed the process.

Develop a plan detailing strategies for facilitating organizational adoption of a new program, policy, or practice.

Strategies for facilitating organizational adoption of a new program, policy, or practice will likely be a set or series of activities that involve communication, meetings, and providing information to specific stakeholders who influence or who make the adoption decision. The selected strategies should be appropriate for the setting. Use Worksheet 3.1 as a template to summarize relevant organizational characteristics and specific strategies to facilitate organizational adoption of a program, policy, or practice by categories of influence on the adoption process.

LEAP Case Illustration

Table 3.3 illustrates the use of Worksheet 3.1 for the adoption plan based on Lifestyle Education for Activity Program (LEAP). Following school district approval to approach schools, the LEAP research team focused adoption efforts on high school principals as the primary decision makers. There were two primary strategies: individual meetings and a collective "kick-off" meeting. The LEAP research team emphasized LEAP's adaptive nature, consistency with state standards, and the partnership approach, as detailed in Table 3.3.

Worksheet 3.1 Template for Summarizing Plan to Facilitate Organizational Adoption of a Program, Policy, or Practice

Organization: _____

Primary decision maker(s): _____

Primary approach to facilitating organizational adoption (i.e., meetings, specific communication strategies, materials, and information): _____

Category and Specific Influence	Relevant Characteristics of Participating Organization	Specific Strategies to Facilitate Adoption
Factors Over Which the Planning Team Has Control		
Characteristics of innovation • Nature of the program (complexity, relative advantage, trialability, observability, uncertainty) • Scope for reinvention (adaptability, flexibility) • Fit with organizational/stakeholder needs, goals, priorities, skills, work practices		
Adoption approach/process • Timing and degree of adopter involvement • Nature of adoption decision		
Factors That Can Be Influenced (to some extent)		
Leadership and support; resources • Establishing priorities, consensus • Investment of resources needed for activities (staff, funding, equipment) • Organizational slack (uncommitted resources available)		
Characteristics of adopters • Awareness/concern related to (specific area addressed by the program, policy, or practice) • Support for issue (e.g., prevention, treatment) • Perceived need		

(Continued)

(Continued)

Category and Specific Influence	Relevant Characteristics of Participating Organization	Specific Strategies to Facilitate Adoption
Important Factors Less Amenable to Influence		
Characteristics of the organization • Features such as maturity (+), size (+), complexity (+), centralization (−), and formalization (−) • Norms, openness to change, risk taking, innovation • System openness, members linked to others outside organization • Expertise in assessment, planning, and evaluation, use of evaluation data, feedback		
External factors • Support from interorganizational networks • Features of networks (structure, homophily, boundary spanners) • Political support or opposition • Intentional spread (dissemination) • Connection to "research system," access to information on "what works"		

Organization: LEAP high schools

Primary decision maker(s): Principal

Primary approach to facilitating organizational adoption (i.e., meetings, specific communication strategies, materials, and information): *Meet with the principal and invite principal, teachers, and appropriate school staff to a centralized LEAP "kick-off" event, attended by all 12 intervention schools*

Category and Specific Influence	Relevant Characteristics of Participating Organization	Specific Strategies to Facilitate Adoption
Factors Over Which the Planning Team Has Control		
Characteristics of innovation • Nature of the program (complexity, relative advantage, trialability, observability, uncertainty) • Scope for reinvention (adaptability, flexibility) • Fit with organizational/ stakeholder needs, goals, priorities, skills, work practices	LEAP was designed to be a flexible, adaptive intervention rather than a curriculum; because this is not a curriculum, initially it may be more challenging to convey to teachers and school staff. LEAP was consistent with the requirements already in place in the school.	Emphasis was placed on the flexible, adaptive nature of LEAP, which should allow a lot of flexibility and autonomy for each school. It was important to develop materials that not only conveyed the essential elements of LEAP (i.e., "How do I know it's LEAP?") but also clearly conveyed the roles and specific activities expected of specific teachers and school staff (e.g., PE teacher, health teacher, and school nurse) as well as the LEAP team (i.e., collective efforts to assess and improve the physical activity–promoting environment within the school). The LEAP project also emphasized the roles and responsibilities of LEAP investigators and staff.
Adoption approach/process • Timing and degree of adopter involvement • Nature of adoption decision	The LEAP principles, basic outline of the innovation, and intervention approach were developed prior to approaching the schools.	The LEAP project emphasized the partnership between the LEAP project and the schools in working together to carry out LEAP. The school teachers and staff were experts in their fields and their setting, and regarding their students, whereas the LEAP project staff were experts in physical activity programs.

(Continued)

Table 3.3 (Continued)

Category and Specific Influence	Relevant Characteristics of Participating Organization	Specific Strategies to Facilitate Adoption
Factors That Can Be Influenced (to some extent)		
Leadership and support • Establishing priorities, consensus	School leadership was supportive in the majority of schools, but most believed that current physical education class meets needs of students.	LEAP set out to cultivate school leadership and champion support from the beginning of the project. LEAP communicated a partnership philosophy and flexible, adaptive approach of LEAP from the beginning of the project. The primary initial strategy was a "kick-off" event in Columbia that involved school administrators, teachers, and staff potentially involved in LEAP (early involvement and input of stakeholders). At the kick-off meeting, the LEAP project team: • Emphasized the flexible, adaptive nature of LEAP and its consistency with standards • Emphasized the value of physical activity (PA) particularly for adolescent girls • Provided an overview of LEAP and expectations concerning participation • Described active involvement and role of LEAP staff and resources that project would provide • Held break-out sessions for specific topic discussions allowing time for concerns to be expressed and potential barriers identified There were also follow up contacts and meetings with administrators, teachers, and staff as needed.

Category and Specific Influence	Relevant Characteristics of Participating Organization	Specific Strategies to Facilitate Adoption
Characteristics of adopters • Awareness/concern related to issue • Support for prevention • Perceived need **Resources** • Organizational resources • Investment of resources needed for activities (staff, funding, equipment)	All schools had physical education teachers; health requirements were taught by different teachers in different schools; some but not all schools had access to a school nurse who could participate in the intervention. The faculty-staff wellness coordinator was a volunteer position that was not present in all schools.	The basic infrastructure needed to implement the instructional components of LEAP were present in all schools, but there was variation in the infrastructure needed for the environmental components; therefore, several of the environmental elements were "recommended" rather than "required" (see Worksheet 3.1). The project team emphasized that LEAP would enhance schools' ability to conduct the activities that it is already conducting in physical education, health education, and school health. LEAP provided a few basic resources (e.g., PE equipment) to facilitate implementation, and LEAP interventionists worked as partners with schools to get LEAP into place.
Factors Less Amenable to Influence		
Characteristics of the organization • Characteristics of the organization that need to be taken into account • Expertise in assessment, planning, and evaluations; use of evaluation data, feedback	• LEAP schools vary in terms of organizational characteristics such as location, school composition, school resources, and priorities placed on physical activity and health of students.	LEAP interventionists conducted detailed formative assessments in each school setting to facilitate planning.
External factors • Support from interorganizational networks • Political support or opposition	LEAP was developed to be consistent with required PE standards and other health-related requirements in the school; there was little or no political opposition.	LEAP ensured that LEAP PE met state standards for PE and also addressed potential legal concerns (i.e., based on Title IX) related to separating boys and girls in physical education (PE) as recommended in one of the LEAP "essential elements."

KEY POINTS FOR FACILITATING PROGRAM, POLICY, AND PRACTICE ADOPTION

- It is important to identify organizational decision makers and to understand how decisions are made prior to facilitating adoption of a new program, policy, or practice.

- Planning for organizational adoption of the program, policy, or practice should be based on factors that are known to influence the adoption process.

- Strategies for facilitating adoption should be tailored to the organizational setting(s).

I wish success could be ordered like delivery pizza, because I'd order take out.

—Jarod Kintz

STEP 4

Establish Complete and Acceptable Delivery/Installation of the Program, Policy, or Practice

You and your planning team should have a very good understanding of the program, policy, or practice and the context into which it will be implemented from Steps 1 and 2, as well as a good plan for facilitating organizational adoption from Step 3. Prior to "jumping in" to carry out the new program, policy, or practice, it is important to define "complete and acceptable delivery/installation" of the innovation or its essential elements—those elements, components, and/or characteristics of delivery that are needed to produce the desired outcomes/impacts by engaging mechanisms through which the program, policy, or practice would produce beneficial effects. For example, evidence-based instructional practice in Head Start was based on responsive teaching and included five characteristics: following a child's lead, interpreting a child's behavior as intent to interact with others, adult contingent responsiveness to child behavior, reciprocal child-adult interactions, and adult efforts to promote and support child behavior elaborations (Dunst, Trivette, & Raab, 2013). Identifying these observable essential elements facilitates practices that will result in desired outcomes and enables the planning team to communicate clearly with change agents and to develop checklists or other measures to assess implementation.

Learning Objectives

By the end of the chapter, you will be able to

1. Describe the components of complete and acceptable delivery/installation in implementation monitoring

2. Identify the crucial components of the program, policy, or practice (completeness)

3. Define program, policy, or practice delivery or installation that is consistent with its conceptual underpinnings (fidelity)

4. Identify who the program, policy, or practice should reach in order to have the desired level of outcomes/ impacts (reach)

5. Define the extent to which participants should engage with, interact with, be receptive to, and/or use materials and recommended resources (dose received)

Describe the components of complete and acceptable delivery/installation in implementation monitoring.

Complete and acceptable delivery/installation in implementation monitoring is based on components of an implementation monitoring plan along with the particulars of a given project. The components of an implementation monitoring plan include implementation **completeness** or **dose delivered**, **fidelity**, and **reach,** and may also include **dose received.** In other words, what constitutes complete and acceptable delivery/installation for a program, policy, or practice within a given setting is based on how fidelity, completeness or dose delivered, and reach are defined for that program, policy, or practice. These implementation monitoring plan components form the essential elements of the program, policy, or practice.

The elements of the comprehensive implementation monitoring plan and their definitions are described below, based on Saunders, Evans, and Joshi (2005) and derived from Steckler and Linnan (2002) and Baranowski and Stables (2000). Most of the models for implementation monitoring to date have focused on program delivery and individual-level conceptualizations of the elements of a process evaluation plan. Both individually and environmentally focused definitions are discussed below.

Completeness or Dose Delivered

Implementation completeness or dose delivered is the amount, number, and/or percentage of intended units of each program, policy, or practice component installed, delivered, or provided, including components, materials, media, content, and activities of sufficient duration by implementers.

Individual Level

In individually focused programs, completeness or dose delivered, is *what* is implemented, or the extent to which all parts of the program are delivered.

Environmental Level

In environmentally focused program, policy, or practice change, delivery is not at the individual level, but rather component installation is at the organizational level. One could potentially look at completeness by assessing the extent to which individuals who spend time in the environment are aware of the changes, but individual awareness is not needed for environments to influence behavior (Cohen, Scribner, & Farley, 2000). The term completeness, rather than dose delivered, is used in this textbook because it is a better fit with the emphasis on organizational or systems change such as change in infrastructure, procedures, or policies.

Fidelity

Fidelity refers to the extent to which program, policy, or practice implementation is consistent with the conceptual framework and/or underlying philosophy or approach.

Individual Level

For programs that are delivered primarily at the individual level, fidelity pertains to *how* the program is implemented including consistency with the conceptual framework, rather than *what* is implemented. Fidelity is the extent to which the mode of delivery reflects the conceptual and philosophical approach. An example is the extent to which theory-based strategies such as demonstration, practice with feedback, encouragement, and reinforcement are used to increase skill development for using software; in contrast, lecturing with little interaction and combining practice with scolding would reflect low fidelity.

Environmental Level

When the focus is policy and environmental change, fidelity pertains to the consistency of such changes with the conceptual framework that guides them. For example, fidelity could be assessed by the extent to which the environment in an organization reflects the guidelines and/or procedures used to create or enhance a health-promoting environment.

Environmental change focuses on the installation of defined environmental elements (e.g., programs, policies, and/or practices) into the setting in which a population of individuals spends time. Therefore, the goal is to install a complete set of appropriate environmental elements based on the conceptual framework. It may be difficult, then, to distinguish between fidelity and completeness in environmental change.

Reach

Depending on the project focus, reach may be defined in one or more ways:

Individual Level

In an individually focused program, reach is usually conceptualized as the *proportion of individuals within the possible population of individuals* who are reached (as reflected by attendance at certain sessions or events) or exposed to elements of the program (such as media messages).

Environmental Level

In an environmentally focused change effort, reach is often conceptualized at the *organizational* or *setting level* with the understanding that the population of interest spends substantial amounts of time in that setting. The key to exposure, then, is creating a changed environment for all participants.

Please note that the *primary distinction* between individually focused and environmentally focused change efforts is *the conceptualization of individuals as the unit of exposure to the innovation versus the environmental setting as the unit of exposure.* An environment should "reach" the population of individuals who spend time there; for example, an environment in a nonprofit organization may include online communities and/or local grassroots groups. Reach may also be conceptualized as the proportion *of change agents* who participate in training compared to all who could have been trained and the proportion *of organizations or units within the organization* that participate, such as the actual number of classrooms within a school that implement a new curriculum compared to the possible numbers of classrooms.

The key feature for all of these is *proportion or numbers reached relative to the possible population*; that is, reach must consider not only the numerator such as individuals, units, and/or organizations participating or exposed, but also the denominator, the possible population. For example, if 10 volunteers (numerator) from a nonprofit organization attend training that was intended for 20 (denominator), then the organizational reach is 50% (10/20). Similarly, if 25 students (numerator) of 100 eligible students (denominator) attend an academic skills program for high-risk students, the reach is 25% (25/100). This encourages the planning team to think about who was *not* exposed to the program, policy, or practice as much as who *was* exposed.

Dose Received

Dose received is traditionally defined at the individual level, but can also pertain to the environmental or organizational level.

Individual Level

At the individual level, dose received refers to the extent to which participants actively engage with, interact with, are receptive to, and/or use materials or recommended resources and can include both "initial use" and "continued use" (Baranowski & Stables, 2000). This includes immediate reactions, such as satisfaction, but can also include follow-up reactions and activities if these are expected as part of the program. For example, to what extent do individuals in a nonprofit professional organization exposed to social media and email messages aimed at encouraging voting actually vote in the election of their leadership?

Environmental Level

At the environmental or organizational level, dose received may pertain to change agents' response to training and their role in planned program, policy, and practice changes including engaging in expected follow-up activities after training. For example, to what extent did change agents who were exposed to training form an action team after returning to their organizations, as recommended in the training?

As shown in Table 4.1, individually focused definitions of fidelity and completeness require adjustment for environmentally oriented change efforts including those that install programs, policies, or practices into organizational settings. Change efforts that have both individually and environmentally focused elements may need to address implementation monitoring from both perspectives depicted in Table 4.1.

The next step is for the planning team to define completeness, fidelity, reach, and dose received for their specific program, policy, or practice. To further define these concepts, the sections below offer issues and questions to engage planning teams in discussion about specific projects.

Identify the crucial components of the program, policy, or practice (completeness).

Program, policy, or practice components constitute *complete* delivery or installation; that is, all of the components, parts, or elements that are important are included. Therefore, complete delivery/installation, sometimes known as dose delivered, reflects the extent to which implementation includes the (1) essential *components and subcomponents* of the program, policy, or practice; (2) essential

Table 4.1 Comparing Definitions of Process Evaluation Plan Components for Individually Focused Versus Environmentally Focused Change Efforts

Plan Component	Individually Focused		Environmentally Focused	
	Definition	Examples	Definition	Examples
Completeness (Dose delivered)	Amount or number of intended units of each program or component installed or delivered/provided by implementers	90% of participants participated in all program components.	Appropriate environmental elements, based on conceptual framework, are reflected; population approach assumes individuals in program, policy, or practice environment are exposed.	90% of the organizational settings installed the recommended physical and social environmental changes to create physical activity opportunities and encouragement to use them, as defined by the framework.
Fidelity (Quality)	Extent to which program was implemented consistent with underlying theory and philosophy.	Program activities are delivered in a manner consistent with improving self-efficacy.		
Dose received (Exposure)	Individuals engage in recommended follow-up actions.	95% of participants enjoyed the program activities; 70% completed between-session "homework."	Dose received and satisfaction often pertain to change agent training and response to planned program, policy, and practice changes.	100% of change agents attended training; 80% reported confidence in ability to change the environment.
(Satisfaction)	Individuals are satisfied with components received.			
Reach (Participation rate)	Number of individuals exposed to/receiving program compared to total population intended	Over the duration of the program, 75% of the possible population was exposed to 80% of program components.	Depending on the project, reach is at the organizational or unit (within the organization) level.	Over the duration of the intervention, 75% of sites made at least 80% of recommended environmental changes.

content to be addressed; (3) core *strategies, activities, methods,* and *media*; and (4) required *timing, sequencing, and duration* of delivery of components, content, and/or strategies, as applicable.

The process for defining completeness of delivery/installation begins with a detailed description and understanding of the program, policy, or practice components:

- List and describe in detail all program components and subcomponents.

- List and describe in detail all content and messages that should be included.

- List and describe in detail all activities, methods, strategies, and events that should be included.

- Describe timing, sequencing, and duration of all elements, as applicable. Note that timing and sequencing of activities and events may be considered a conceptual matter in some instances and would, therefore, be regarded as part of the fidelity definition.

Most innovations will have multiple components, and perhaps subcomponents, with content and/or messages, activities/methods, and strategies that may be unique to each. These may also differ in timing, sequencing, and duration. It is likely that the initial list of elements to be delivered and/or installed will be very lengthy. *Your task at this phase is to pare this list down to the absolutely critical components, messages, strategies, and other elements: that is, those elements that are required to produce the intended intervention outcomes/impacts.* This can be very challenging at this stage, as the planning team tends to believe that all of the elements, strategies, and messages are equally important and that all are needed. It is unlikely, however, that this is the case.

Furthermore, it is unlikely that it will be feasible to implement all elements into the real-world settings. Without clear priorities of what is important from the planning team, implementers will select the elements that they are most comfortable or familiar with to implement when they run short of time or face other challenges. Therefore, it is important to provide guidance to implementers up front about priorities. When possible, work with change agents and other setting stakeholders to ensure feasibility through preliminary trials, pilot testing, and feasibility assessments prior to full implementation of a program, policy, or practice (Campbell et al., 2000).

Define program, policy, or practice delivery or installation that is consistent with its conceptual underpinnings (fidelity).

Acceptable delivery/installation is synonymous with fidelity and pertains to program, policy, or practice delivery or installation that reflects its philosophical and/or conceptual underpinnings. This section will include challenges of distinguishing between completeness and fidelity in practice and will also address the tension between adaptation and maintaining high levels of fidelity.

To define fidelity for a specific innovation, consider how the program is supposed to work conceptually, which may be explicit (stated) or implicit (unstated) (King, 1987; Saunders et al., 2005). The goal is to identify the "active ingredients, core elements, and mechanisms of change" that specify the theoretically important components of innovations and to assess how well these are delivered and/or altered during implementation (Durlak & DuPre, 2008, pp. 341–342). To develop fidelity criteria, identify the critical indicators or elements of a given model based on structure and process considerations, as well as the conceptual framework, logic model, and program philosophy. Implementation fidelity can be defined by the extent to which the

- program, policy, or practice *model* is implemented;

- program, policy, or practice reflects *prescribed conceptual elements* (and lacks nonprescribed elements);

- services are carried out in the manner and "spirit" *intended* based on the conceptual framework;

- implementers adhere to conceptually informed intervention delivery protocol;

- implementation reflects the intervention goals, theory, and/or philosophy; and

- environmental change reflects the *conceptual framework* for an optimal environment.

The goal is to identify a list of observable characteristics or traits that reflect implementation fidelity. If the innovation is being delivered and/or installed in a manner that is consistent with the underlying theory, conceptual framework, and/or philosophy, an informed observer should be able to observe and identify these essential elements. In practice, it can be very difficult to separate completeness (i.e., complete delivery of all components, subcomponents, strategies, messages, etc.) from fidelity (i.e., appropriate delivery that is consistent with the underlying conceptual model and philosophy), although conceptually they are very different in programs that target individual behavior change. In individually focused programs, the planning team should strive to distinguish between *what* is to be implemented (completeness or dose delivered) from *how* it is to be delivered or installed (fidelity). Ultimately, it is up to the project team and collaborating stakeholders to define completeness and fidelity for a given program, policy, or practice.

It may not be feasible or even desirable to completely separate completeness and fidelity for policy, practice, and other environmental changes. In these cases, one may fully describe complete and acceptable delivery by identifying the conceptual elements that describe the optimal physical and/or social environment. Fidelity and completeness, together, are assessed by measuring the extent to which environmental change is consistent with the identified framework.

Durlak and DuPre (2008) also noted that adaptation (i.e., changes to the program, policy, or practice) and fidelity can co-occur and that adaptation is inevitable and can be beneficial. Adaptation is at least benign to the extent that the changes made do not interfere with the underlying mechanisms that are responsible for the program, policy, or practice producing the desired effects on outcomes of interest. Beneficial adaptations are more likely when the core or essential elements are identified prior to implementation and are clearly communicated to change agents and other stakeholders. In this way, modifications that improve innovation–setting fit do not inadvertently alter or eliminate an essential element.

Below are some strategies to identify the indicators or critical components of a program, policy, or practice that has not been implemented or has been newly implemented. This can be particularly challenging because sometimes it is difficult to know what these are without some pilot work or previous experience with the program, policy, or practice in the setting (King, 1987).

- Review the program proposal and conceptual model; note important activities or characteristics that may be listed, referred to repeatedly, and/or reflected in the budget; be alert for assumptions that are crucial but unstated and implications of conceptual approaches that are not detailed.

- Consider peoples' opinions, including those of program planners or developers and experts in the field.

- Make observations, including direct observation of program activities.

The following guidelines pertain to defining implementation fidelity for programs that have already been implemented (Mowbray, 2003):

- Consult expert opinions, including literature and/or surveys of experts.

- Conduct qualitative work by obtaining opinions of users, advocates, and other stakeholders and conducting interviews, site visits, etc.

- Draw from a program model with proven efficacy, effectiveness, or acceptance (published reports, manuals, etc.).

- Make observations, including direct observation of program activities.

It is important that discussions about fidelity (based on active ingredients, core components, and critical features), as well as decisions about appropriate adaptations, take place prior to adoption by the implementing organization (Meyers, Durlak, & Wandersman, 2012).

Identify who the program, policy, or practice should reach to have the desired level of impacts/outcomes (reach).

Reach refers to the proportion of desired populations that are exposed to the innovation and can have multiple levels in program, policy, and practice change efforts. The levels include the population of individuals within a given setting, such as employees in worksite settings; the population of change agents who will work with the planning team to implement the program, such as the number of change agents who completed training relative to those who were signed up; and the number of organizations reached relative to the possible population of organizations, such as the number of worksites that participated relative to the population of worksites that were approached for participation in the program, policy, or practice change.

Acceptable reach is defined as reaching a predefined percentage or proportion of the intended priority audience or population over time, whether those are individual participants, change agents, and/or organizations. An appropriate value for a predefined proportion will vary by project; for example, in some cases contextual factors may make 50% an appropriate value whereas in other cases 80% may be more appropriate. As previously noted, reach into the population of individuals may be defined differently for environmental change efforts. For change efforts targeting the physical, social, or policy environment, the population of individuals who spend time within that environment are presumed to be reached if environmental change has been implemented. It is important to design environmental changes to ensure that the population of interest has broad exposure and that there is complete and acceptable installation of the environmental changes. For example, for a no smoking policy to have population impact, the policy should be fully implemented and enforced, and should apply to all of the affected population.

Define the extent to which participants should engage with, interact with, be receptive to, and/or use materials and recommended resources (dose received).

Dose received typically refers to the extent to which individual participants (i.e., the recipients of dose delivered) actively engage with, interact with, are receptive to, and/or use materials and recommended resources; it may also apply to the extent to which individuals exposed to a program, policy, or practice engage in recommended follow-up behavior. For instance, how do students in a physical activity afterschool program react to the program? To what extent do they engage in follow-up activity outside the program, as recommended by the program staff? For another example, do adults who have been exposed to a media campaign about cancer screening follow up with getting the appropriate screening tests done? As a final example, do clinic staff members who have been trained to follow different client intake procedures use the new procedures when they return to work?

In innovations that target program, policy, or practice change within organizational settings, members of the planning team may deliver training or other support for internal change agents who then deliver or install the program, policy, or practice into the setting. In this case, one can define dose received as the extent to which change agents are prepared to carry out implementation (that is, have the confidence and skills needed). In essence, there are two innovations: one that the project staff deliver to change agents and one that the change agents deliver within the setting. Therefore, a project can have a planning staff completeness or dose delivered and fidelity (e.g., deliver the full training or capacity development innovation) and change agent completeness or dose delivered and fidelity (e.g., implementation or delivery/installation of the program, policy, or practice in the organizational setting). As will be covered in Step 5, many factors influence change agent implementation (Durlak & DuPre, 2008); prominent among them are response to the training as well as training-instilled confidence and skills (Kealey, Peterson, Gaul, & Dinh, 2000).

Where to Begin?

Defining complete and acceptable delivery/installation is best done as a collaborative discussion of the planning team and, ideally, change agents and other setting stakeholders. In this step, you are defining the optimally implemented *intervention-in-context*. This is more challenging to do than simply describing the program, policy, or practice components or elements, as it requires knowledge of the context or setting in which the program, policy, or practice will be implemented. Below is a question that can be used to begin the discussion to identify complete and acceptable delivery/installation:

> What would observers, who know nothing of planning or theory, actually see if they were to observe the program, policy, or practice in operation in its ideal form in the setting?

Use Worksheet 4.1 as a template for summarizing the essential elements of the program, policy, or practice, describing complete and acceptable delivery/installation of the program, policy, or practice after working through the questions and issues. It may be necessary to refine or update the project conceptual model after articulating complete and acceptable delivery/installation to ensure that the crucial conceptual elements are reflected in the conceptual model.

LEAP Case Illustration

A Lifestyle Education for Activity Program (LEAP) illustration of a completed Worksheet 4.1 is provided in Table 4.2. Prior to implementation, the LEAP planning team identified the ideal characteristics of LEAP based on theory, evidence, and team experience (Saunders, Ward, Felton, Dowda, & Pate, 2006). These essential elements, as they were known, were believed to be the mechanisms through which the innovation would produce beneficial effects on girls' physical activity.

Worksheet 4.1 Template for Describing Complete and Acceptable Delivery/Installation of Program, Policy, or Practice in an Organizational Setting

Element	Planning Team Discussion Questions	Description of Elements That Are Essential for Program Success
Completeness (dose delivered): Amount or number of intended units of each component installed or delivered/provided by implementers	– What are the program components? – What will the interventionists deliver for each program component? – What content, materials, strategies, and activities should be included for each component? – When should these be delivered? – How long should each take? – How should they be sequenced?	
Fidelity: Extent to which program, policy, or practice was implemented, consistent with underlying theory and philosophy	– What theory, constructs, or conceptual elements guide the program, policy, or practice – What is the philosophy of the program, policy, or practice? – What are the implications of the theory and philosophy for *what* is done during implementation? For *how* things are done? – What implementer behaviors and/or environmental components will convey the conceptual elements and philosophy?	
Reach: Proportion of the intended target groups that participate in the program, policy, or practice at appropriate levels (e.g., individual participants, organizational units, organizations)	– Who are the target groups at multiple levels as applicable (describe)? – How many participants and/or organizations are in the target groups? – What level of attendance is expected in training (if applicable)? – For individual participants, what level of attendance is expected in each program component? Sessions within components? How much attendance is needed to get the intended benefit of the program or training?	

(Continued)

(Continued)

Element	Planning Team Discussion Questions	Description of Elements That Are Essential for Program Success
Dose received: Extent to which participants, change agents, and/or organizations actively engage with, interact with, are receptive to, and/or use materials or recommended resources	– What are the expectations for participant involvement? – What are the expected reactions of participants? – What follow-up behaviors are expected (e.g., use materials and activities, make contacts and identify resources, make changes in behavior, implement policies, etc.)? – What is the expected timeline?	

Source: Adapted from Saunders, Evans, and Joshi (2005).

Table 4.2   LEAP Example for Describing Complete and Acceptable Delivery/ Installation of Program, Policy, or Practice in an Organizational Setting

Organization: LEAP high schools

Element	Description of Elements That Are Essential for Program Success
Completeness (dose delivered): Amount or number of intended units of each component installed or delivered/ provided by implementers and **Fidelity:** Extent to which program, policy, or practice was implemented, consistent with underlying theory and philosophy	LEAP was conceptualized as an environmental intervention that targeted both instructional practices as well as the healthy school environment. It was guided by the "essential elements" that defined fidelity and completeness, described below*: *School environment* • **Support for PA promotion from the school administrator** • **Active school physical activity team** • **Messages promoting physical activity are prominent in the school** • Faculty/staff health promotion provides adult modeling of physical activity • Community agency involvement • Family involvement • Health education reinforces messages • School nurse involved in PA • PA opportunities outside of PE

Element	Description of Elements That Are Essential for Program Success
	Instructional practice • **Gender-separated PE classes** • **Classes are fun** • **Classes are physically active** • **Teaching methods are appropriate** • **Behavioral skills are taught** • **Lifelong PA emphasized** • **Noncompetitive PA included in PE** * **Boldface = "Required" element**; other elements were "Recommended."
Reach: Proportion of the intended target groups that participate in the program, policy, or practice; often measured by attendance	Reach in LEAP was assessed at the organizational level, as LEAP was conceptualized as an environmental, public health intervention. It was expected that the population of students who spend time in the school environment would be exposed to LEAP.

Source: Adapted from Ward et al. (2006).

Your Turn: Defining Completeness, Fidelity, and Reach

Your job is to facilitate a planning team discussion to define completeness, fidelity, and reach for a specific project and setting that is the current focus of your planning team. Describe the approach you would take with your team including how you would introduce the discussion. Using Worksheet 4.1 and other resources, select and adapt the questions that you would pose to the team.

KEY POINTS FOR DESCRIBING COMPLETE AND ACCEPTABLE DELIVERY OF A PROGRAM, POLICY, OR PRACTICE

- Complete and acceptable delivery for a program, policy, or practice comprises completeness, fidelity, reach, and sometimes, dose received.

- Completeness pertains to the crucial components of the program, policy, or practice.

- Fidelity addresses how the program, policy, or practice should be delivered or installed in such a way as to reflect philosophical and/or conceptual underpinnings.

- Reach described the proportion of individuals, organizations, or other units that should be present or exposed to the program, policy, or practice in order to have the desired level of outcomes/impacts.

- Dose received pertains to the extent to which participants engage with, interact with, are receptive to, and/or use materials and recommended resources.

Establishing complete and acceptable delivery for a program, policy, or practice entails the following steps:

- Identify the components and philosophical or conceptual underpinnings of the program, policy, or practice crucial to achieve the desired outcomes/impacts.

- Create project-specific definitions for

  o Completeness (or dose delivered)

  o Fidelity

  o Dose received

- Identify the optimal reach of the program at multiple levels, as applicable (e.g., population of individuals, organizations, and/or units within organizations).

- Adjusting the definitions of completeness, fidelity, dose received, and reach as needed for change efforts targeting organizational or environmental rather than individual change.

Whatever failures I have known, whatever
errors I have committed, whatever follies
I have witnessed in private and public
life have been the consequence of action
without thought.

-Bernard M. Baruch

STEP 5

Develop Strategies for Facilitating Program, Policy, or Practice Implementation and Sustainability

Program, policy, and practice adoption, implementation, and sustainability are desirable from the planning team's perspective, but they cannot be taken as a given. Adoption does not automatically lead to implementation, and implementation does not automatically result in sustainability. There are some influences that are common to all three phases, but there are also some influences that are unique to each phase. Furthermore, different stakeholders may be influential at different phases and, therefore, should be engaged in each of the three phases. Facilitating adoption was addressed in Step 3; the focus of Step 5 is facilitating implementation and sustainability.

Implementation at the organizational level involves execution of a policy or practice change within a particular setting or program delivery to the intended target audience. Implementation reflects the shift from an organizational decision to adopt a new program, policy, or practice to a series of actions that require full cooperation from key stakeholders including implementers or change agents within the implementing setting. Implementing programs, policies, and practices within organizational settings is a complex process, and it often requires providing training as well as technical assistance and ongoing support. The organizational assessment, discussed in Step 2, may have revealed other capacity issues as well. For example, the Lifestyle Education for Activity Program (LEAP) had a component that assumed the availability of a school nurse in each intervention school; this became a "recommended" rather than "required" element when it became clear that most schools did not have access to a school nurse in the manner needed for that component.

Learning Objectives

By the end of this chapter, you will be able to

1. List the steps needed to facilitate program, policy, or practice implementation

2. Develop a plan to facilitate implementation of a specific program, policy, or practice in an organizational setting

3. List the steps needed to facilitate program, policy, or practice sustainability

4. Develop a plan to facilitate sustainability of a specific program, policy, or practice in an organizational setting

Sustainability refers to the degree to which an innovation is continued over time after the formal intervention ends (Rogers, 2003, p. 476). Additional definitions include continuing to deliver beneficial services to clients at the individual level; maintaining the program and/or its activities in an identifiable, though possibly modified, form at the organizational level; and maintaining capacity to deliver program activities (Scheirer, 2005). It is important to begin planning for sustainability early, along with planning for adoption and implementation. Delaying sustainability planning reduces the likelihood of sustainability, in part because some factors that influence sustainability begin with adoption and implementation (Pluye, Potvin, & Denis, 2004; Pluye, Potvin, Denis, Pelletier, & Mannoni, 2005).

Working with stakeholders to plan and carry out strategies to facilitate implementation and sustainability processes is essential. Developing a plan to facilitate implementation and sustainability of a program, policy, or practice in an organizational setting entails identifying influences on each phase, identifying and engaging appropriate stakeholders at each phase, and identifying and using appropriate strategies at each phase. Specific steps for the implementation and sustainability phases are provided below. To facilitate clear presentation of the material, implementation and sustainability will be presented separately; however, planning for implementation and sustainability should be concurrent as the implementation process itself influences sustainability. Note that sustainability may not always be desirable as an endpoint if the program or policy is not effective or is a poor fit for the setting.

List the steps needed to facilitate program, policy, or practice implementation.

Steps to Facilitate Implementation

The following steps are used to facilitate the implementation process:

1. Define what constitutes implementation for the setting. How will you know when implementation has taken place? This should be based on complete and acceptable delivery as defined in Step 4.

2. Identify the implementer(s) within the setting such as internal change agents or planning team agents tasked with carrying out the program, policy, or practice and other key stakeholders such as supervisors or managers, as appropriate.

3. Identify specific influences on implementation by category (discussed below and listed in Table 5.1).

4. Develop strategies for facilitating implementation at individual, organizational, and collaborative levels, as appropriate, based on identified factors that influence implementation in this setting.

5. Summarize the implementation plan (see Worksheet 5.1).

6. Develop an implementation action plan (Step 6) and carry it out (Step 9).

To facilitate implementation of a program, policy, or practice, it is necessary to describe influences on implementation and select corresponding strategies based on the implementation goals.

Influences on Program, Policy, and Practice Implementation and Suggested Strategies

Implementation occurs when an innovation is put into use within the organizational setting (Rogers, 2003, p. 474). Factors associated with program, policy, and practice implementation are presented in Table 5.1 along with questions to guide the planning process (Bopp, Saunders, & Lattimore, 2013). This list of influence factors was derived from multiple sources including Roger (2003), Greenhalgh (2004), and Durlak and DuPre (2008) (Bopp et al., 2013). The factors are organized into three categories: (1) factors that implementers can control (implementation approach/processes and innovation characteristics); (2) factors that can be influenced or nudged (organizational leadership and support, adopter/implementer characteristics: resources); and (3) factors that are important to know but less amenable to influence (organizational characteristics and external factors). Some of the same influences apply to both adoption and implementation: early involvement of stakeholders, organizational characteristics, perceived need, openness to change and innovativeness, expertise in/use of evaluation, organizational leadership and support, organizational resources, connections with other organizations and organizational networks, and characteristics of the program, policy, or practice (Bopp et al., 2013). There are some additional factors associated with implementation as shown in Table 5.1 and discussed below (Bopp et al., 2013). This is due in part to the fact that different stakeholders such as front-line staff are usually involved in implementation compared to adoption, which typically involves decision makers and administrators, and is also due to the fact that the needed actions differ. Table 5.1 emphasizes those elements that are new, important, and/or modifiable.

Characteristics of Program, Policy, or Practice

Characteristics of the program, policy, or practice to be implemented are within the control of the planning team. As discussed in Step 3, the planning team can develop the program, policy, or practice to ensure that it is not overly complex, is advantageous compared to current practices, fits with current practices, is observable, can be tried out first, and has clear uses and effects. Several of these characteristics hinge upon an understanding of current implementing organizational practices. Similarly, the program, policy, or practice can be designed with reinvention in mind, such as the process-oriented approach discussed in Step 2.

In some cases, the issue is how the characteristics or nature of the program, policy, or practice is *communicated* to implementers, rather than the innovation design per se. The planning team should have a *clear* description of the program, policy, or practice, an understanding about what conceptually should make it work, and a list of its essential elements that constitute complete and acceptable delivery/installation. To facilitate implementation, planners must communicate this in an effective manner and without jargon to implementers and stakeholders. During this process, it will be important to examine how stakeholders perceive the innovation because the perceived characteristics of the program, policy, or practice itself are very important in the implementation process. In essence, it doesn't matter how well a program, policy, or practice is developed and conceptualized if the planning team is unable to clearly communicate it in a manner that implementers and stakeholders will understand and find acceptable.

Implementation Approach/Process

The approach to implementation is particularly important at this phase. Implementers ideally should have input and/or be involved earlier rather than later in the process, be provided training through active forms of learning, receive ongoing support and clear communication, and have structures such as workgroups or teams for accomplishing required tasks within the organization. As discussed in previous chapters, this requires the formation and maintenance of effective working relationships between the planning team and the implementers as well as other internal stakeholders. These relationships should be characterized by shared decision making and trust. Implementation is more likely if mutual adaptation of the program, policy, or practice is possible. That is, implementers need flexibility to make adjustments in the program, policy, or practice to ensure fit with the setting practices and the population served. If the planning team and stakeholders have agreed on what constitutes complete and acceptable delivery/installation, they will be able to focus on what is important as adaptations are made. Flexible, adaptive innovations with standardized processes may be optimal as they are designed for adaptation while maintaining the characteristics of complete and acceptable delivery/installation.

An effective internal change agent will have access to the decision-making mechanisms of the implementing organizations either directly or indirectly through other stakeholders, including champions, within the setting. Therefore, the selection of internal implementers or change agents is important; the implementing organization will need to understand enough about the purpose and scope of the program, policy, or practice to be able to identify an appropriate change agent to work with the planning team. A change agent with limited access to the decision-making mechanisms within the organization may be successful if an innovation has a very limited scope and involves minimal systems change. But in most cases, the change agent needs to know how to get things done within the organization. In an unfortunate scenario, the head of an organization can ensure, either consciously or unconsciously, that a particular change effort will not be successful by identifying a change agent who is either inexperienced or lacking in the necessary skills or knowledge to work within the organization to "get things done."

Leadership and Support and Resources

Organizational leadership and support need to go beyond support for adoption of the program, policy, or practice to ensure their implementation is an organizational priority. At the organizational level, there should be some incentive for staff to participate (or at least not costs including social disadvantages for participation) along with support from managers and/or supervisors. For example, there should be clear expectations and recognition for participating, and support from managers or supervisors should be tangible rather than just verbal.

The presence of an internal advocate or **champion** is positively associated with implementation, and this role can be cultivated. A champion is a "charismatic individual who throws his or her weight behind an innovation, thus overcoming indifference or resistance that any new idea might provoke an organization" (Rogers, 2003, p. 473). As previously mentioned, additional *resources* in the form of funding or personnel may also be needed for the implementation process, especially if the organization does not have sufficient resources. The planning team can include resources to seed implementation as part of a grant and/or can work with community partners to address the need for additional resources. However, if the planning team provides extensive resources or pays for services in a manner that is not sustainable, the program, policy, or practice may not be maintained beyond the initial funding period.

Table 5.1 Implementation Process: Engaging Internal Change Agents in Implementation With Focus on Influences Beyond Adoption and/or Important and Modifiable Factors

Category (boldface) and Specific Influences (bulleted)	Questions for Planners to Facilitate Planning
Factors Over Which Planning Teams Have Control	
Characteristics of program, policy, or practice • Nature of the program, policy, or practice (complexity, relative advantage, trialability, observability, uncertainty) • Scope for reinvention (adaptability, flexibility) • Fit with organizational/stakeholder needs, goals, priorities, skills, work practices	– How do we describe the program, policy, or practice in terms of complexity, advantages/disadvantages over current practices, and flexibility? – What are likely reactions from participants and others? – How does it fit with the priorities, goals, and the way things are done day-to-day in the organization? – How will it affect the implementers' jobs and daily tasks? – What is the best way for us to communicate what is important in and about this program? – What adaptations to the innovation would make it more feasible for use in this setting?
Implementation approach/process • Timing and degree of implementer involvement • Providing training, active forms of learning • Providing ongoing technical assistance support • Clear communication • Shared decision making, positive relationships, trust • Extent of adaptation/reinvention • Mutual adaptation • Formulation for tasks (workgroups, teams, etc.)	– What is our approach to implementation, and how might it affect implementation? – How will we facilitate clear communication with implementers on an ongoing basis? – How will we ensure quality training characterized by active forms of learning? – How can we ensure provision of useful and ongoing technical assistance and support? – How can we ensure the development of effective working relationships that are characterized by trust, positive relationships, and shared decision making? – How can we ensure that structures appropriate to the setting for getting tasks done are in place? – How can we work with stakeholders to ensure that appropriate adaptations are made?
Factors That Can Be Influenced (to some extent)	
Leadership and support; resources • Presence of advocate, champion	– How can we best identify advocates, champions, and implementers (i.e., change agents) within the setting to support the program, policy, or practice?

Category (boldface) and Specific Influences (bulleted)	Questions for Planners to Facilitate Planning
• Establishing priorities, consensus, managing implementation process • Organizational incentive for participating staff (vs. costs) • Managerial/supervisory/administrative support • Investment of resources needed for activities (staff, funding, equipment) • Organizational slack (uncommitted resources available)	– How can we work with administrators, management, supervisors, and other leadership from within the organization to ensure that the program, policy, or practice is a priority? – How can we work with leadership to ensure that participating staff are appropriately incentivized? – How can we best facilitate use of existing organizational resources? – What additional resources are needed to seed activities for implementation?
Characteristics of implementers • Perceived need • Perceived benefits • Self-efficacy • Capability (skill proficiency)	– How can we ensure that implementers and other key stakeholders understand the need for and benefits of the program, policy, or practice? – What is the current level of implementer self-efficacy and capability? – What type of training, staff development, technical assistance, and ongoing support should we provide to develop implementer self-efficacy and capability?
Factors Less Amenable to Influence	
Organizational characteristics • Integration of program, policy, or practice with existing programs and services • Effective intraorganizational communication	– How can we work with stakeholders to ensure that the innovation is integrated with existing programs, practices, and services? – How does communication take place within the organization? – Is it sufficient to facilitate communication about the program, policy, or practice to all implementers and other key stakeholders associated with the organization?
External factors • Political support or opposition • Consistency with federal, professional mandates, social policies, and guides	– To what extent will political support or opposition for the program, policy, or practice be a factor? – In what ways can this be addressed? – To what extent is the program, policy, or practice consistent with government and professional mandates and requirements, and do we need to make adjustments for better consistency with them?

Source: Content from Bopp, Saunders, and Lattimore (2013).

For example, the planning team may provide or pay for transportation services in an afterschool program for middle school students. If transportation is funded by grant funds that will not continue beyond the funding period, student participation in the program will likely not be sustainable beyond that period.

Characteristics of Implementers and Features of the Organization

Implementers are more likely to carry out implementation tasks if they perceive a need for and benefits of the change—that is, if they are sufficiently motivated. Implementers also need the self-efficacy and skills required to put the program, policy, or practice into place. Often, planning teams make assumptions about the setting and implementers' backgrounds that need to be identified and examined, particularly if these assumptions about the implementers' skills and experiences are essential for successful program implementation. For example, if classroom teachers are expected to integrate physical activity breaks into their schedules, the planning team may make positive but unfounded assumptions about classroom teachers' prior experiences with physical activity, which may have actually been negative; their confidence, which may be low; and their skills needed to conduct the activities, which may be underdeveloped. In addition, there may be barriers to integrating these physical activity breaks into the school day, including other subjects that have already been scheduled and organizational priorities that may value academics over nonacademic activities.

Peterson (2013) discusses the influences on implementation in early childhood education interventions from a "readiness" perspective. In this context, implementing evidence-based practices often requires that implementers, such as early childhood teachers, shift attitudes, beliefs, and reflective capacities that underlie how they interact with young children. This goes beyond learning *how to* and may require a journey of self-discovery and personal development.

Staff development focused on carrying out the program, policy, or practice should be characterized by active learning strategies and should also develop implementer motivation as well as confidence and skills or capacity to carry out the innovation (Kealey, Peterson, Gaul, & Dinh, 2000). The specific skills needed depend on the program, policy, or practice and the implementing setting. For example, if the innovation calls for a team approach within the organization to change practices or policies, it should first be determined if this is the way the organization operates. That is, are organizational activities or changes accomplished via committees or team efforts? If this is the case, training can likely focus on skill development for the specific tasks in which the team will need to engage. On the other hand, if the organization does not operate through committees, it may be necessary to examine organizational processes to see if a team approach is feasible, and if so, training may be needed to enable implementers to work within a team, in addition to training about innovation-specific skills and tasks.

For example, in a school that is very committee oriented, it may be feasible to integrate a team approach into daily operations, assuming implementers understand the rationale for doing this. In a school that does not operate by committee, it may be difficult to schedule times for team members to get together, and furthermore, individuals may not be comfortable working in teams or may lack the skills necessary for teamwork. In this case a team approach may require addressing school norms, processes, and scheduling, as well as potential lack of confidence and skills related to teamwork among teachers and staff who are not accustomed to working in teams. Similarly, in a nonprofit setting that does not operate by committee, it may be necessary to address norms, processes, and procedures as well as a potential lack of confidence and skills among volunteers and staff who are not accustomed to working in groups. This may be of particular importance if, within the volunteer structure of a nonprofit organization, the lack of volunteers results in committees made up of one individual.

If implementers were not involved in defining complete and acceptable delivery/installation, it is important to convey this to them to ensure their full understanding and acceptance; this is a process that takes time! Complete and acceptable delivery/installation is the planning team's best understanding of what will make the program effective; that is, if implementers follow these guidelines, it will increase the chances that the program will produce positive effects and desired outcomes. The planning team should deliver clear messages about what is important. Otherwise, during the messy implementation process when time grows short and things don't go as planned, implementers will make adjustments "on the fly," which may or may not reflect the elements of the project that are important to project outcomes/impacts.

Peterson indicates the importance of understanding the implementers' current situation and experiences as a prelude to collaboratively identifying "what is possible" within the implementing setting rather than focusing on "what should happen." Furthermore, in early children education, this often takes place in a context characterized by low pay, high turnover, low levels of education, and low levels of perceived support in the work environment (Peterson, 2013).

It is important to integrate the program, policy, or practice into existing programs and services. This is more challenging to accomplish, but is a worthy goal. It is also important to be mindful of internal communication mechanisms in the implementing organization as this influences implementation, even though addressing the communication infrastructure within the implementing organization may be beyond the scope of the intervention.

External Factors

Factors such as political support and the extent to which the organization is connected to outside organizations and networks (including access to research information about evidence-based approaches) are positively associated with successful implementation. Again, it may be difficult to change some of these factors, but this information can be used in planning the appropriate strategies to build support from outside the implementing organization. Prior actions at higher levels are sometimes needed to support implementation. For example, endorsement of and support for a particular program at the district level may play an important role in facilitating school-level implementation. Advocacy with professional associations may facilitate uptake of a new policy among affiliated nonprofit organizations. In cases where a base of political support needs to be developed, coalition formation may be an important strategy. Similarly, the program, policy, or practice is more likely to be implemented if it is consistent with federal and/or professional mandates and/or guidelines. Finally, bear in mind that the new program, policy, or practice will likely face competition from existing programs, policies, and practices, as well as competing innovations.

Develop a plan to facilitate implementation of a specific program, policy, or practice in an organizational setting.

Use Worksheet 5.1 to summarize the plan to facilitate organizational implementation.

LEAP Case Illustration

Table 5.2 depicts the LEAP approach to facilitating implementation using Worksheet 4.1. LEAP focused on instructional practice and environmental change at the school level and was designed with implementation and sustainability in mind. Effective implementation depended on clearly communicating about the LEAP essential elements, providing staff development for teachers and staff who implemented LEAP, and facilitating and maintaining organizational support for LEAP practices. The LEAP intervention was also

Worksheet 5.1 Template for Summarizing Plan to Facilitate Organizational Implementation of a Program, Policy, or Practice

Organization: _____

Implementation approach (e.g., insider versus outsider delivery/installation and process- versus product-oriented innovation): _____

Change agents (if applicable) and positions: _____

Primary strategies to develop capacity of organization and implementers to implement the program, policy, or practice (i.e., training sessions, technical assistance, communication strategies, provision of ongoing support, site visits): _____

Category (boldface) and Specific Influences (bulleted)	Relevant Characteristics of Participating Organization	Specific Strategies to Facilitate Implementation
Factors Over Which Planning Teams Have Control		
Characteristics of program, policy, or practice • Nature of the program (complexity, relative advantage, trialability, observability, uncertainty) • Scope for reinvention (adaptability, flexibility) • Fit with organizational/stakeholder needs, goals, priorities, skills, work practices		
Implementation approach/process • Timing and degree of implementer involvement • Providing training, active forms of learning • Providing ongoing technical assistance, support • Clear communication • Shared decision making, positive relationships, trust • Extent of adaptation/reinvention • Mutual adaptation • Formulation for tasks (workgroups, teams, etc.) *Unique to sustainability:* • Early planning for sustainability • Implementation with quality		

(Continued)

(Continued)

Category (boldface) and Specific Influences (bulleted)	Relevant Characteristics of Participating Organization	Specific Strategies to Facilitate Implementation
Factors That Can Be Influenced (to some extent)		
Leadership and support • Leadership establishing priorities, consensus, managing implementation process • Presence of advocate, champion • Organizational incentive for participating staff (vs. costs) • Managerial/supervisory/administrative support *Unique to sustainability:* • Development of organizational infrastructure, policies, and procedures to codify routines • Sharing cultural artifacts		
Resources • Investment of resources needed for activities (staff, funding, equipment) *Unique to sustainability:* • Standardization, stabilization of organizational resources needed for program/policy • Obtain funding from other resources • Program used low-cost approaches and/or volunteers		
Characteristics of implementers • Perceived need • Perceived benefits • Self-efficacy • Capability (skill proficiency) *Unique to sustainability:* • Support for prevention		

Category (boldface) and Specific Influences (bulleted)	Relevant Characteristics of Participating Organization	Specific Strategies to Facilitate Implementation
Factors Less Amenable to Influence		
Characteristics of the organization • Integration of program with existing programs and services • Effective intraorganizational communication • Expertise in assessment, planning, and evaluation; use evaluation data, feedback		
External factors • Support from interorganizational networks • Coordination with other organizations • Political support or opposition • Consistency with federal, professional mandates, social policies, and guides		

consistent with state curriculum standards to ensure a better fit with existing school practices. Finally, LEAP was designed to be flexible and adaptive, and the LEAP team worked in collaboration with school teachers and staff to install LEAP in each school setting.

Table 5.2   LEAP Plan to Facilitate Organizational Implementation of a Program, Policy, or Practice

Organization: LEAP high schools

Implementation approach (e.g., insider versus outsider delivery/installation and process- versus product-oriented innovation): *Process-oriented innovation with insider installation*

Change agents (if applicable) and positions: Primarily physical education and health education teachers plus school nurse, faculty staff wellness coordinator, media specialist, and others interested in improving physical activity to serve on LEAP team

(Continued)

Table 5.2   (Continued)

The primary implementers are teachers and staff. LEAP staff will work with teachers and school staff in a collaborative, partnership approach in which their professional expertise and contextual knowledge is respected. Teachers and staff will need organizational support to carry out LEAP.

Optimal individual teacher and staff roles include the following:

- The principal will provide tangible support for LEAP.

- The PE teacher(s) will implement LEAP PE with fidelity and completeness as indicated by attainment of LEAP PE criteria.

- The health education teacher will implement LEAP health education as indicated by attainment of LEAP health education criteria.

- The school nurse will promote physical activity in the health room.

- Other school staff (e.g., wellness coordinator, media specialists, etc.) will implement appropriate LEAP components.

Team Role

A LEAP team will be formed to develop a plan for promoting physical activity in the school as documented by a written plan. Team membership will include administrator, teachers, and other appropriate staff.

Specific implementation expectations include the following:

PE teacher example: The PE teacher will

- participate in central workshops with LEAP staff;

- participate in local workshop with LEAP staff;

- make changes in PE to make it LEAP PE; and

- be active on the LEAP team.

Team example: The LEAP team will

- have appropriate representation (e.g., teachers and school staff);

- meet/communicate on a regular basis;

- develop a plan to promote PA in the school; and

- implement the plan.

Primary strategies to develop capacity of organization and implementers to implement the program, policy, or practice: Centralized and local training sessions and ongoing technical assistance; regular communication in person, electronically, and via newsletter; provision of ongoing support and regular site visits.

Category (boldface) and Specific Influence (bulleted)	Relevant Characteristics of Participating Organization	Specific Strategies to Facilitate Implementation
Factors Over Which Planning Teams Have Control		
Characteristics of program, policy, or practice • Nature of the program (complexity, relative advantage, trialability, observability, uncertainty) • Scope for reinvention (adaptability, flexibility) • Fit with organizational/ stakeholder needs, goals, priorities, skills, work practices	LEAP was designed to be a flexible, adaptive intervention rather than a curriculum; because this is not a curriculum, it may be more challenging to convey to teachers and school staff. LEAP is consistent with the requirements already in place in the school.	LEAP is a flexible, adaptive intervention that will be carried out in a way that "fits" each school.
Implementation approach/process • Timing and degree of implementer involvement • Providing training, active forms of learning • Providing ongoing technical assistance, support • Clear communication • Shared decision making, positive relationships, trust • Extent of adaptation/ reinvention • Mutual adaptation • Formulation for tasks (workgroups, teams, etc.) *Unique to sustainability:* • Early planning for sustainability • Implementation with quality	The LEAP principles in the basic outline of the intervention approach were developed prior to approaching the schools.	The LEAP team will communicate a partnership philosophy and the flexible, adaptive approach of LEAP from the beginning of the project. The primary strategy will be a "kick-off" event in Columbia that will involve school administrators as well as teachers and staff potentially involved in LEAP (early involvement and input of stakeholders). The team will • emphasize the flexible, adaptive nature of LEAP and its consistency with standards; • emphasize the value of PA particularly for adolescent girls; • provide an overview of LEAP and expectations concerning participation; • describe active involvement and role of LEAP staff as well as resources that the project will provide; and

(Continued)

Table 5.2 (Continued)

Category (boldface) and Specific Influence (bulleted)	Relevant Characteristics of Participating Organization	Specific Strategies to Facilitate Implementation
		• hold break-out sessions for specific topic discussions allowing time for concerns to be expressed and potential barriers identified. LEAP staff will work with teachers and school staff in a collaborative, partnership approach in which their professional expertise and contextual knowledge is respected. See also training, technical assistance, and other support activities described below under "characteristics of implementers."
Factors That Can Be Influenced (to some extent)		
Leadership and support • Leadership establishing priorities, consensus, managing implementation process • Organizational incentive for participating staff (vs. costs) • Managerial/supervisory/ administrative support *Unique to sustainability:* • Development of organizational infrastructure, policies, and procedures to codify routines • Sharing cultural artifacts	The LEAP schools vary in the extent to which the school administrator will provide tangible support for LEAP.	LEAP will cultivate the presence of an advocate or champion for physical activity and LEAP within the school, assess leadership and support, communicate with administrators, and hold administrator meetings.
Resources • Investment of resources needed for activities (staff, funding, equipment) *Unique to sustainability:* • Standardization, stabilization of organizational resources needed for program/policy	All schools have physical education teachers; health requirements are taught by different teachers in different schools; some but not all schools have access to a school nurse who can participate in the intervention.	LEAP will ensure that basic resources are available to schools for required elements and provide minimal resources to facilitate implementation (i.e., small equipment and mini-grants). The basic infrastructure needed to implement the instructional components of LEAP is present

Category (boldface) and Specific Influence (bulleted)	Relevant Characteristics of Participating Organization	Specific Strategies to Facilitate Implementation
• Obtain funding from other resources • Program used low-cost approaches and/or volunteers		in all schools, but there is variation in the infrastructure needed for the environmental components; therefore, several of the environmental elements are "recommended" rather than "required" (e.g., school nurse, faculty/staff wellness, and family/community involvement components).
Characteristics of implementers • Perceived need • Perceived benefits • Self-efficacy • Capability (skill proficiency) *Unique to sustainability:* • Support for prevention	LEAP PE and health education teachers were initially apprehensive due to the absence of the curriculum. Many of the schools are not accustomed to working in a committee format as recommended by the LEAP team approach. Therefore, it is likely that many of the change agents may initially lack self-efficacy and some degree of capability. Teachers and school staff see the need for a program such as LEAP.	LEAP staff will provide training, technical assistance, and ongoing support so that PE teachers will: • see the need for and benefits of LEAP • have specific skills to implement LEAP PE: selection of activities, classroom management, methods of teaching, activity skills (e.g., how to teach kickboxing) • have confidence in ability to implement LEAP PE • receive reinforcement and social support from LEAP staff and other LEAP schools *For PE*: A series of workshops will be held including Sport Education, LEAP criteria and strategic plans, LEAP physical activity behavioral skills, LEAP resistance training, and LEAP introduction to self-defense. Workshops will be structured to include some brief lecture/discussion, demonstration of skills, guided practice with feedback, and sharing among participants.

(Continued)

Table 5.2 (Continued)

Category (boldface) and Specific Influence (bulleted)	Relevant Characteristics of Participating Organization	Specific Strategies to Facilitate Implementation
	Factors Less Amenable to Influence	
Characteristics of the organization • Integration of program with existing programs and services • Effective intraorganizational communication • Expertise in assessment, planning, and evaluation; use evaluation data, feedback	The intraorganizational communication infrastructure and effectiveness varies by school that will be documented through formative assessment; no schools have existing expertise in planning and evaluation.	LEAP was designed to be integrated with existing programs and services, consistent with its flexible, adaptive approach. LEAP interventionists will tailor organizational communication strategies to the needs and infrastructure of the specific school. Primary contact will be made with the LEAP champion, who will serve as the liaison between the school and the LEAP project.
External factors • Support from interorganizational networks • Coordination with other organizations • Political support or opposition • Consistency with federal, professional mandates, social policies, and guides	LEAP was developed to be consistent with required PE standards and other health-related requirements in the school; there is little or no political opposition.	LEAP will ensure that LEAP PE meets state standards for PE and is consistent with recommendations of the State PE Professional Association.

List the steps needed to facilitate program, policy, or practice sustainability.

Steps to Facilitate Sustainability

Use the following steps to facilitate program sustainability:

1. Define the sustainability goal (Scheirer, 2005).

2. Identify key agents and actions. (What is to be sustained, how or by whom, how much, and by when?)

3. Identify influences on the sustainability process.

4. Develop strategies for facilitating sustainability based on identified factors that influence sustainability in this setting.

5. Summarize the sustainability plan (Worksheet 5.2).

6. Develop an implementation action plan (Step 6) and carry it out (Step 9).

The important first step in planning for sustainability is for the planning team and stakeholders to discuss and come to agreement about the definition of sustainability for the specific program, policy, and practice and setting(s). In general, sustainability refers to continuation of the program in part or whole after the end of the formal intervention period. However, this may include continuing to deliver beneficial services to clients at the individual level; maintaining the program and/or its activities in an identifiable though possibly modified form at the organizational level; institutionalization or incorporating the program, policy, or practice into organizational routines; and/or maintaining capacity to deliver program activities (Scheirer, 2005).

Influences on Program, Policy, and Practice Sustainability and Suggested Strategies

To facilitate sustainability of a program, policy, or practice, you must describe appropriate influences on sustainability and select corresponding strategies based on the sustainability goal. Factors associated with program, policy, and practice sustainability include many of the same factors associated with implementation (see Table 5.2) (Bopp et al., 2013). These include presence of an internal advocate; perceived benefits of program, policy, or practice; integration with existing programs and services; support from leadership, manager, and supervisors; organizational incentives for participating; skills and capability of implementers; clear communication, early involvement, positive working relationships, and support from planning team; characteristics of the program and program adaptation; investment of resources; and support from interorganizational networks, political support, and consistency with requirements. This suggests that processes begun during implementation have a strong effect on sustainability and that effective implementation processes are also beneficial to sustainability.

There are some unique factors that affect only sustainability, as well; these include organizational capacity to sustain the program, policy, or practice; development of infrastructure and procedures to codify routines; early planning for sustainability; obtaining additional funding or resources; sharing cultural artifacts; and quality implementation (Bopp et al., 2013). Each of these is discussed briefly below. See Table 5.3 for an overview of the factors influencing sustainability, as well as questions to guide discussions among the planning team and setting stakeholders. See also Johnson and colleagues' (Johnson, Hays, Center, & Daley, 2004) sustainability planning model for a planning approach that focuses specifically on sustainability.

Implementation Process and Leadership and Support

If the program, policy, or practice has received little organizational support and is a low organizational priority, both implementation and sustainability are less likely to occur. Even if there is organizational support, it is important that the implementation process goes well, as poor implementation will likely result in poor outcomes, which precludes the need for sustainability. Few organizations will want to sustain a program, policy, or practice that has been poorly implemented and/or does not have positive effects. Accordingly, investment in implementation is an investment into sustainability. Sharing cultural artifacts related to the program, policy, or practice change such as recognizing "anniversaries" is also a good indicator of sustainability and one that can be cultivated.

Organizational Characteristics and Resources

To continue the program, policy, or practice on an ongoing basis, the organization needs capacity as well as infrastructure to integrate the program, policy, or practice into organizational procedures that are part of daily routines. It is best to facilitate both capacity development and infrastructure development by early and explicit planning for sustainability, as these take time. In some cases additional funding or resources may be needed; in this case the planning team can work with implementers to obtain funds, identify partners who may be able to access resources, or use other strategies to minimize and cover costs.

LEAP Case Illustration

LEAP did not develop an explicit sustainability plan from the beginning of the project; however, the sustainability tasks were largely a continuation of the tasks listed in implementation, as were the determinants. To foster sustainability, LEAP focused on developing the skills of individuals, organizational support and capacity, integration of LEAP practices into the school routine, and connections to community resources to promote physical activity in girls.

Table 5.3 Sustainability Process: Engaging Decision Makers and Internal Change Agents in Sustainability

Category (boldface) and Specific Influences (bulleted)	Questions for the Planning Team to Facilitate Sustainability Planning
Factors Over Which Planning Teams Have Control	
Characteristics of the program, policy, or practice • Nature of the program (complexity, relative advantage, trialability, observability, uncertainty) • Scope for reinvention (adaptability, flexibility) • Fit with organization and stakeholder needs, goals, priorities, skills, work practices	– How can we ensure fit of the program, policies, or practices as the implementing organization evolves over time?
Implementation approach/process • Timing and degree of implementer involvement • Nature of relationship with change agency • Providing training, active forms of learning • Providing ongoing technical assistance and support • Clear communication • Shared decision making, positive relationships, trust • Extent of adaptation/reinvention *Unique to sustainability:* • Early planning for sustainability • Quality implementation	– How can we best work from the beginning to plan for sustainability and to ensure quality implementation? – How can we ensure the development of effective working relationships from the beginning? – How can we link the organization with other sources of staff development, ongoing technical assistance, and support for sustainability?
Factors That Can Be Influenced (to some extent)	
Leadership and support; resources • Presence of advocate, champion • Support for establishing priorities, consensus, managing implementation • Organizational incentive for participating staff (vs. costs) • Managerial/supervisory/administrative support	– How can we best facilitate enduring, internal advocates or champions? – How can we ensure ongoing and tangible support from administrators and organizational leadership? – How can we best facilitate the development of infrastructure, policies, procedures, and routines consistent with the program, policy, or practice?

(Continued)

Table 5.3 (Continued)

Category (boldface) and Specific Influences (bulleted)	Questions for the Planning Team to Facilitate Sustainability Planning
Unique to sustainability: • Development of organizational infrastructure, policies, and procedures to codify routines • Sharing cultural artifacts • Standardization, stabilization of organizational resources needed • Obtain funding from other resources • Low-cost approaches and/or volunteers	– How can we ensure stabilization of resources needed for ongoing implementation and sustainability? – How can we best enable the organization to obtain funding as well as to use volunteers, partners, and other resources from the beginning?
Characteristics of implementers • Perceived benefit • Capability, skill proficiency	– How can we work with the organization to ensure ongoing staff development and new staff orientation?
Important Factors Less Amenable to Influence	
Organizational characteristics • Integration of program with existing programs and services • Effective intraorganizational communication • System openness, members linked to others outside organization • Expertise in assessment, planning, and evaluation; use evaluation data, feedback • Existing organizational capacity	– How can we ensure innovation integration into the setting from the beginning? – How can we ensure that the organization is linked to appropriate external organizations including those that can provide support and resources after the formal project is over? – Does the organization have sufficient capacity to sustain activities after the formal project is over?
External factors • Support from interorganizational networks • Coordination with other organizations • Political support or opposition • Consistency with federal, professional mandates, policies, guides • Connection to research system, access to info on "what works"	– How can we ensure linkages with partners and other resources to provide support for ongoing implementation and sustainability? – What partnerships or coalitions are needed to provide ongoing, external support?

Source: Content from Bopp, Saunders, and Lattimore (2013).

Develop a plan to facilitate sustainability of a specific program, policy, or practice in an organizational setting.

Use Worksheet 5.2 to summarize the sustainability plan.

Worksheet 5.2 Template for Summarizing Plan to Facilitate Organizational Sustainability of a Program, Policy, or Practice

Category (boldface) and Specific Influence (bulleted)	Relevant Characteristics of Participating Organization	Specific Strategies to Facilitate Implementation
Factors Over Which Planning Teams Have Control		
Characteristics of program, policy, or practice • Nature of the program (complexity, relative advantage, trialability, observability, uncertainty) • Scope for reinvention (adaptability, flexibility) • Fit with organizational/stakeholder needs, goals, priorities, skills, work practices		
Implementation approach/process • Timing and degree of implementer involvement • Providing training, active forms of learning • Providing ongoing technical assistance, support • Clear communication • Shared decision making, positive relationships, trust • Extent of adaptation/reinvention • Mutual adaptation • Formulation for tasks (workgroups, teams, etc.) *Unique to sustainability:* • Early planning for sustainability • Implementation with quality		

(Continued)

(Continued)

Category (boldface) and Specific Influence (bulleted)	Relevant Characteristics of Participating Organization	Specific Strategies to Facilitate Implementation
Factors That Can Be Influenced (to some extent)		
Leadership and support • Leadership establishing priorities, consensus, managing implementation process • Presence of advocate, champion • Organizational incentive for participating staff (vs. costs) • Managerial/supervisory/administrative support *Unique to sustainability:* • Development of organizational infrastructure, policies, and procedures to codify routines • Sharing cultural artifacts		
Resources • Investment of resources needed for activities (staff, funding, equipment) *Unique to sustainability:* • Standardization, stabilization of organizational resources needed for program/ policy • Obtain funding from other resources • Low-cost approaches and/or volunteers		
Characteristics of implementers • Perceived need • Perceived benefits • Self-efficacy • Capability (skill proficiency)		

Category (boldface) and Specific Influence (bulleted)	Relevant Characteristics of Participating Organization	Specific Strategies to Facilitate Implementation
Factors Less Amenable to Influence		
Characteristics of the organization • Integration of program with existing programs and services • Effective intraorganizational communication • Expertise in assessment, planning, and evaluation; use evaluation data, feedback		
External factors • Support from interorganizational networks • Coordination with other organizations • Political support or opposition • Consistency with federal, professional mandates, social policies, and guides		

Your Turn: Planning for Sustainability

Several members of your planning team argue that sustainability planning should not begin until there is evidence that the intervention is effective. However, many experts recommend beginning sustainability planning very early in the process since some adoption and implementation actions affect sustainability. Using material in this step and other resources, outline the argument that you would present to your planning team for planning for sustainability early in the adoption and implementation process.

KEY POINTS FOR FACILITATING IMPLEMENTATION AND SUSTAINABILITY

Below are some suggestions and considerations to facilitate implementation and sustainability of programs, policies, and practices based on influences at this stage of the process.

Implementation Key Points

Actions Over Which Planning Teams Have Control

• Involve stakeholders early in the process and form positive working relationships that are characterized by trust, empathy, and shared decision making; be flexible and encourage appropriate adaptation.

• Maintain an awareness that characteristics of the program, policy, or practice will influence the process, and program design should proceed accordingly; similarly, be aware that innovations that can be adapted and that have a good fit with the organizational setting are more likely to be implemented.

• Ensure that the program, policy, or practice is consistent with mandates, policies, and guides already in place.

• Provide active and skills-based training and ongoing technical assistance and support, as needed, for implementation.

Actions That Can Be Positive Influences

• Identify or cultivate an internal program champion for the program, policy, or

practice who can work to integrate it with existing programs and services.

• Strive to develop and maintain support from all levels of the organization and to ensure that there are organizational incentives for participating.

• Invest the needed resources to facilitate implementation, particularly to ensure that implementers are motivated (e.g., aware of the needs and benefits) and have the self-efficacy, skills, and materials or equipment needed to carry out the program, policy, or practice.

• Seek or facilitate the development of support from outside of the organization (e.g., similar organizations, coalitions, professional groups), particularly if there is political opposition.

• Ensure effective communication within the organization and facilitate structures to get the work done (e.g., committees, teams, workgroups).

Important to Know

• Understand the characteristics and features of the organization and how these might influence the implementation process.

Sustainability Key Points

Actions Over Which Planning Teams Have Control

• Plan for sustainability from the very beginning of the adoption and implementation process; ensure quality implementation.

- Share information on benefits and successes.

- Involve stakeholders from early on in the process and form positive working relationships that are characterized by trust and shared decision making; be flexible and encourage appropriate adaptation.

- Maintain awareness that characteristics of the program, policy, or practice will influence the process, and proceed with program design accordingly; similarly, innovations that can be adapted and that have a good fit with the organizational setting are more likely to be adopted.

- Ensure that the program, policy, or practice is consistent with mandates, policies, and guides that are already in place.

Actions That Can Be Positive Influences

- Identify or cultivate an internal program champion for the program, policy, or practice who can work to integrate it with existing programs and services.

- Strive to develop and maintain support from all levels of the organization and to ensure that there are organizational incentives for participating and to share cultural artifacts.

- Work to develop organizational infrastructure and procedures to codify routines.

- Identify sources for long-term resources, both from within and outside of the implementing setting; design the innovation with use of low-cost approaches and/or sustainable volunteers.

- Seek or facilitate the development of support from outside of the organization (e.g., similar organizations, coalitions, professional groups), particularly if there is political opposition.

Important to Know

- Be mindful of the organizational capacity (i.e., extent to which the organization can accomplish its basic mission) and the additional requirements from the program, policy, or practice.

The key to implementation of sustainable practices is following a long-term program based on persistence, not insistence.

−Christopher Uhl, professor,
Pennsylvania State University

Develop or Update the Action Model, Action Plan, and Logic Model to Integrate Planning

In this step, you and your planning team will consolidate the planning from earlier steps into an action model, action plan, and finally, a logic model. The **action model** depicts "a systematic plan for arranging staff, resources, settings and support organizations in order to reach a target population and deliver intervention services" (Chen, 2015, p. 23), whereas the **action plan** is a more detailed document that describes actions needed to deliver and/or install the program, policy, or practice. The action plan identifies detailed actions, persons responsible, and time frames needed to deliver/install and to facilitate adoption, implementation, and sustainability of the program, policy, or practice. The **logic model** provides a graphical portrayal of the framework that demonstrates the relationships between the resources and inputs, activities, outputs, and outcomes of a program (Bucher, 2009). Optimally, the logic model was developed earlier in the planning process (Step 1), and should be revisited and revised in this step as needed.

In Step 2, you described the program, policy, or practice, the change or conceptual model, implementation approach, and the organizational context into which the program, policy, or practice is to be implemented. In Step 3, you developed an adoption plan that included strategies to facilitate the adoption process. In Step 4, you identified the conceptually based "essential elements" of the program, policy, or practice that are expected to produce program effects; these also describe complete and acceptable delivery/installation. In Step 5, you described a plan to address influences on the implementation and sustainability processes to facilitate program, policy, or practice uptake in the organizational setting.

Learning Objectives

By the end of the chapter, you will

1. Develop the action model

2. Draft an initial action plan

3. Develop or update a logic model that incorporates change and action model elements

It is now time to integrate these plan elements into an action model that graphically depicts actions and resources of stakeholders and partners, to develop an action plan that describes action details for carrying out the plan, and to update or develop the logic model that integrates the action and change models. The integrated logic model will also serve as the framework for the implementation monitoring plan in later chapters. The approach to the action model in this textbook is based on Chen's approach to program theory (Chen, 2015), which describes explicit and implicit assumptions about what actions are needed to solve a social problem and why the problem will respond to this action.

Develop the action model.

The action model describes how the planning team will work with implementers and other stakeholders within the implementing organization(s) to facilitate implementation, based on Chen's approach to program theory (Chen, 2015). The action model includes prescriptive assumptions about what needs to be done to activate the change model to produce desired outcomes/impacts.

Figure 6.1 provides a conceptual presentation concerning how planning teams can partner with implementing organizations via change agents and stakeholders to facilitate systems change within the implementing organizations and to enhance outcomes/impacts. This conceptualization draws from program theory in evaluation (Chen, 2015), approaches to changing environments (Commers, Gottlieb, & Kok, 2007), and conceptualization of mechanisms through which environments influence behavior (Kremers et al., 2010). As shown in Figure 6.1, the planning team, in collaboration with implementing organizations, identifies and works with change agents from within the organization who implement the innovation guided by the intervention and service delivery protocols required to install the program, policy, or practice in a given setting. The planning team engages other partners and provides training and other capacity development activities within the implementing organizations, as needed. The change agents within the implementing setting take actions to change selected aspects of the organizational environment or system—that is implement new programs, policies, or practices—which results in environmental change (not shown on Figure 6.1).

To illustrate, an external university planning team may partner with a school serving as the implementing setting and with a recreation commission serving as a key organizational partner, supplying recreation leaders to provide an

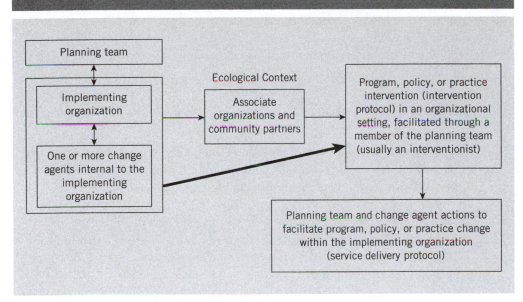

Source: Adapted from Chen (2015).

afterschool physical activity program for young people. The intervention plan or method would describe details of the afterschool program, including how workers would collaborate to plan, how the implementers would be prepared to deliver the program, and how it would be delivered to the target population. The interventionist from the planning team would work with the school and recreation staff serving as change agents (implementers) to carry out the program, which would change environmental conditions.

In the action model, it is important to identify all resources, partners, and stakeholders to be included in some aspect of the intervention process. Elements of the action model include the implementing organization; intervention protocol and service delivery protocol for the program, policy, or practice; implementers or change agents; community partners; and ecological context. These have been addressed in previous chapters and are explained below. Use the sections below to develop action model components (Worksheet 6.1) and identify actions from previous worksheets to expand into the action plan (Worksheet 6.2).

Implementing Organization

Chen (2015) emphasized the role of the implementing organization for providing basic infrastructure crucial to the program, policy, or practice. You described characteristics of the implementing organization in Step 2, Worksheet 2.2, and characterized organizational leadership, support, and resources for adoption in Step 3, Worksheet 3.1. You also described characteristics of the implementing organization for implementation and sustainability, in Step 5, Worksheets 5.1 and 5.2.

Intervention Protocol

Intervention protocol includes the major activities, events, and strategies that are part of the intervention over time, based on the program, policy, or practice description (Step 2 and Step 4). The intervention protocol, which is often described independently of the implementation context, is the description of the program, policy, or practice and of how, when, and to whom it should be delivered in a general sense. For example, in the Lifestyle Education for Activity (LEAP) intervention protocol, the action model indicates that LEAP PE, one LEAP component, should have certain instructional elements without considering school variations.

Implementers, Community Partners, and Service Delivery Protocol

Implementers, service delivery protocol, and community partners are discussed together because in the change agent approach to action planning, it is optimal to consider together the roles and activities of all stakeholders in the implementing setting. Implementers, also known as change agents or environmental actors, as well as other stakeholders, including community partners with key roles in the intervention, were identified in Steps 1, 3, and 5. These individuals or groups have primary responsibility for implementation, so their motivation and capability for carrying out the intervention are very important. They also need guidance, provided by the service delivery protocol; ideally, the service delivery protocol is developed collaboratively with change agents since they are the experts in the implementing setting and population.

The service delivery protocol addresses what must be done in the setting(s) to deliver/install the program, policy, or practice. Steps needed prior to implementation may include developing materials and communication messages, attending meetings, and providing training and/or technical assistance. The action plan is context dependent; that is, it necessarily depends on the motivation, skills, and availability of setting change agents and key stakeholders.

This was addressed in Steps 3 and 5 in relation to adoption, implementation, and sustainability. In LEAP, the service delivery protocol describes how the essential elements were put into place within the school settings (shown in Figure 6.2) and includes consideration of the flexible, adaptive intervention approach, working relationships with the schools, provision of materials and resources, and provision of training and ongoing support and technical assistance.

Ecological Context

The ecological context refers to the broader context in which the intervention takes place, also known as external factors in Table 3.2 (Step 3) and Tables 5.1 and 5.3 (Step 5) when examining influences on adoption, implementation, and sustainability.

Worksheet 6.1 provides a template for developing or updating the action model. The planning team compiles key elements from previous worksheets to complete this worksheet.

LEAP Case Illustration

An example action model, based on LEAP, is provided in Figure 6.2.

The next step is to develop a more detailed action plan that specifies who does what, and when, to operationalize the action model.

Draft an initial action plan.

Draft an initial action plan for program, policy, or practice delivery/installation and for facilitating adoption, implementation, and sustainability. An action plan is a document that describes actions needed to deliver and/or install the program, policy, or practice; it identifies all key stakeholders, roles, and activities, and summarizes the strategies used to facilitate adoption, implementation, and sustainability. The action plan operationalizes the service delivery protocol in more depth than is possible in the graphic format of the action model. Successful delivery/installation of the program, policy, or practice depends on multiple influences on the implementation process beyond the issues addressed in the service delivery protocol. Therefore, the action plan incorporates the service delivery protocol (or "doing the intervention") as well as the adoption, implementation, and sustainability plans from Steps 3 and 5 that describe strategies to facilitate the implementation and sustainability processes, which are organized by the components of the action model.

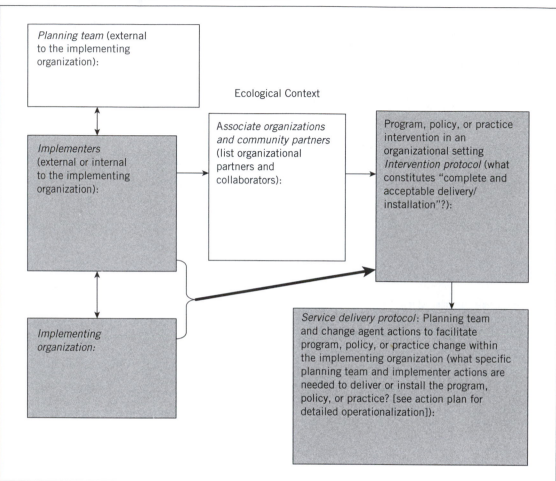

The details of the action plan will address what communication, materials, staff development, and other interactions are needed for each stakeholder or stakeholder group and how these will be delivered to each stakeholder or stakeholder group over time. It will specify action details such as *who, what, when,* and *where.* That is, it should describe who is responsible for what actions, as well as when and where these actions should take place. It is best to draft the plan early and to expect it to evolve over time as the planning team learns more about the setting and the stakeholders.

Facilitating both *service delivery/installation protocol* and *adoption, implementation, and sustainability* depend on establishing and maintaining good working

Figure 6.2   Action Model Based on LEAP

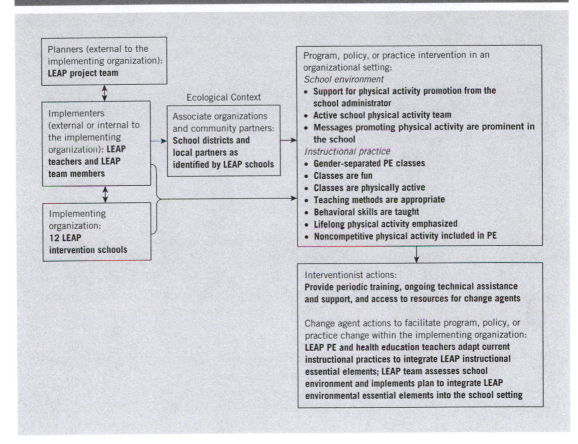

relationships with change agents and stakeholders. Actions to support implementing and evaluating the intervention must be established at multiple levels including participants; stakeholders who may control access to participants, such as parents of participants, implementers, organizational administrators, and supervisors; other stakeholders who are affected by the intervention; and stakeholders outside of the setting, all of whom may be influential on the process.

For example, in a school setting, an adoption decision is often made at the district and school level by the superintendent and principal, respectively, and may also require approval of the school board. Similarly, in worksite settings, an adoption decision may be made by the CEO, with approval also required by the board of directors. Having support for adoption from the head of the organization, however, is just the beginning. The planning team must have the support of middle managers and work supervisors, as well as the frontline workers serving as change agents and program, policy, or practice implementers. Other employees may be affected by the intervention directly or indirectly and may act accordingly. As discussed in Step 1, the planning team must establish and maintain effective working relationships with change agents and provide training, technical assistance, ongoing communication, and support to ensure competency and commitment. Also important is a mutual understanding of roles, responsibilities, and tasks related to implementing the program, policy, or practice. This requires effective interpersonal communication (i.e., conveying respect) and professional communication (i.e., conveying clear expectations).

Furthermore, the planning team will need to work appropriately within the setting to accomplish this. For example, mechanisms for regular communication with change agents (e.g., teachers and school staff who are the implementers) and key stakeholders (e.g., curriculum coordinators, assistant principal, principal, and parents in school settings) will need to be established. The best approach (e.g., in-person visits, meetings, email, telephone, newsletters) may vary by stakeholder within a given organization and across organizations within the same system (e.g., for schools within the same school district).

Use Worksheet 6.2 for action planning that integrates previous planning elements. Worksheet 6.2 is a generic planning tool that will need to be tailored for each project and setting. It includes identification of stakeholders, resources, timeframe, actions needed, and responsible parties.

Develop or update a logic model that incorporates change and action model elements.

In this step, you will update or develop a logic model that incorporates elements from both the change and action models and serves as the organizing framework for the implementation monitoring plan. A logic model provides a graphical portrayal of the framework used throughout program planning, implementation, and evaluation and demonstrates the relationships between the resources and inputs, activities, outputs, and outcomes of a program (Bucher, 2009). It is a graphic way to organize information, display thinking, and describe planned actions with expected results (Knowlton, 2013). Logic models are useful for summarizing the structure of a program visually (McDavid, Huse, & Hawthorn, 2013) and can take multiple forms (Knowlton, 2013). The focus of this textbook

Worksheet 6.2 Action Planning Template Based on Action Model

(Develop from actions indicated on worksheets from previous steps—multiple sheets are likely needed)

Category	Collaborating stakeholders	Actions needed	Resources, materials, skills, training, etc. needed	Details (who, what, when, and where)
Implementing organization (characteristics, leadership, support, resources)				
Intervention protocol (intervention description, change model, complete and acceptable delivery/ installation, characteristics of intervention)				
Implementers, community partners, service delivery protocol (intervention approach, characteristics of implementers, implementation process, stakeholders)				
Ecological context (context, external factors)				

will be on using logic models to integrate action and change models and to organize the comprehensive implementation monitoring plan.

It is beyond the scope of this textbook to address constructing logic models from scratch; rather, the reader is referred to other resources such as the Knowlton and Phillips' textbook *The Logic Model Guidebook* (Knowlton, 2013), and Chapter 2, "Understanding and Applying Program Logic Models," in the McDavid, Huse, and Hawthorn's textbook *Program Evaluation and Performance Measurement: An Introduction to Practice* (McDavid et al., 2013).

The content needed for the logic model comes from the implementation planning process discussed thus far in this textbook. First you will select an appropriate logic model template, provided in this section, then update or develop the logic model that will be used in subsequent chapters to organize the evaluation plan.

Selecting a Logic Model Template

A general logic model template is provided in Table 6.1. This model includes inputs, or resources that enable the production of program activities resulting in outputs, and outcomes, within a specific context.

The logic model is organized into three major categories/columns: inputs, which describe funding and other resources including partners; outputs, which describe activities, who is reached, and expected effects; and outcomes, which include intervention outcomes/impacts, as well as mediating and moderating factors that reflect the change model. For change to take place, the change model must be activated through implementation of the program, policy, or practice,

Table 6.1 General Logic Model Format

Inputs	Outputs			Outcomes		
Resources	Activities	Who is reached	Results of activities	Short-term outcomes/ impacts	Medium-term outcomes/ impacts	Long-term outcomes/ impacts
Funding and partners	What we do	Individuals in groups we reach	Immediate effects	Short-term effects (e.g., change in mediating variables)	Medium-term effects (e.g., change in behavior)	Long-term effects (e.g., change in outcome variables)

guided by the action model and action plan. The change model includes causal assumptions and descriptive theory that articulate the important influences on the outcomes of interest (Chen, 2015). The goal of the change model is to link cause and effect, that is, to understand through what mechanisms the program produces results (Astbury & Leeuw, 2010).

The input column reflects stakeholder involvement, relationship development, and/or collaboration with partner organizations if these are applicable to your program, policy, or practice, as they are often the most valuable resources for many real-world interventions. The output columns reflect implementation of the innovation and will be evaluated with corresponding implementation monitoring elements to be discussed in subsequent chapters. Finally, the outcome columns reflect the expected outcomes and impacts of the intervention, are guided by the change model, and are assessed by effectiveness evaluation approaches.

The number of columns and details of what goes into each column in the logic model depend on a number of factors including the intervention approach and primary outcomes/impacts. Below, three example logic models are provided that illustrate (1) a program, policy, or practice implemented by change agents with a primary environmental outcome and a secondary individual behavior outcome; (2) a program, policy, or practice implemented by change agents with a primary individual behavior outcome and a secondary environmental outcome; and (3) a program, policy, or practice implemented by outsiders to the setting with an individual behavior outcome. Each example has an accompanying worksheet for planning; *select the one worksheet that "fits" best with your project, or design your project-specific model.*

Provided with each worksheet template is an illustration of how to "read" the change-of-events logic model from left to right in the second row, a set of guiding questions to help the planning team fill in the content for each column in the third row, and an indication of type of planning model and evaluation (e.g., action model and implementation monitoring or change model and outcome/impact) in the fourth row.

Sample Logic Model Templates

The Environmental Interventions in Children's Homes (ENRICH) project illustrates a logic model for a program, policy, or practice delivered by change agents with a primary emphasis on environmental change and a secondary emphasis on individual behavior change (Table 6.2) (Saunders et al., 2013). The inputs column for ENRICH combined resources, activities, and who

Table 6.2 ENRICH Logic Model

	Inputs	Immediate Impact	Short-Term Impact	Organizational Outcome	Individual Behavior Outcome
Logic Model	Developing effective working relationships with the RCHs, providing training and consultation, facilitating access to local resources for wellness team, and securing administrative support from chief executive officer in RCHs . . .	will facilitate the development of skills and confidence among wellness team members for creating a healthier home environment that, with a supportive organizational environment, . . .	will result in the development and implementation of effective wellness team plans that . . .	will result in an RCH environment that promotes and supports PA and eating FV by (1) providing more opportunities for PA and eating FV; (2) ensuring that opportunities are appealing (i.e., fun and tasty); (3) strengthening social support and adult modeling for PA and FV; (4) developing, strengthening, and/or enforcing policies supporting PA and FV; (5) increasing positive media messages related to PA and FV; and (6) strengthening organizational structures to support these changes that . . .	will result in increased PA and improved dietary practices in RCH residents ages 11–18 years: (1) Meets PA recommendation: 60 minutes of MVPA on 5 or more of previous 7 days; (2) Meets dietary guideline: 5 servings of FV per day.
Evaluation	ACTION MODEL Implementation monitoring			CHANGE MODEL Outcome/Impact assessment	

Source: Saunders et al. (2013).

Abbreviations: FV = fruits and vegetables; MVPA = moderate-to-vigorous physical activity; PA = physical activity; RCH = residential children's homes; WT = wellness teams

was reached and reflected the ENRICH emphasis on working effectively with stakeholders. ENRICH provided training and technical assistance to Wellness Teams, who served as change agents within children's homes. The immediate effect of working with Wellness Teams was Wellness Teams returning to their organizations to assess their residential children's home environments and develop and carry out a plan to create a health-promoting environment. The primary organizational outcome, based on Cohen's structural ecologic model (Cohen et al., 2000) was the health-promoting environment that encourages physical activity (PA) and nutrition as the primary study outcome. For the secondary study outcome, this changed environment was expected to have a positive impact on physical activity and eating fruits and vegetables for children residing in the homes (Table 6.3). Note that ENRICH did not have a mediating factors column in the outputs section. Worksheet 6.3 provides a logic model planning template for projects similar to ENRICH.

Table 6.3 depicts the LEAP outcomes logic model as an example of an innovation delivered by change agents where individual behavior is the primary outcome with mediating factors and long-term health outcomes are part of the change model (Dishman et al., 2005, 2009; Pate et al., 2005). LEAP provided training and support to LEAP team members, who served as change agents in the schools (Ward et al., 2006). The LEAP teams changed instructional practices and the school environment to promote physical activity in girls. The changed environment was expected to positively impact physical activity enjoyment, self-efficacy, social support, and connections to outside opportunities, which results in increased physical activity. The change model was based on the social ecological framework informed by social cognitive theory. Long-term health outcomes were not assessed in LEAP.

Note that organizational change in LEAP was considered a process variable, whereas in ENRICH, the organizational change variable was considered the primary outcome. Accordingly, the LEAP logic model had four rather than three columns in the outputs component. Worksheet 6.4 provides a logic model planning template for projects similar to LEAP.

The final logic model template provided here depicts intervention delivery by outsiders to the setting with an individual behavior outcome and is illustrated by the Active Winners project, which was an afterschool physical activity program for middle school youth (Pate et al., 2003). The Active Winners program was delivered by an interventionist who was an outsider to the setting, hired by the research team (Table 6.4). The change model was based on social cognitive theory and Pender's health promotion model (Pender, Smith, & Vernof, 1987; Nola J. Pender, 2011). The afterschool program was designed to be fun and participatory for middle school students and was expected to change self-efficacy and social support, resulting in increased physical activity among students. Worksheet 6.5 provides a logic model planning template for projects similar to Active Winners.

Worksheet 6.3   General Logic Model With Questions to Guide Development

(Innovation delivered by change agents with a primary environmental and secondary individual behavior change focus)

	Inputs		Outputs			Outcomes/Impacts	
	What We Invest	What We Do	Who Is Reached and Expected Effects	Changes Made by Change Agent	Organizational Outcome	Mediating Factors	Individual Behavior Outcome
Logic Model	Resources provided enable us to . . .	conduct certain activities that will . . .	reach the "change agents" and provide them the tools and skills needed to . . .	work on environmental policy and changes that will result in . . .	environmental change, which will influence the . . .	mediating factors through which the environment influences . . .	behavior of individuals who spend time in the changed environment.
Guiding Questions	What are the primary resources? What do you have to invest?	What are the primary activities that work toward achieving project goals?	Who serves as the change agent? How will your activities enable the change agent to carry out intervention?	What do you expect the change agent to do? What actions will change the environment (intervention)?	What are the expected results of change agent activity? What structural changes are expected in the environment?	What are the mediating factors affecting how environment influences behavior?	What changes are expected in population behavior as a result of the changed environment?
Template							
Evaluation	ACTION MODEL Process evaluation/Implementation monitoring				CHANGE MODEL Outcome/Impact evaluation		

Table 6.3 The LEAP Outcomes Logic Model

Logic Model	Inputs	Outputs				Outcomes/Impacts		
	What We Invest	**What We Do**	**Who Is Reached**	**Expected Effects: Change Agent Actions**	**Expected Effects: School Change**	**Short-Term Changes, Impact on Influence Variables**	**Medium-Term Change on Individual Behavior Outcome**	**Long-Term Change on Health Outcomes**
	Two intervention staff . . .	provided training and support to . . .	LEAP team members who went back into the school environment . . .	and changed instructional practices in physical education and the school environment to promote physical activity . . .	that resulted in change to the school environment	that resulted in increased enjoyment, self-efficacy, social support, and connections to outside physical activity opportunities . . .	that resulted in increased physical activity among high school girls.	[Not assessed in LEAP]
	ACTION MODEL					CHANGE MODEL		
	Implementation monitoring					Outcome/Impact evaluation		

137

Worksheet 6.4   General Logic Model With Questions to Guide Development

(Innovation delivered by change agents with individual behavior change as the primary focus)

| | Inputs | Outputs | | | Outcomes/Impacts | | |
	What We Invest	What We Do	Who Is Reached and Expected Effects	Changes Made by Change Agent	Short-Term Changes, Impact on Influence Variables	Medium-Term Change on Individual Behavior Outcome	Long-Term Change on Outcomes
Logic Model	Resources provided enable us to . . .	conduct certain activities that will . . .	reach the change agents and provide them with tools and skills needed to . . .	carry out the intervention, which will result in . . .	change in influence variables, which will influence the . . .	behavior of individuals reached by intervention which, if sustained, will . . .	have positive effects on outcomes.
Guiding Questions	What are the primary resources? What do you have to invest?	What are primary activities that work toward achieving project goals?	Who serves as the change agent? How will your activities enable the change agent to carry out intervention?	What do you expect the change agent to do? What activities constitute carrying out intervention?	What are expected intervention impacts on influence variables?	What changes are expected in behavior as a result of the intervention?	What problems are impacted by behavioral factors?
Template							
Evaluation	ACTION MODEL Process evaluation/Implementation monitoring				CHANGE MODEL Outcome/Impact evaluation		

Table 6.4 Outcomes Logic Model for the Active Winners Project

	What We Invest	What We Do	Who Is Reached and Expected Immediate Effects	Short-Term Changes, Impact on Influence Variables	Medium-Term Change on Individual Behavior Outcome	Long-Term Change on Health Outcomes
Logic Model	Providing a staff person, equipment, and transportation . . .	for a physical activity (PA) afterschool program will result in . . .	middle school students participating and enjoying the program, which will result in . . .	changes in PA self-efficacy and social support, which will result in . . .	increased PA among middle school children.	[Not assessed in Active Winners]
	ACTION MODEL			CHANGE MODEL		
	Implementation monitoring			Outcome evaluation		

139

Worksheet 6.5   General Logic Model Template With Questions to Guide Development

(Innovation delivered by outsiders with individual behavior change as the primary focus)

	What We Invest	What We Do	Who Is Reached and Expected Immediate Effects	Short-Term Changes, Impact on Influence Variables	Medium-Term Change on Individual Behavior Outcome	Long-Term Change on Health Outcomes
Logic Model	Resources provided enable us to . . .	carry out the intervention that will . . .	reach the program participants, which will result in . . .	change in influence variables, which will influence . . .	behavior of individuals reached, which will . . .	have positive effects on health outcomes.
Guiding Questions	What are primary resources? What do you have to invest?	What are primary activities of the intervention?	Who is the priority audience? Are there expected follow-up activities or other reactions?	What are expected intervention impacts on influence variables?	What changes are expected in population behavior as a result of the intervention?	What health problems are impacted by behavioral or environmental factors?
Template						
Evaluation	ACTION MODEL Implementation monitoring			CHANGE MODEL Outcome evaluation		

Summary

· ·

At the completion of this step, the planning team will have an action model, action plan, and logic model that should provide a very clear sense of program, policy, or practice details, stakeholder involvement and roles, and action steps needed to put the program, policy, or practice into place. This step builds on and adds detail to previous steps, in which the innovation, its context, and strategies for facilitating adoption, implementation, and sustainability were developed. This completes Phase II. In Phase III, the planning team will develop the plan for monitoring the implementation process.

KEY POINTS FOR INTEGRATING PLANNING

- Effectively planned and implemented innovations have well-designed action and change models.

- The action model includes intervention protocol and service delivery protocol, as well as consideration of the implementers, the implementing organization, and the ecological context of the innovation.

- Effectively planned and implemented interventions have a detailed action plan that describes a context-specific work plan. This plan involves change agents and other stakeholders as well as the detailed steps of the service delivery protocol (i.e., program, policy, or practice delivery/installation) and strategies to facilitate adoption, implementation, and sustainability.

- A logic model can be used to integrate both action and change models.

Implementation Monitoring Planning

This section of the textbook guides the reader through implementation monitoring planning. In this phase consisting of two steps, the reader will develop implementation monitoring questions for each element of the implementation monitoring plan and select quantitative and qualitative evaluation methods, as appropriate, to address the implementation monitoring questions. This phase culminates in the development of the final implementation monitoring plan.

Figure III.1 The Implementation Planning and Monitoring Process, With Phase III, Implementation Monitoring Planning, Highlighted

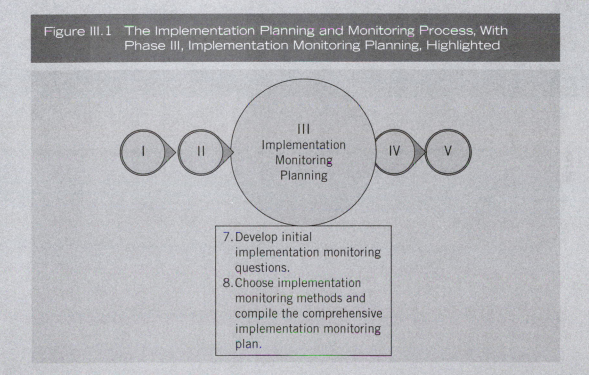

When you translate a dream into reality,
it's never a full implementation. It is
easier to dream than to do.

-Shai Agassi

Develop Initial Implementation Monitoring Questions

In this step, you and your planning team are ready to begin developing the implementation monitoring plan. You will state general formative and/or summative purposes for using implementation monitoring data, develop potential implementation monitoring questions or objectives for each component of the implementation monitoring plan, and begin organizing the evaluation plan according to a logic model.

Articulate the general purposes for conducting implementation monitoring for a specific program, policy, or practice change.

It is important to articulate the general purposes for conducting implementation monitoring for a specific program, policy, or practice change. General purposes for conducting implementation monitoring refer to **formative** and **summative uses** of the data. Formative uses of implementation monitoring data include keeping the program "on track" (Devaney & Rossi, 1997; Helitzer, Yoon, Wallerstein, & Dow y Garcia-Velarde, 2000; Scriven, 1967) by instituting early, corrective action as needed. For example, implementation monitoring data might reveal problems with personnel, scheduling, access to space, and/or participant transportation that might have serious effects on completeness, fidelity, and/or reach of program, policy, or practice implementation. If intervention staff members are absent, scheduling precludes intervention activities, program space is not available, and/or participants cannot get to and from the program; then the program cannot proceed as planned. If this information is known and acted upon in a timely manner, these problems can likely be fixed prior to causing much "damage." If, however, these problems persist for weeks or months before corrective action is taken, the damage to completeness, fidelity, and/or reach may be extensive and affect project outcomes. Formative use of implementation monitoring data can prevent serious implementation problems such as a "Type III error," in which the planned program is not implemented (Green & Kreuter, 1999). More extensive coverage on uses of formative implementation monitoring data is provided in Step 9.

Summative uses of implementation monitoring data entail making a judgment about the extent to which the program, policy, or practice was implemented completely, with fidelity, and with adequate reach. Summative data, in turn, can be used to interpret and explain program outcomes, analyze how a program works, and provide input for future planning (Baranowski & Stables, 2000).

At this point in the planning process, the focus is to determine the extent to which implementation monitoring data will be used for formative and/or summative purposes, as well as what those purposes are. This should be decided based on planning team and stakeholder needs and will depend, in part, on resources available. There are three overlapping resource-related issues to consider when determining priorities concerning formative and/or summative uses of implementation data: collection of data by measurement and/or intervention staff; separate versus the same data systems for formative and summative purposes; and turnaround time for making data available, especially for formative purposes.

There are often challenges to making implementation monitoring data available to interventionists in a timely fashion to enable early, corrective action. It is much faster for the interventionist to collect some data to use for formative purposes; however, collecting data will likely distract the interventionist from implementation tasks, and the data will be less objective. Objectivity may be inadvertently affected by interventionist expectations and socially desirable behavior on the part of implementers and/or participants. Measurement staff, not involved with the carrying out the innovation, are more objective data collectors, but usually require greater turnaround time to collect, enter, and report the information for formative purposes, which can potentially limit its usefulness.

It is possible, of course, to have a dual approach in which interventionists collect some limited amount of data, such as documenting their activities, and measurement staff who are not involved in intervention activities collect objective data with adequate turnaround times for formative feedback; however, this requires planning and resources including trained staff, as well as project priorities that support these activities. In dual approaches, the formative and summative systems for collecting data can be completely independent, or they may use the same data collection tools and possibly the same or similar data collection procedures.

As shown in Table 7.1, each recommended element of an implementation monitoring plan—fidelity, completeness, dose received, reach, recruitment, and context—can be used for both formative and/or summative purposes (Baranowski & Stables, 2000; Saunders, Evans, & Joshi, 2005; Steckler & Linnan, 2002). Ideally, process data would be used for both purposes (Bartholomew et al., 2006).

The formative use of implementation monitoring data is to keep a defined program on track as it is happening. In contrast, **formative evaluation** is frequently defined as obtaining data to inform a program that is being developed or refined. In this textbook, the phrase "formative uses of process evaluation" refers to a program that has already been developed and is in the process of being carried out, not to an evolving program in which data is being used for informing the development of the program.

LEAP Case Illustration

The Lifestyle Education for Activity (LEAP) provides an example of formative and summative uses of implementation monitoring. The LEAP planning team reported seven purposes for collecting implementation monitoring data: (1) documenting completeness of LEAP staff activities including training and all contacts with schools; (2) documenting reach at the teacher, school staff, and student levels; (3) getting feedback from teachers, school staff, and students; (4) providing feedback on change agent implementation (completeness, fidelity, and reach for corrective action by LEAP staff); (5) monitoring fidelity and completeness of LEAP implementation by change agents; (6) monitoring the organizational-level implementation of LEAP components in intervention schools; and (7) monitoring environmental and policy factors in intervention and secular trends in control schools that could potentially affect program outcomes (Saunders, Ward, Felton, Dowda, & Pate, 2006; Ward et al., 2006).

The functions outlined in purposes one through four above were administered by the interventionists, and the data were used primarily for formative purposes and were recorded by interventionists and presented at project staff meetings; these are reported by Ward and colleagues (Ward et al., 2006). This information was also used in a summative manner to document what happened in LEAP. The

Table 7.1 Process Evaluation Plan Elements With Formative and Summative Applications

Plan Component	Purpose	Formative Uses	Summative Uses
Fidelity (quality)	Extent to which program, policy, or practice was implemented consistently with underlying theory and philosophy	Monitor and adjust program implementation as needed to ensure theoretical integrity and program quality	Describe and/or quantify fidelity of program, policy, or practice implementation
Dose delivered (completeness)	Amount or number of intended units of each component delivered or provided by interventionists	Monitor and adjust program implementation to ensure all components of program, policy, or practice are delivered	Describe and/or quantify the dose of the program, policy, or practice delivered
Dose received (exposure)	Extent to which participants actively engage with, interact with, are receptive to, and/or use materials or recommended resources; can include "initial use" and "continued use"	Monitor and take corrective action to ensure participants are receiving and/or using materials/resources	Describe and/or quantify how much of the program, policy, or practice was received
(Satisfaction)	Participant (primary and secondary audiences) satisfaction with program and interactions with staff and/or investigators	Obtain regular feedback from primary and secondary targets and use feedback as needed for corrective action	Describe and/or rate participant satisfaction and how feedback was used
Reach (participation rate)	Proportion of the intended priority audience that participates in the program, policy, or practice; often measured by attendance; includes documentation of barriers to participation	Monitor numbers and characteristics of participants; ensure sufficient numbers of target population are being reached	Quantify how much of the intended target audience participated in the program, policy, or practice; describe those who participated and those who did not
Recruitment	Procedures used to approach and attract participants at individual or organizational levels; includes maintenance of participant involvement in intervention and measurement components of study	Monitor and document recruitment procedures to ensure protocol is followed; adjust as needed to ensure reach	Describe recruitment procedures

Source: Taken from Saunders, Evans, and Joshi (2005).

data pertaining to purposes five through seven were collected by independent measurement staff, used for summative purposes, summarized annually for the research team, and used in data analysis. Using summative information in outcome data analysis revealed greater intervention effects in schools with higher levels of implementation; that is, schools with higher levels of implementation had a larger percentage of girls engaging in vigorous physical activity compared to other schools (Saunders et al., 2006). In LEAP, the same data collection forms were used to assess completeness and fidelity of change agent implementation for both formative and summative purposes; data collection procedures were similar, as well.

Use Worksheet 7.1 to conduct preliminary planning for broad purposes of implementation monitoring for a specific project. Specific purposes of implementation monitoring data are defined by the implementation monitoring questions addressed in the next section. A LEAP example of Worksheet 7.1 is provided in Table 7.2.

Select components of the implementation monitoring plan and draft implementation monitoring questions.

In addition to completeness, fidelity, reach, and dose received described in Step 4, the comprehensive implementation monitoring plan may include *context* and *recruitment*, described below.

Context encompasses the organizational, community, or greater environment that may influence program, policy, or practice implementation or study outcomes. Contextual factors encompass characteristics of the organization including existing structures, interorganizational connections, and external factors such as the history, events, political factors, and controversy that are concurrent with the program (Scheirer, Shediac, & Cassady, 1995; Viadro, Earp, & Altpeter, 1997; Zapka, Goins, Pbert, & Ockene, 2004).

This includes broader events in the environment and media unrelated to intervention activities, also known as **secular trends,** which could influence either implementation processes or outcomes. These may be community specific, such as a media campaign by a local nonprofit on the same issue as the innovation, or broader in scope, such as national media events or related federal policies. Federal policies or professional guidelines are issued periodically and may be consistent or inconsistent with the guidelines provided as part of a specific innovation. This category also includes contamination, or the extent to

Worksheet 7.1 Purposes of Implementation Monitoring

Purpose (formative, summative, or both)	Who Collects	When It Is Collected	Who Receives Information	Turnaround Time

Table 7.2 Purposes of Implementation Monitoring in LEAP

Purpose (formative, summative, or both)	Who Collects	When It Is Collected	Who Receives Information	Turnaround Time
Formative	LEAP intervention staff	Periodic observation of instructional practices and environment; end of year surveys with teachers and high school girls	LEAP intervention team	Immediate for staff; team meets weekly
Summative	Process evaluator (not involved in intervention)	Two observations of instructional practices and environment per class per semester; record reviews and interviews once per year	LEAP investigator team	End of year; full summary at end of intervention

which the control group was inadvertently exposed to intervention activities. Of course, the control group can also be influenced by secular trends. Because of the importance of context for program, policy, and practice change, it is essential to monitor contextual factors in both intervention and control groups throughout the intervention process.

Recruitment refers to organized and systematic efforts to obtain participants including individuals, change agents, and organizations. Recruiting and maintaining participants and organizations are crucial to the success of the program, policy, or practice but may also be a challenge. Recruitment entails identifying the potential population to be recruited based on the sampling frame, which is usually dictated by study design, application of eligibility criteria, and engagement in the recruiting process (Elder et al., 2008). In organizational settings, recruitment is a multilevel process; for example, in schools, recruitment efforts are directed at the district, school, and classroom, and at individual students and parents/guardians. Effective recruitment efforts are culturally relevant, use appropriate incentives for each level, use strategies such as personal contact, and provide clear communication about the consenting process, expectations, and benefits (Elder et al., 2008). Effective recruiters demonstrate caring and altruism and respect privacy and confidentiality; furthermore, the program, policy, or practice is endorsed by an internal advocate (Elder et al., 2008).

For implementation monitoring, the planning team documents the procedures used to approach and attract participants at individual and organizational levels. This includes participant involvement in both the intervention and measurement components of the study. Protecting human subjects is essential, so organizational and professional guidelines that protect the rights of human subjects and that guide ethical practice should be followed; see http://eval.org/ for American Evaluation Association website ("AEA—American Evaluation Association: Home," n.d.).

One or more questions should be included for each plan element—fidelity, completeness, dose received, reach, context, and/or recruitment—and for each component of the innovation. Not all plan components will apply to all innovations; however, a minimum of fidelity, completeness, and reach are recommended. Implementation monitoring questions should be based on a combination of what has been defined as complete and acceptable delivery/ installation by the planning team in collaboration with stakeholders, and consensus on priority issues, and should be guided by modeling questions such as those in Table 7.3 or other sources.

There is a tendency for the planning team to pose too many questions, especially given the limited resources often available to address them. Part of the planning process involves setting priorities about what is important to know during implementation, which should be informed largely by what information will be used within the project and shared with stakeholders on a regular basis.

The specific evaluation questions are likely to be as varied as the projects themselves. See the appendix in King, Morris, and Fitz-Gibbon (King, 1987, pp. 129–141) for an extensive list of potential process evaluation and implementation monitoring questions to use as models. In addition, see Table 7.3 for broadly stated model implementation monitoring questions, adapted from Saunders et al. (2005).

Table 7.3 Sample Questions for Each Component in an Implementation Monitoring Plan

Plan Element	Sample Implementation Monitoring Questions
Fidelity	• To what extent was the program, policy, or practice implemented consistently with the underlying theory and philosophy? • To what extent was training for change agents provided as planned (consistent with the underlying theory and/or philosophy)? • In what ways was program, policy, or practice implementation consistent with or not consistent with the underlying theory and philosophy? (qualitative)
Completeness (dose delivered)	• To what extent were all of the intended units or components of the program, policy, or practice provided to program participants? • To what extent were all materials (written and audiovisual) designed for use in the change effort used? • To what extent was all of the intended content covered? • To what extent were all of the intended methods, strategies, and/or activities used? • To what extent were all components of the policy and/or environment addressed or included? • What adjustments were made to program, policy, or practice components, materials, content, activities, and/or policies in specific settings? (qualitative)
Dose received (exposure-individual participants; exposure-change agents; satisfaction)	• To what extent were participants present at intervention activities engaged in the activities? • To what extent did participants engage in recommended follow-up behavior? • To what extent do change agents feel confident to institute policy change following training? • How did participants react to specific aspects of the program, policy, or practice or training? (qualitative)
Reach (participation rate)	• What proportion of the priority target audience attended each program session? How many participated in at least three quarters of possible sessions? • What proportion of the possible organizations had representatives participate in all of the program, policy, or practice workshop series for skill development?

Plan Element	Sample Implementation Monitoring Questions
Recruitment (assessed qualitatively)	• What planned and actual recruitment procedures were used to attract individuals, groups, and/or organizations? • What were the barriers to recruiting individuals, groups, and organizations? • What planned and actual procedures were used to encourage continued involvement of individuals, groups, and organizations? • What were the barriers to maintaining involvement of individuals, groups, and organizations?
Context	What factors in the organization, community, social/political context, or other situational issues could potentially affect either program, policy, or practice implementation or the intervention outcome? (qualitative)

Source: Adapted from Saunders, Evans, and Joshi (2005).

A template for drafting implementation monitoring questions for a three-component innovation can be found in Worksheet 7.2.

LEAP Case Illustration

An example of implementation monitoring questions from LEAP is provided in Table 7.4. The components represented are dose delivered, which pertained to the training, technical assistance, and support that LEAP staff provided to change agents (i.e., members of the LEAP team); reach into the change agent population for training; and dose received by change agents, which pertained to their preparation to carry out LEAP. Fidelity and completeness questions related to the extent to which the LEAP instructional and environmental essential elements were implemented by change agents. Contextual factors were assessed annually through an interview with the assistant principal, and recruitment was also documented.

Organize implementation monitoring plan questions according to the logic model.

The components of the implementation monitoring plan can be organized by the logic model columns. In Step 6, the action and change models were reflected in the different "halves" of the logic model. The action model corresponds to the implementation monitoring component; additional rows can now be added to reflect implementation monitoring plan components and implementation

Worksheet 7.2   Drafting Implementation Monitoring Questions for a Three-Component Innovation

	Evaluation Questions
Component A:	
Completeness	
Fidelity	
Reach	
Context	
Recruitment	
Component B:	
Completeness	
Fidelity	
Reach	
Context	
Recruitment	
Component C:	
Completeness	
Fidelity	
Reach	
Context	
Recruitment	

Source: Based on Saunders, Evans, and Joshi (2005).

Table 7.4   Example LEAP Implementation Monitoring Questions

Instructional Practices and Healthy School Environment	
	Evaluation Questions
Dose delivered	To what extent did LEAP staff provide all innovation components, materials, and equipment through training, technical assistance, and ongoing support?

Instructional Practices and Healthy School Environment	
	Evaluation Questions
Reach	To what extent did LEAP team members attend training?
Dose received	To what extent did LEAP team members have the confidence and skills needed to carry out LEAP in their school?
Completeness and fidelity	To what extent did LEAP team members install all seven instructional and four environmental essential elements (physical activity–promoting environment)?
Context	What contextual factors are present that could affect the outcome (school policies and practices in intervention and control groups)?
Recruitment	What recruitment procedures were used at the school, teacher/school staff, and student levels? What recruitment procedures were most effective?

monitoring questions. Worksheet 7.3 provides a template for organizing the implementation monitoring components in your draft plan along with your associated evaluation questions. Note: Use a logic model template from Step 6 that is appropriate for your project.

LEAP Case Illustration

Table 7.5 illustrates LEAP implementation monitoring questions for dose delivered, reach, dose received, and fidelity and completeness, organized into the logic model columns. For LEAP, dose delivered pertains to training and other resources that project staff delivered to the change agents. Reach was at the organizational level; therefore, reach pertains to reach into the organizations and the change agents from the organizations. Dose received refers to the confidence and skills that change agents obtained from training, technical assistance, and perceptions of ongoing support provided by the project staff. Fidelity and completeness refer to changes made by change agents to policies, practices, and the environment: in short, implementation of the program, policy, or practice.

The planning team now has a draft list of implementation monitoring questions and has begun to organize the implementation monitoring plan. Finalizing this list of questions is an iterative process that will continue as we consider implementation monitoring methods in the next step.

Worksheet 7.3   Template for Organizing Implementation Monitoring Plan Using a Logic Model

	Inputs	Outputs			Outcomes/Impacts		
	What We Invest	What We Do	Who Is Reached and Expected Effects	Changes Made by Change Agent	Short-Term Changes, Impact on Influence Variables	Medium-Term Change on Individual Behavior Outcome	Long-Term Change on Health Outcomes
Logic Model	Resources provided enable us to . . .	conduct certain activities that will	reach the change agents and provide them with tools and skills needed to . . .	carry out the program, policy, or practice, which will result in . . .	change in influence variables, which will influence the	behavior of individuals reached by the program, policy, or practice, which, if sustained, will . . .	have positive effects on health outcomes.
Evaluation and Questions	Dose delivered		Reach and dose received	Fidelity and completeness	Outcome/ impact: influence variables or determinants	Outcome/impact: individual behavior	Outcome: health issue or problem
	ACTION MODEL—Implementation monitoring				CHANGE MODEL—Outcome evaluation		

156

Table 7.5 LEAP Logic Model to Organize the Implementation Monitoring Plan

	Inputs	Outputs			Outcomes/Impacts		
	What We Invest	**What We Do**	**Who Is Reached and Expected Effects**	**Changes Made by Change Agent**	**Short-Term Changes, Impact on Influence Variables**	**Medium-Term Change on Individual Behavior Outcome**	**Long-Term Change on Health Outcomes**
Logic Model	Resources provided enable us to . . .	conduct training and other activities that will . . .	reach the change agents and provide them with tools and skills needed to . . .	carry out the program, policy, or practice, which will result in . . .	change in influence variables, which will influence the . . .	behavior of individuals reached by the program, policy, or practice, which, if sustained, will . . .	have positive effects on health outcomes.
Evaluation Elements and Sample Questions	Dose delivered		Reach and dose received	Fidelity and completeness	Outcome/impact: influence variables or determinants	Outcome/impact: individual behavior	Outcome: health issue or problem
	To what extent did LEAP staff provide all program, policy, or practice components, materials, and equipment through training, technical assistance, and ongoing support? To what extent did LEAP team members have the confidence and skills needed to carry out LEAP in their school?		To what extent did LEAP team members attend training? To what extent did LEAP team members have the confidence and skills needed to carry out LEAP in their school?	To what extent did LEAP team members install all seven instructional and four environmental essential elements?			
	ACTION MODEL—Implementation monitoring				CHANGE MODEL—Outcome evaluation		

Source: Based on Saunders, Ward, Felton, Dowda, and Pate (2006).

Your Turn: Ethics of Excessive Data Collection

Less is more (or is it?): There is often a tendency in implementation monitoring to ask a large number of evaluation questions, which will result in collecting large amounts of data without considering what is most important and what can realistically be used. If all of the question suggestions listed in Table 7.3 were used, the planning team would have a total of 20 questions, which would require considerable resources, and data could be burdensome to collect. What are the potential practical and ethical issues for collecting more data than feasibly can be used? To develop your response, see the American Evaluation Association's Guiding Principles for Evaluators at http://www.eval.org/p/cm/ld/fid=51.

KEY POINTS FOR DEVELOPING IMPLEMENTATION MONITORING QUESTIONS

- It is important to have formative and summative purposes for implementation monitoring.

- Early planning limits barriers to timely use of formative information.

- The implementation monitoring plan includes fidelity, completeness, and reach; it may also include dose received, context, and recruitment.

- The implementation monitoring questions and the plan are drafted for each component or element of the plan.

- A logic model can be used to organize the comprehensive evaluation plan.

Here's the thing: If you're monitoring every single thing that goes on in a given culture, if you have all the information that is there to be had, then that is the equivalent of having none of it. How are you going to process that amount of information?

—Alan Moore

STEP 8

Choose Implementation Monitoring Methods and Compile the Comprehensive Implementation Monitoring Plan

In this step, you and your planning team will review evaluation methods applied to implementation monitoring, select specific methods to address implementation monitoring questions, and organize the methods into a plan using a logic model.

Consider options for implementation monitoring design and methods.

This step consists of reviewing and considering options for implementation monitoring design and methods, including data sources, sampling, design, data collection tools, data collection procedures, criteria for evidence of implementation, triangulation, data management, and data analysis/synthesis. A comprehensive plan ideally will use both *qualitative* and *quantitative methods* and multiple data sources, within the confines of available implementation monitoring resources. Internal Review Board (human subject) issues must also be considered and addressed prior to any data are collected; these will be discussed more fully in Step 10 when the data collection plan is carried out.

Qualitative and Quantitative Methods

Qualitative methods involve an inductive approach to gathering information about the *how* and *why* of human behavior through observation, interviews, focus groups, storytelling, and open-ended interview

Learning Objectives

By the end of the chapter you will

1. Consider options for implementation monitoring design and methods

2. Select multiple implementation monitoring methods for each implementation monitoring question

3. Compile the comprehensive implementation monitoring plan

4. Organize the implementation monitoring plan using a logic model

questions, in contrast to surveys with close-ended questions. Conversely, **quantitative methods** entail collecting data that are in numerical form or can be changed to numerical form for mathematical/statistical analysis. McDavid, Huse, and Hawthorn (2013) compared qualitative and quantitative approaches to evaluation, summarized in Table 8.1. The quantitative column is heavily oriented toward outcome/impact evaluation, which does not apply directly to implementation monitoring. Many of the principles expressed, however, do apply to the quantitative approaches recommended in this textbook. The quantitative focus of this textbook should be evident by now with its emphasis on conceptual and logic models, implementation monitoring questions, and quantitative data collection tools. This is in large part an attempt to create balance with the long tradition of using largely qualitative approaches in process evaluation including program, policy, or practice implementation monitoring. It is essential, however, to use both qualitative and quantitative methods.

The quantitative methods provide numerical data to specify level of implementation based on predefined program, policy, or practice elements and can be used in outcome analysis to adjust for level of implementation. Qualitative approaches enable the planning team to fully understand the setting, stakeholders' perceptions of the innovation, adaptations to the innovation, and both positive and negative unintended effects of the implementation process. Quantitative methods are well suited to capture expected elements, whereas qualitative methods are very useful for unexpected elements including some contextual factors; both are needed in a comprehensive approach.

Common qualitative data collection methods include, but are not limited to, open-ended questions in interviews, focus groups, direct observation, and content analysis of video. Common quantitative methods include, but are not limited to, surveys, checklists, attendance logs, self-administered forms, and project archives (Steckler & Linnan, 2002). Baranowski and Stables (2000) presented both qualitative and quantitative aspects of data collection for each of the components of implementation monitoring. Qualitative aspects are largely descriptive and document types of approaches including messages and incentives used to recruit and maintain participants, contextual factors, quality and depth of program, policy, or practice delivery, barriers experienced, changes or adjustments made to the program, policy, or practice during implementation, and participant reactions and preferences, whereas quantitative elements are numerical, including counts and levels. The approach taken in this textbook builds on these quantitative approaches.

	Qualitative Work Characteristics	Quantitative Work Characteristics
Overall approach	Inductive approach to data gathering, interpretation, and reporting	Hypotheses and questions, which may be embedded in logic models, are tested.
Perspective	Holistic approach that looks to understand the context and implementation process and to interpret results	Finding patterns that either corroborate or disconfirm hypotheses and/or answer evaluation questions
Understanding	The subjective lived experiences of stakeholders (their truths)	How social reality as assessed by the evaluator corroborates or disconfirms hypotheses and answers evaluation questions
Data	Natural language throughout the process	Measurement procedures that lend themselves to numerical representations of variables
Data collection	In-depth, detailed, and focused	Representative samples
Sample size	Purposive sampling, small samples to examine a specific phenomenon in detail	Larger sample sizes, to gather evidence for overall implementation
Data collection tools	Evaluator as primary measuring instrument, qualitative interview, and focus group guides	Measuring instruments are quantitative and constructed to be valid and reliable
Approach to setting	Naturalistic, does not explicitly manipulate the setting	Evaluator control to improve objectivity

Source: Adapted from McDavid, Huse, and Hawthorn (2013, p. 201).

Methods and Design Elements for Implementation Monitoring

Methods and design elements include data sources, sampling, design, data collection tools, criteria for evidence of implementation, data collection procedures, data management, and data analysis/synthesis. These are reviewed and summarized in Table 8.2, which presents qualitative and quantitative examples.

Data Sources

Data sources refer to *from where* or *from whom* information will be obtained; the selection of data sources may be related to, but is not the same as, sampling.

Table 8.2 Examples of Qualitative and Quantitative Implementation Monitoring Method Components

Methodological Component	General Definition	Quantitative Examples	Qualitative Examples
Data sources	Source of information (e.g., who and/or what will be surveyed, observed, interviewed, etc.).	Possible data sources include participants, teachers, or other staff delivering the program, policy, or practice, records, the environment, written policies, etc.	
Sampling	How participants, settings, and/or activities will be chosen, as well as how many will be chosen.	Quantitative sampling is optimally designed to be representative (ideally, random sampling).	Qualitative sampling is generally purposive (select specific cases for an in-depth view).
Design	Timing of data collection: when and how often data are to be collected and from what group(s) (e.g., intervention, control, or both) data are collected.	Observing intervention and control classroom activities at least twice per semester with at least 2 weeks between observations.	Conducting focus groups with participants in the last month of the program.
Data collection tools or measures	Instruments, tools, and guides used for gathering data.	Surveys, checklists, observation forms, interview guides, etc.	
Data collection procedures	Protocols for how the data collection tool will be administered.	Detailed description of how to do environmental observation, record reviews, face-to-face or phone interviews, mailed surveys, focus groups, etc.	
Criteria for evidence of implementation	Values on rating scale, percentages, or indices that indicate acceptable level of implementation.	Applies primarily to quantitative indicators; a rating of 3 or higher on a 4-point scale; 80% of participants with "agree" or "strongly agree" responses; index score of at least 8 out of 10.	In some cases, presence of theme may serve as qualitative evidence.
Data management	Procedures for collecting and entering data from field; quality checks on raw forms and data entry.	Staff turn in participant sheets weekly; implementation monitoring coordinator collects and checks surveys and gives them to data entry staff.	Interviewers transcribe information and turn in tapes and complete transcripts at the end of the month.
Data analysis/synthesis	Statistical and/or qualitative methods used to analyze and/or summarize data.	Statistical analysis and software that will be used (e.g., frequencies and chi squares in SAS, SPSS).	Type of qualitative analysis and/or software that will be used (e.g., NUD*IST, InVIVO).

Source: Adapted from Saunders, Evans, and Joshi (2005).

Data sources include individuals who are reflecting their own perspectives and reactions and organizations reporting on their environmental policies or practices. Data sources may also include observation of environments and/or activities as well as reviews of organizational records. A new program, policy, or practice is experienced by many stakeholders and can be viewed from multiple perspectives; therefore, it is often recommended that multiple data sources be used to examine important elements (Bouffard, Taxman, & Silverman, 2003; Helitzer, Yoon, Wallerstein, & Dow y Garcia-Velarde, 2000; Resnicow et al., 1998). For example, ENRICH focused on enhancing the physical activity and nutrition environment in children's residential homes and sought to understand the perspectives of multiple stakeholders including children, implementing staff, direct care staff, and organizational administrators (Saunders et al., 2013).

Identifying the people, locations, and/or records to interview, observe, and/or review is largely a project-specific activity, but King and colleagues (King, 1987) provided several pointers. These include focusing on key people or sources who have the information in which you are interested, such as implementers, participants, and others who have active roles, and asking stakeholders to nominate individuals and other sources who are likely to have the information that is needed.

Identifying data sources that reflect organizational level perspectives can be challenging. There are several common approaches used to assess organizational policy, including reviewing written documents, interviewing or surveying organizational informants, and interviewing or surveying many people within the organization. Each approach has strengths and weaknesses, as well as its appropriate uses. For example, reviewing written documents is an effective way to assess formal policies (McGraw et al., 2000), but it may not capture informal practices and the extent to which policies are enforced, which may require interviewing. Interviewing or surveying an organizational informant as a representative of the organizational perspective is a common practice; however, it is important to select an informant who has the appropriate policy and/or practice perspective. Finally, interviewing or surveying many respondents within an organization may be appropriate for some organizational measures, such as climate or culture; however, for understanding policy, this approach may yield a diversity of opinions rather than a unified perspective. This diversity of opinion is informative in its own right, but it may be difficult to create a coherent variable from these data.

Obtaining information from a variety of data sources will likely require a great deal of cooperation from the stakeholders (King, 1987). It is essential to maintain positive and effective working relationships with all stakeholders by being mindful of potential respondent burden when collecting implementation monitoring data. To ignore the potential burden is to jeopardize relationships, quality of the collaboration, quality of the data, and the program, policy, or practice itself.

Sampling

Sampling refers to *how* participants—including individuals and organizations, settings such as classrooms and other environments, and/or activities such as specific sessions or events that provide information about the implementation process—will be selected, as well as *how many* will be selected. For many change efforts that target change in programs, policies, or practices, sampling will need to be done at multiple levels that may include coalitions, organizations, groups, specific settings, and/or individuals. If there are multiple organizations with multiple settings and multiple individuals within each setting, sampling becomes somewhat more complex as the planning team will need to determine how to sample as well as how many participants to sample at each level. For example, what are the strategies for sampling if there are 48 recreation centers, each with multiple outdoor playgrounds and play areas, all operated by multiple personnel? How many of the organizations should be sampled? How does one select the specific observation areas at each site? How should staff be selected for interviews? These decisions are ideally driven by data sources needed to address the implementation monitoring question and are often constrained by available resources.

The manner in which the sample is selected should enable the planning team to draw meaningful conclusions about the question being examined. For most quantitative applications, the planning team is not interested in a single perspective about a program per se, but rather, a reflection of intervention participants in general. For example, a single individual's satisfaction or dissatisfaction with training may be less informative than the level of satisfaction of all or most participants who attended training. Similarly, from an intervention perspective, one policy environment is potentially an interesting case study, but the planning team is often interested in patterns or results involving many policy environments.

As with outcome evaluation, the evaluator using quantitative methods should avoid sampling in ways that create bias, particularly systematic bias. For example, if training takes place in multiple sessions over time and attendance drops over time, assessing only those present at the final training session may inadvertently select for those favorably predisposed because those who were dissatisfied may not be present. Ideally, sampling should be structured in a manner to reflect the full population or group. If it is not possible to sample every individual and population or group, which is frequently the case, the optimal approach is random sampling, as this increases one's ability to generalize to the population, though in practice random sampling may be challenging.

In some cases, it may also make sense to take a stratified sample based on features of sites at the organizational level or demographic characteristics at the individual level that could affect how the program is implemented (King, 1987). For example, if organization size is an important influence on implementation and/or outcomes, stratifying by and sampling from both large and small organizations is a reasonable strategy. Having a full understanding of organizational and community factors will facilitate decisions along these lines. Similarly, at the individual level, if gender is known to have an influence on outcomes, then sampling should ensure perspectives of both genders for implementation monitoring. Having a full understanding of the program, policy, or practice focus and population of interest is essential for sampling at the individual level.

For example, level and type of physical activity, as well as influences on physical activity, vary by sex at nearly all ages. This means that boys and girls participating in the same afterschool physical activity intervention may have very different experiences. Fully understanding population reach and how the afterschool program was received will require sampling males and females.

To address qualitative evaluation questions, purposive sampling may be appropriate. For example, if the planner or evaluator wishes to understand nonparticipation from the perspective of nonparticipants in an initiative, sampling should draw from organizations and/or individuals who have not participated and who are willing to share their perspectives. Often qualitative approaches may call for understanding the perspectives of a limited number of participants in far greater depth; these are not intended to be generalizable, but rather to paint a very detailed picture that is generally unobtainable with quantitative approaches.

Design

Design refers to *when* and *from what groups* data are to be collected. From what groups data are collected in implementation monitoring refers to the intervention and control or comparison conditions; in contrast, sampling refers to how specific units of interest are selected into either condition, as described above. It is very common in implementation monitoring to collect data only from the intervention or program condition, and this may be appropriate in many cases;

however, if resources allow, it is advisable to collect the same or analogous information in control or comparison conditions as well. This will enable the planning team to examine the role of specific organizational and broader community factors as well as secular trends on implementation and outcomes in both conditions. Collecting implementation monitoring data in the control condition necessitates using language that does not require awareness of the program, policy, or practice. For example, rather than asking about the Lifestyle Education for Activity (LEAP) team, which is specific to the innovation, the planning team would ask about a "committee that plans or coordinates activities related to physical activity."

Monitoring contextual factors in intervention and control conditions is important because contextual and external influences can have positive or negative effects on implementation processes and study outcomes in both groups. Outside influences on the intervention group could be confounded with intervention effects. An example of a positive influence would be increased federal funding at the state level or new federal regulations that promote policies or practices similar to those promoted in the innovation. Examples of negative influences include staff turnover, construction, or disasters. Similarly, contextual and external influences can affect the control condition positively, mimicking the program, policy, or practice and reducing the distinction between the intervention and control conditions, or negatively. If these influences are assessed in both conditions, it is possible to document and describe them objectively in real time and to control for them analytically.

Concerning when data should be collected, baseline or preimplementation data ideally should be collected in both the intervention and control or comparison conditions within the same time frame. Depending on the implementation monitoring question and the implementation process, it may make sense to collect data periodically during the implementation process or at a single point later in the intervention timeline. The exact timing of the data collection depends on the question being answered as well as feasibility issues. If the purpose of data collection is to assess level of implementation, consideration needs to be given to at what points in time implementation can be best reflected. For example, if full implementation of a policy change in a nonprofit organization is expected to take 3 months, it would not make sense to collect data after 1 month. Similarly, if implementation is expected to result in organizational or environmental change, the time frame in which this is likely to occur needs to be considered as part of timing of data collection. King and colleagues (King, 1987, p. 51) provided a series of useful questions concerning timing of data collection:

- Do you wish to look at the program periodically in order to monitor whether the program implementation is on schedule?

- Do you intend to collect data from any individual site more than once?

- Do you have reasons to believe that the program will change over the course of the evaluation?

- If so do you want to write a profile of the program throughout history that describes how it evolved or changed?

Data Collection Tools

Data collection tools refer to all instruments, measures, checklists, observational tools, and interview/focus group guides used for gathering implementation monitoring data. Quantitative data collection tools for implementation monitoring differ from other quantitative measures only in their application to implementation monitoring; therefore, all measurement considerations such as validity and reliability apply to these scales (McDavid et al., 2013, Chapter 4). It is difficult to find standardized tools in implementation monitoring that have established validity and reliability, in large part because most implementation monitoring instruments are specific to the program, policy, or practice intervention under investigation (McGraw et al., 2000).

King and colleagues (King, 1987) described instrument validity in innovation implementation as a four-part question that addresses the extent to which the description of the program presented by the instrument is accurate, relevant, representative, and complete. An accurate instrument creates a picture of the program that is very close to what one would see on-site. Relevant measures focus on the most critical features of programs, those that are most likely related to the program outcomes. A representative depiction of the program presents a typical feature of the program and variations across sites and over time. And, finally, a complete picture includes all relevant and important program features. Table 8.3, adapted from King (1987) compares four common methods for collecting implementation data: examining records, conducting observations, using self-administered questionnaires, and conducting interviews. In a comparison of methods to assess school-based curricula, Resnicow and colleagues (1998) reported that implementer self-report was not related to outcomes, but that multiple observation and interviews were.

Table 8.3 Comparing Four Methods for Collecting Implementation Data

Method	Advantages	Disadvantages	Examples
Examine records	– Can be collected without additional demand on participants – Often viewed as objective and more credible – Sets down events at the time of occurrence that increases credibility	– May be incomplete – May be time-consuming to extract relevant information – May be ethical or legal constraints – May be burdensome if not routinely collected	Systematic accounts of regular occurrences, often part of the organization's record keeping; may also include records (e.g., field notes and other documentation) kept by project staff
Conduct observations	– May be seen as highly credible when collected by trained, objective observer – Observers provide a point of view that is different than those connected to the program.	– May alter what takes place – Time is needed to develop instruments and train observers. – Conducting observations is time-consuming. – May encounter scheduling problems	One or more trained observers use a checklist or other instrument to observe events, activities, and/or the environment.
Use self-report measures: questionnaires	– May address a variety of questions – May be answered anonymously – May allow respondent time to think before responding – May be given to many people at distant sites and simultaneously – May impose uniformity on information obtained	– Are not flexible – May limit people's ability to express themselves and capture unique circumstances – Getting surveys returned may be difficult.	A written tool administered in person, electronically, or via mail to which participants or staff respond, often using a rating scale (quantitative); open-ended responses are options (qualitative).
Use self-report measures: interviews	– May be used with a variety of people who have difficulty with written questions – Permits flexibility and ability to pursue anticipated responses	– Time-consuming – Interviewer may inadvertently influence responses.	Participant responds to questions in person or over the telephone; it may be open-ended (qualitative) or close-ended (quantitative).

Source: Content adapted from King, Morris, and Fitz-Gibbon (1987).

Ideally, the quantitative data collection tools used to monitor implementation are conceptually based, reflecting the conceptual framework of the program, policy, or practice—that is, reflecting complete and acceptable delivery/installation. Therefore, at a minimum, it should be possible to establish content and/or face validity and, with sufficient resources, to establish concurrent, predictive, and construct validity. Similarly, reliability for checklists, surveys, observational tools, record review instruments, and other measures may be established through test-retest methods or interrater reliability (DeVellis, 2012; King, 1987). All data collection tools should be pilot tested prior to use in data collection.

Qualitative methods have alternate criteria for judging quality and credibility. McDavid and colleagues (McDavid et al., 2013) compared traditional positivist/postpositivist quantitative and interpretivist/constructivist and critical change qualitative approaches. The qualitative criteria clearly reflect subjectivity openly as well as the necessity of social, political, moral, and/or historical values in context. The emphasis is on trustworthiness, authenticity, and representation of multiple perspectives in contrast to measurement validity and reliability. See Chapter 5 in McDavid et al. (2013) for more in-depth coverage of the use of qualitative methods in program evaluation.

Data Collection Procedures

Data collection procedures used in quantitative approaches refer to the detailed protocols for the administration of data collection tools. It is important that all procedures are clearly documented and that all data collectors are trained to administer the tools systematically. In large projects with ongoing data collection, data collectors may need periodic "recertification" to ensure systematic and high-quality data collection. Data collection procedures should be pilot tested in similar conditions prior to use in data collection. Data collection features for qualitative approaches should be consistent with the theoretical perspectives of the qualitative approach, as discussed in McDavid et al. (2013).

Criteria for Evidence of Implementation

Criteria for evidence of implementation refers to standards that are set for complete and acceptable delivery and that may include values on rating scales, percentages, or indices that indicate desirable levels of implementation. For quantitative data, it is optimal to set standards for desirable levels that provide evidence of implementation prior to data collection. What constitutes an acceptable level will vary by project and setting; this should be discussed and agreed on by the planning team and stakeholders. Establishing criteria for acceptable levels of implementation prior to data collection may prevent problems such as collecting data that are not applicable or are difficult to interpret and therefore have little meaning or use.

At the most basic level, the planning team can set criteria for acceptable levels of implementation on individual quantitative data collection tools by determining acceptable score(s) on the rating scale. This should be informed by the meaning of the response options on the form. For example, in LEAP, there was a 4-point response scale that examined records for evidence of implementation of essential elements: 0 = not found in records; 1 = some activity documented; 2 = organized activity documented; and 3 = organized activity highly consistent with LEAP philosophy and theory. The planning team, working with stakeholders, set acceptable levels at 2 or higher, that is, any organized activity. Criteria for evidence of implementation may be revisited with caution in the analysis phase. It is not acceptable to manipulate criteria for evidence of implementation after-the-fact to create a more or less favorable report of implementation. However, if the collected data have a restricted or skewed range so that reported ratings are 2s and 3s with no 0s and 1s, the planning team may wish to revisit the definition of the evidence level.

If there are multiple data sources with corresponding data collection tools examining the same program, policy, or practice element, the planning team will next examine or **triangulate** multiple data sources/tools that provide multiple perspectives on one program element. **Data triangulation** refers to using two or more data sources to examine evidence of implementation. Similarly, if the program, policy, or practice has multiple elements within a component, criteria for evidence of implementation will need to be established at this level as well. In other words, the acceptable level of overall implementation when multiple data elements are triangulated must be determined to examine implementation of a program component (see Figure 8.1). Figure 8.1 illustrates how multiple tools can be used to assess each element of the program, policy, or practice, and then how multiple elements can contribute to understanding overall innovation implementation. Criteria for evidence of implementation are needed at each of these levels.

The approach described above enables the planning team to determine implementation for program, policy, or practice components using multiple data sources and tools to assess evidence for complete and acceptable delivery/ installation of program, policy, or practice core elements. The purpose here is to illustrate the importance of thinking about criteria for evidence of implementation in a manner that reflects the complexity of the data.

Evidence of implementation can be determined for each component of a program (e.g., most to least implemented elements) and for each organization or organizational unit (e.g., school- or classroom-level implementation). For example, in LEAP, we reported the most (Emphasizes lifelong physical) to least (Family involvement) implemented innovation elements, and classified each school into a "higher" and "lower" implementing category (Saunders, Ward, Felton, Dowda, & Pate, 2006).

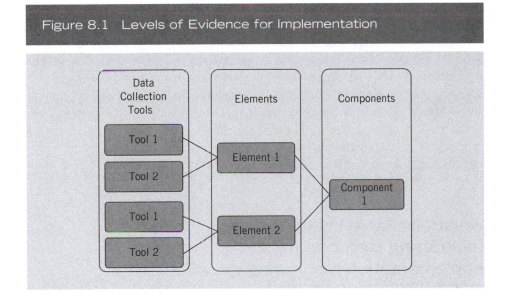

Figure 8.1   Levels of Evidence for Implementation

Data Management

Data management refers to the process of getting raw data, collected in the field, through the data entry process and into summarized form. It is important to plan carefully for this aspect of methodology, as poor data management can create tremendous amounts of unnecessary work. In the worst cases, poor data management can compromise data quality, rendering data useless. It is important in the planning stages, therefore, to determine preliminary procedures to ensure the needed resources are in place when data collection begins. These largely pertain to having sufficient time and qualified personnel. Data management will be discussed in more depth in Step 9.

Data Analysis/Synthesis

Quantitative **data analysis and synthesis** will be discussed in depth in Step 11. For planning purposes, it is important to determine preliminary approaches to conducting data analysis and synthesis. The specific analysis or synthesis approach depends on the implementation monitoring questions, but often begins with descriptive data and basic statistical operations such as calculating means of multi-item scales, summing index scores, and triangulating multiple data sources (illustrated in Tables 8.5 and 8.6). Attention to this step prior to data collection can prevent collection of data that are difficult to summarize and can prompt planning about ways to meaningfully combine and synthesize large volumes of information. If large amounts of data accumulate prior to addressing this, the planning team will likely be overwhelmed.

After data are analyzed or synthesized, they should be put into a "digestible" form for stakeholders. Reporting and using data entails a description of how the information will be summarized, to whom it will be distributed, and for what specific purposes it will be used. Although reporting data to project staff and stakeholders and using the information are not methods per se, it is essential to think about how the data will be used as part of the planning process for methods. Thinking carefully about how this step can prevent collection of unnecessary information that will never be used.

Select multiple implementation monitoring methods for each implementation monitoring question.

The recommended elements of the implementation monitoring plan for each component of the program, policy, or practice include at a minimum fidelity, completeness, and reach, and may also include dose received, recruitment documentation, and contextual factor documentation. Each program, policy, or practice component may have different implementation monitoring plan elements and different methods; therefore, each must be addressed in the implementation monitoring plan. For example, in a school-based program, one component may target students, and another, the students' parents/guardians. The elements that constitute fidelity, completeness, reach, and context, as well as approaches to recruitment, will likely differ between these two components of the innovation.

Planning begins with an implementation monitoring question and consideration of complete and acceptable delivery/installation. The final implementation monitoring plan is the culmination of an iterative process in which the planning team considers implementation monitoring resources, program characteristics, and setting characteristics as implementation monitoring questions and methods are refined and prioritized (see Figure 8.2).

This section will highlight developing data collection tools and establishing criteria for evidence of implementation, as the planning team often finds these elements of the comprehensive plan challenging.

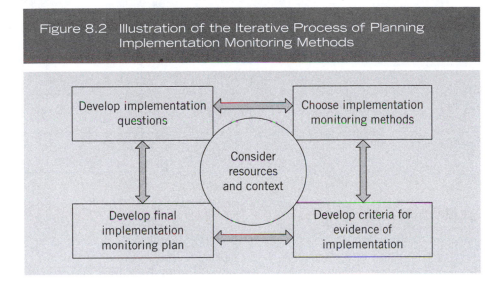

Figure 8.2 Illustration of the Iterative Process of Planning Implementation Monitoring Methods

Data Collection Tools

The identification or development of data collection instruments should be guided by complete and acceptable delivery/installation. In LEAP, the essential elements that characterized LEAP PE and the healthy school environment were assessed using multiple quantitative data collection tools including rating scales, checklist observation of the environment and classroom activities, and review of written records and documentation using a rating scale (Saunders et al., 2006). In essence, the LEAP essential elements, which reflected complete and acceptable installation of the LEAP intervention, served as a framework for instrument development. For example, one of the essential elements for instructional practice was gender separation in physical education (PE). Accordingly, items appropriate to staff rating scales, observational checklists, and record review rating scales were developed based on this item (see Table 8.4). Multiple data collection methods and sources are recommended due to the complexity of settings and the genuinely varying perspectives of different stakeholders (Bouffard et al., 2003; Helitzer et al., 2000; Resnicow et al., 1998). Prior to use, all instruments should be pilot tested and all data collectors trained in their use.

Worksheet 8.1 provides a template for choosing and summarizing data sources and tools, including rating scales for implementation monitoring, based on the conceptual definition of complete and acceptable delivery/installation.

Worksheet 8.1   Data Sources, Sampling, and Tools Based on the Definitions of Complete and Acceptable Delivery/Installation of the Innovation

Element and Definition of Complete and Acceptable Delivery/Installation	Data Sources/ Sampling	Tools and Rating Scale	Sample Items
Component A—Fidelity			
Component A—Completeness			
Component B—Fidelity			
Component B—Completeness			

LEAP Case Illustration

Table 8.4 summarizes data sources and tools used in the LEAP project; all tools were based on the LEAP essential elements (Saunders et al., 2006).

Criteria for Evidence of Implementation

Criteria for what constitutes evidence of implementation are established through a series of steps that begin with determining the criteria for a single data source and then for multiple data sources used to monitor implementation of an essential or core program, policy, or practice element, defined by complete and acceptable delivery/installation. If an innovation component is made up of multiple elements, then criteria must be set at this level, also. This process is repeated for all components; criteria can also be set for the number of components that define complete and acceptable overall implementation.

LEAP Case Illustration

This sequence of steps will be illustrated by the assessment of long-term implementation or sustainability of instructional practices in LEAP (Saunders et al., 2012). There were seven essential elements comprising complete and acceptable delivery/installation of instructional practice in LEAP. Specifically, the LEAP PE elements were gender separation, fun classes, physically active classes, appropriate teaching methods, teaching behavioral skills, lifelong physical activity emphasis, and noncompetitive physical activity included.

Table 8.4 LEAP Data Sources and Tools Based on the Definitions of Complete and Acceptable Delivery/Installation of the Innovation

Element and Definition of Complete and Acceptable Delivery/Installation	Data Sources	Tools and Rating Scale	Sample Items
LEAP PE: Characterized by – Gender separation – Fun classes – Physically active classes – Appropriate teaching methods – Teaching behavioral skills – Lifelong physical activity emphasized – Noncompetitive physical activity included	Written records maintained by LEAP staff including training activities, training attendance, field notes, school files, and communication	*Record Review* (35-item rating scale) 0 = not found in records 1 = documents indicate some activity 2 = documents indicate organized activity 3 = documents indicated organized activity that is highly consistent with LEAP theory	Rate evidence for: *Instruction* – Lifelong physical activity is emphasized – Teaching behavioral skills *Environment* – School physical activity team – Administrative support for physical activity
Healthy School Environment: Characterized by – School administrator support for physical activity promotion – Active school physical activity team – Physical activity-promoting messages in the school	Observation of physical education (PE) class and school environment	*Observational checklist* (25 items) 0 = no or none 1 = sometimes 2 = most of the time 3 = all of the time	*Instruction* – Students are organized into small, enduring groups *Environment* – Girls are linked to out-of-class physical activity opportunities via school media messages.
	LEAP staff made systematic assessments based on observation and results documented in written records.	*LEAP Criteria* (36-item rating scale) 0 = no 1 = partially 2 = yes, completely	*Instruction* – Are noncompetitive activities included in PE? *Environment* – Does school have an active wellness team?

Source: Adapted from Saunders et al. (2006).

The active LEAP intervention had concluded several years prior to this implementation assessment; therefore, LEAP intervention staff were not available as data sources. Instead, the LEAP planning team used both qualitative and quantitative methods to tap into evidence of possible sustained implementation. Specifically, qualitative methods included interviews of PE teachers and focus groups of ninth-grade girls currently in PE classes. Many, but not all, of the PE teachers were involved with LEAP in prior years. As expected, none of the ninth-grade girls interviewed during the follow-up period had been exposed to the LEAP intervention during its active phase. The observational tool used to observe the ninth-grade PE class was identical to the quantitative tool used for the active intervention.

Single Data Collection Tool

An essential element was considered to be present if it was observed "most" or "all" of the time (i.e., rated 2 or 3 on the observational checklist) or identified in transcripts of focus groups or interviews by two independent coders.

Multiple Data Collection Tools

An instructional essential element was considered to be present in the school if two of the three data sources (observational checklist, focus groups, interviews) identified the element.

Multiple Essential Elements

LEAP-like instructional practices were considered to be present in a school if a majority (four out of seven) of the instructional essential elements were present.

Figure 8.3 applies this multilayer, multistep process illustrated in Figure 8.1 to LEAP.

Showing the results of this process will illustrate how to define criteria for evidence of implementation. Presenting data in tables and applying the criteria are part of data analysis/synthesis and will be discussed in more depth in Step 11. Table 8.5 presents the data from the three data sources (numbered 1, 2, and 3) by school (lettered A through K) and by essential element (left-hand column). A check is placed in each cell column when data from a data collection tool provides evidence of implementation using the criteria described above. From this table, the patterns of implementation by school and by component become clear. For example, in School A, for the essential element "gender separation in physical education," the PE teacher interview, former LEAP team players interview, and ninth-grade PE observation met the criteria and therefore provided evidence for implementation of this element at follow-up.

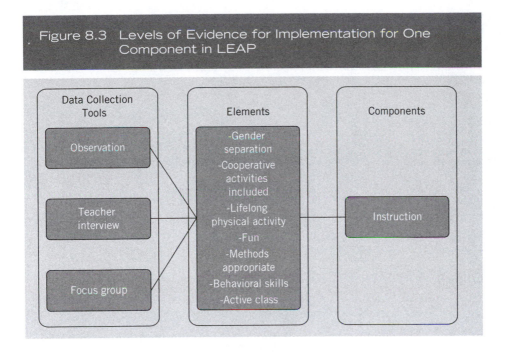

Figure 8.3 Levels of Evidence for Implementation for One Component in LEAP

Data Collection Tools: Observation, Teacher interview, Focus group

Elements:
-Gender separation
-Cooperative activities included
-Lifelong physical activity
-Fun
-Methods appropriate
-Behavioral skills
-Active class

Components: Instruction

If the planning team requires only an assessment of overall implementation at the organizational level, without consideration of specific essential elements or components, another strategy is to use information from all data sources to rank order organizations based on scores on quantitative data collection tools. LEAP implementation assessment at the close of the active intervention illustrates this approach (Ward et al., 2006). Multiple data sources and quantitative data collection instruments were used to assess instructional practices as well as the school environment.

Each school received a mean scale score for each of four data collection tools with all items combined, and schools were ranked based on the scores; that is, each school received four rankings, one for each data source. These data were considered ordinal rather than numeric. Therefore, criteria for evidence of implementation was defined as the top two-thirds of schools for a given data source; schools consistently ranked in the top two-thirds were considered "higher implementers," whereas schools consistently ranked in the bottom third were considered "lower implementers." The results of this process illustrate the application of criteria for evidence of implementation (see Table 8.6). Note that the school codes presented in Table 8.6 are not the same as the school codes in Table 8.5, although many of the same schools were involved.

Table 8.5 Using Multiple Data Sources to Establish Evidence of Implementation for Instructional Component of LEAP by School

Essential Element	A			B			C			D			E			F			G			H			I			J			K		
Schools (A–K) and Data Sources (1–3)	1	2	3	1	2	3	1	2	3	1	2	3	1	2	3	1	2	3	1	2	3	1	2	3	1	2	3	1	2	3	1	2	3
Gender-separate physical education (PE) classes		✓	✓	✓							✓																				✓	✓	
Cooperative activities are included		✓	✓		✓	✓			✓	✓	✓												✓			✓	✓	✓			✓	✓	✓
Lifelong physical activity is emphasized		✓	✓		✓						✓												✓			✓	✓				✓	✓	✓
Classes are fun and enjoyable	✓	✓	✓	✓	✓					✓	✓		✓			✓			✓	✓		✓				✓		✓			✓	✓	✓
Teaching methods are appropriate	✓	✓			✓	✓														✓			✓			✓		✓		✓		✓	✓
Behavioral skills are taught	✓	✓			✓							✓			✓						✓			✓			✓					✓	
At least 50% of class is active	✓	✓		✓					✓				✓		✓			✓				✓	✓	✓			✓	✓					

Source: From Saunders et al. (2012).

1 = PE teacher interview; 2 = former LEAP team players interview; 3 = ninth-grade PE observation

✓ = evidence for presence of the indicated element for a given data source

Shaded = strong evidence for implementation

Table 8.6 LEAP Intervention Schools (*n* = 12) Ranked From Highest to Lowest Index Score for Level of Implementation of Essential Elements (Year 2) Using Multiple Data Sources

Rank	Record Review	PE Observations	LEAP Criteria	LEAP Criteria PE
1	G	G	I	C, G, L
2	C	L	G	B, J
3	A, B	F	C, J	A, F
4	F	A	B, L	H
5	D*	B	F	K*
6	J, L	D*	A	I*
7	H*	J	D*	E*
8	K*, E*	C	K*	D*
9	I*	I*	H*	
10		H*	E*	
11		K*		
12		E*		

Source: From Saunders et al. (2006).

Note: Schools ranked in the lower third are shaded. Schools with an asterisk are assigned to low implementation group.

Compile the comprehensive implementation monitoring plan.

The planning team is now ready to compile the final comprehensive implementation monitoring plan, considering the level of resources, program characteristics, and setting characteristics. Resource considerations include the availability of qualified staff to develop and implement all aspects of the implementation monitoring, as well as the time needed for planning; pilot testing instruments and protocols; and collecting, entering, analyzing, and reporting data. It is also important to consider how data collection might be disruptive to program, policy, or practice implementation or the organization's regular operations and might create excessive staff and/or respondent burden. Greater amounts of resources, including time, are needed for large and complicated innovations characterized by multiple components, large numbers of collaborators, and multiple geographic sites. It is best to be realistic about the amount of data that can be collected and used, given the level of resources available and the context.

In practice, elements of the implementation monitoring plan are developed individually and then summarized into a final, comprehensive plan. The draft plan will include a description of data sources, sampling, tools and procedures, timing of data collection, data synthesis, criteria, and reporting. Worksheet 8.2 provides a template for a comprehensive implementation monitoring plan.

LEAP Case Illustration

Table 8.7 provides a LEAP example of a comprehensive implementation monitoring plan.

Organize the implementation monitoring plan using a logic model.

This is an optimal time to use the logic model to organize the comprehensive evaluation plan. To do this, an additional row that specifies measures identified in the comprehensive implementation monitoring plan is added to the logic model figure from previous chapters. Use Worksheet 8.3 as a template for summarizing the comprehensive evaluation plan using the logic model. Anything that is worth evaluating should be in the logic model, and anything in the logic model should be evaluated.

LEAP Case Illustration

The LEAP logic model with rows for the comprehensive implementation monitoring plan is presented in Table 8.8.

Worksheet 8.2 Template for Draft of Final Implementation Monitoring Plan

	Implementation Monitoring Question	Sampling	Data Sources	Tools and Procedures	Timing of Data Collection	Criteria for Evidence of Implementation	Analysis/ Synthesis	Reporting
Fidelity								
Dose delivered								
Dose received								
Reach								
Recruitment								
Context								

Table 8.7   LEAP Summative Implementation Monitoring Plan Example (partial)

Project Definition of Complete and Acceptable Delivery/Installation		Evaluation Question	Sampling and Design	Data Sources	Tools and Procedures	Timing	Criteria	Analysis/ Synthesis	Report
Complete-ness and fidelity	Instructional essential elements*	To what extent were instructional essential elements implemented?	All intervention school PE classrooms	Instruction activities	Independent process evaluator observed classes	At least 2 visits per class per year (fall and spring)	Rated 2 or 3 on 0–3 scale	Mean score	Data from multiple data sources were triangulated in a summative report for investigators, funder, and publication
	Environment essential elements**	To what extent were environmental essential elements implemented?	All intervention school environments	Physical environment	Independent process evaluator observed physical environment	At least 2 visits per school per year (fall and spring)	Rated 2 or 3 on 0–3 scale	Mean score	
	Instructional and environment essential elements	To what extent were all essential elements installed?	All documents on intervention schools	Records	Independent process evaluator rated documentation for essential elements	Once per year	Rated 2 or 3 on 0–3 scale	Mean score	

Project Definition of Complete and Acceptable Delivery/Installation		Evaluation Question	Sampling and Design	Data Sources	Tools and Procedures	Timing	Criteria	Analysis/Synthesis	Report
Organization change (process outcome)	Instructional and environment essential elements	To what extent did instructional practices and the school environment reflect essential elements?	All intervention and control school PE classrooms and environments	Assistant principal	Process evaluator interviewed assistant principal	Once per year (spring)	Not applicable (process outcome, rather than indicator)	Mean score	Examined relationship between implementation and organizational outcome in publication

*LEAP PE—characterized by:

-Gender separation

-Physically active classes

-Teaching behavioral skills emphasized

-Noncompetitive physical activity included

-Fun classes

-Appropriate teaching methods

-Lifelong physical activity

**Healthy School Environment—characterized by:

-School administrator support for physical activity promotion

-Active school physical activity team

-Physical activity–promoting messages in the school

Worksheet 8.3   Template for Summarizing and Organizing an Evaluation Plan Using a Logic Model

	Inputs	Outputs			Outcomes/Impacts		
	What We Invest	What We Do	Who Is Reached and Expected Effects	Changes Made by Change Agent	Short-Term Changes, Impact on Influence Variables	Medium-Term Change in Individual Behavior Outcome	Long-Term Change on Health Outcomes
Logic Model	Resources provided enable us to . . .	conduct certain activities that will . . .	reach the change agents and provide them with tools and skills needed to . . .	carry out the program, policy, or practice, which will result in . . .	change in influence variables, which will affect the . . .	individual behavior, which, if sustained, will . . .	have positive effects on health outcomes.
Evaluation Question							
Evaluation Component and Measures							
	ACTION MODEL—Implementation monitoring				CHANGE MODEL—Outcome evaluation		

Table 8.8 LEAP Outcomes Logic Model, Illustrating Use of Logic Model to Organize Implementation Monitoring Plan

	Inputs	Outputs			Outcomes/Impacts		
	What We Invest	**What We Do**	**Who Is Reached and Expected Effects**	**Changes Made by Change Agent**	**Short-Term Changes, Impact on Influence Variables**	**Medium-Term Change in Individual Behavior Outcome**	**Long-Term Change on Health Outcomes**
Logic Model	Resources provided enable us to	conduct certain activities that will	reach the change agents and provide them with tools and skills needed to	carry out the program, policy, or practice, which will result in	change in influence variables, which will affect the	individual behavior, which, if sustained, will	have positive effects on health outcomes.
Evaluation Question	To what extent did LEAP staff provide all innovation components, materials, and equipment through training, technical assistance, and ongoing support?		To what extent did LEAP team members attend training? Have the confidence and skills needed to carry out LEAP in their school?	To what extent did LEAP team members install all 11 LEAP instructional and environmental essential elements?			
Evaluation and Measurement	Dose delivered		Reach and dose received	Fidelity and completeness	Influence variables (e.g., self-efficacy)	Individual behavior: physical activity	N/A
	Documentation		Attendance records, training evaluation	Observation, record review, LEAP staff rating	LEAP outcome/impact assessment		
	ACTION MODEL—Implementation monitoring				CHANGE MODEL—Outcome evaluation		

Your Turn: Qualitative and Quantitative Methods

Your planning team is debating about whether to use qualitative or quantitative methods for implementation monitoring, and you have been asked to make a recommendation to the team. There are members on your planning team who feel that the philosophical differences between quantitative and qualitative approaches are such that these methodologies are not compatible (see Table 8.1), yet this textbook recommends using both. Make a persuasive argument to your planning team that both methods are needed, providing specific examples to make your case.

KEY POINTS FOR CHOOSING IMPLEMENTATION MONITORING METHODS

- Ideally, both qualitative and quantitative methods are used in implementation monitoring.

- Implementation monitoring methods include considering data sources, design, data collection tools or measures, data collection procedures, criteria for evidence of implementation, data management, and data analysis/synthesis.

- Planning implementation monitoring methods is an iterative process.

- Evidence of implementation will likely need to be established at multiple levels.

- The final implementation monitoring plan must consider available resources, characteristics of the program, and characteristics of the setting.

- The comprehensive implementation monitoring plan can be organized by the logic model.

Implementation

Phase IV consists of two steps: implementing the program, policy, or practice and carrying out the implementation monitoring plan. The intervention and the implementation monitoring plan are based on planning from Phases II and III.

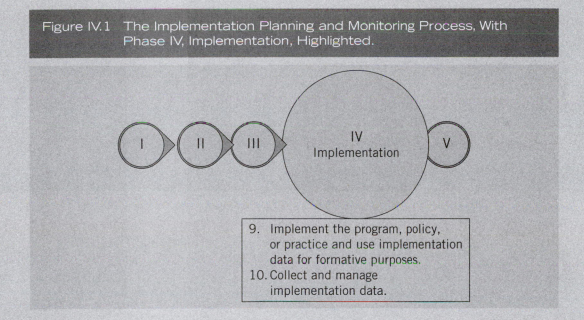

Figure IV.1 The Implementation Planning and Monitoring Process, With Phase IV, Implementation, Highlighted.

Every great inspiration is but an experiment—though every experiment we know, is not a great inspiration.

—Charles Ives

Implement the Program, Policy, or Practice and Use Implementation Data for Formative Purposes

The purposes of this step are to review the issues involved in carrying out the program, policy, or practice, particularly when things do not go as planned, and to address steps and practical issues involved in using implementation data in a formative manner.

Apply concepts from implementation frameworks to understand implementation.

Implementation of programs, policies, and practices in the real world is messy, due in part to the complexity of the setting. Even though you have identified and planned for factors that affect the adoption, implementation, and sustainability process, you will likely encounter unanticipated challenges as you carry out your action plan. There are a number of frameworks that describe and provide guidance for the implementation process, including the Fixsen framework (Fixsen, Naoom, Blase, Friedman, & Wallace, 2005), Normalisation Process Theory (Murray et al., 2010), MRC Framework (Campbell et al., 2000; Campbell et al., 2007; Craig et al., 2008), Replicating Effective Programs Framework (Kilbourne, Neumann, Pincus, Bauer, & Stall, 2007), and Concerns Based Adoption Model (Hall & Hord, 2015) (see Resource Box 9.1). These frameworks were developed to facilitate the uptake of evidence-based programs that have been previously developed, evaluated, and found to be effective. Because these programs are typically tested in optimal and controlled conditions, they often face implementation challenges

Learning Objectives

By the end of the chapter you will

1. Apply concepts from implementation frameworks to understand implementation

2. Understand the innovation and implementation from the perspective of setting stakeholders

3. Review implementation cases: When things don't go as planned

4. Be able to discuss practical issues for using implementation data in a formative manner

5. Develop a plan for using implementation monitoring data in a formative manner to keep a project on track

that these frameworks seek to address. Meyers, Durlak, and Wandersman (2012) have synthesized many of these and other frameworks addressing the implementation process to create the Quality Implementation Framework (QIF). The QIF identifies steps and actions in four temporal phases comprising quality implementation (see Resource Box 9.1) (Meyers et al., 2012).

The elements emphasized in these frameworks have been described in previous chapters, including the importance of being able to describe the program, policy, or practice and context into which it will be implemented (Steps 2 and 4); having a plan with specific strategies for facilitating adoption and implementation including working with stakeholders (Steps 3, 5, and 6); and having a detailed plan for implementation monitoring (Steps 7 and 8). Consistent with the program life cycle perspective used in this textbook, these implementation frameworks identify phases or stages for the implementation process. Additional common elements between these frameworks and the approach in this textbook include an emphasis on the importance of fully describing the innovation and the innovation-setting fit, as well as understanding how it should work conceptually. Most frameworks also identify the ubiquity of adaptation and hence the need for flexibility, implementation support, and monitoring of the implementation process.

Resource Box 9.1
Frameworks for Innovation Implementation

Resource	Key Points	Citation
Fixsen framework	*The stages of the implementation process include:* (1) exploration and adoption; (2) program installation; (3) initial implementation; (4) full operation; (5) innovation; and (6) sustainability	Fixsen, Naoom, Blase, Friedman, and Wallace (2005)
	The core implementation components to facilitate uptake of an innovation include: (1) selection; (2) preservice training; (3) consultation and coaching; (4) staff evaluation; (5) program evaluation; (6) facilitative administrative supports; and (7) systems interventions.	
	Organization context and external influences will have an impact on any program or policy and implementation.	

Resource	Key Points	Citation
Normalisation Process Theory (NPT)	NPT emphasizes the *work that individuals and groups do to establish (i.e., "normalize") an intervention* within a setting. There are *four main components* that work together within the implementing context to improve implementation of complex interventions and translating research into practice: (1) coherence (or sense-making); (2) cognitive participation (or engagement); (3) collective action (work done to enable the intervention to happen); and (4) reflexive monitoring (formal and informal appraisal of the benefits and costs of the intervention). NPT poses a series of questions exploring the following issues and more to facilitate implementation: (1) ability to communicate clearly about the intervention; (2) clearly defined purpose of the intervention for all participants with valued benefits; (3) implementer motivation and skills needed for implementation; (4) fit of the intervention with the organization goals; (5) fit with work practices and daily routines; (6) two-way communication about the intervention once it is in use; and (7) adaptability of the intervention.	Murray et al. (2010)
MRC framework	MRC defines *complex interventions* as those with (1) multiple interacting components within all conditions (intervention/control); (2) multiple and/or different behaviors required by either the interventionist or participants; (3) number of groups and/or organizational levels in the intervention; (4) number and range of outcomes; and (5) level of flexibility and adaptability of the intervention. To *develop and evaluate complex interventions*, developers must (1) use theory to create and understand the intervention; (2) include process evaluation to understand study outcomes; (3) use multiple, as well as qualitative and quantitative, measures; (4) monitor context to check for unintended consequences; (5) use flexible and adaptive interventions; and (6) understand that randomized designs may not always be feasible or acceptable or necessary.	Campbell et al. (2000), Campbell et al. (2007), Craig et al. (2008)

(Continued)

(Continued)

Resource	Key Points	Citation
Replicating Effective Programs (REP) framework	*There arc four steps in the REP process:* 1. Preconditions: Identify the need for the intervention; identify appropriate intervention for the particular context/setting including barrier analysis; translate intervention into common language and identify essential elements and supplemental elements of the intervention. 2. Preimplementation: Select the Community Working Group and refine intervention and essential elements in context; pilot test the intervention and have an orientation with identified implementation setting organizations. 3. Implementation: Provide training, support, feedback, and technical assistance to implementers; refine intervention based on feedback. 4. Maintenance and evolution: Refine intervention based on feedback and disseminate intervention into other settings.	Kilbourne, Neumann, Pincus, Bauer, and Stall (2007)
Quality Implementation Framework (QIF)	*There are four phases in the QIF:* 1. Making initial considerations about the host setting including conducting assessments and building capacity 2. Creating a structure for implementation including developing a plan and creating teams 3. Providing ongoing implementation supports and monitoring with feedback during the implementation process 4. Learning from experience for the future	Meyers, Durlak, and Wandersman (2012)
Concerns Based Adoption Model (CBAM)	Implementers have personal feelings and perceptions: *Stages of Concern.* Implementers progress from nonuse, to novice to expert: *Levels of Use.* There will be a range from high to low fidelity in terms of the Critical Components: *Innovation Configurations.* Change leadership is highly correlated with implementation success: *Change Facilitator Styles.*	Hall and Hord, (2015)

In practical terms, these frameworks suggest that the planning team and others can expect the following:

- Planning for implementation and implementation monitoring to make a positive difference.

- Program fit with the setting and setting "readiness" and capacity to carry out the program to be important: *Consider the context.*

- Implementation to proceed in a nonlinear manner: *Two steps forward, one step back, and repeat.*

- Every place to be unique in how it moves through this process: *One size will not fit all.*

- The program, policy, or practice to be adapted locally; stakeholders and implementers in each setting *will* make adjustments to the program, policy, or practice: *Adaptation is ubiquitous.*

- The implementation process to take more time than anticipated; plan for this: *Time is the scarcest resource.*

- The unexpected; be prepared to *be flexible.*

For example, during the 5 years of the Environmental Interventions in Children's Homes (ENRICH) project (Saunders et al., 2013), which was designed to enhance health-promoting environments for child residents, participating organizations experienced staff turnover and staff layoffs, organizational mergers, changes in funding for providing services and resulting changes in services provided, accreditation demands, and changes in federal nutrition policies. This does not even consider the day-to-day challenges of working with a population of youth who have been abused or neglected or who experience mental health or juvenile justice problems. It is challenging to facilitate health-promoting environments in such turbulent environments!

Given the complexity of the setting and its broader context and the inherent challenges of implementation, it is very important to know what innovation elements are essential to its success. Facilitators external to the implementing setting must develop and work throughout the project to maintain effective working relationships with implementers and other setting stakeholders. These relationships may very well be the "glue" that holds the intervention together until implementers and setting stakeholders understand and buy into the proposed changes to their setting. It is also essential to provide ongoing support and technical assistance beyond providing initial information and training. Provided in isolation, the initial training is likely not sufficient to facilitate change. Finally, it is important to monitor the implementation process and to provide feedback to implementers and setting stakeholders.

Understand the innovation and implementation from the perspective of setting stakeholders.

It is important to understand the innovation and the implementation process from the perspective of setting stakeholders. Conversations with leaders, implementers, participants, and/or other key people in an intervention setting enable the planning team to understand the program, policy, or practice and the implementation process from the "insider" perspective, which may facilitate efforts to implement the program, policy, or practice. Equally important, these conversations with stakeholders provide an opportunity to further develop and maintain effective working relationships. Worksheet 9.1 provides general questions that can be used to guide informal conversations with key people within the implementing setting. Issues to be explored include stakeholders' descriptions of the program, policy, or practice and its purpose; perceived costs and benefits of the innovation; perceived fit of the innovation with organizational goals and day-to-day activities; level of commitment and willingness to invest time, energy, and work to carry out the program, policy, or practice; and changes implementers or others have made to the program, policy, or practice during the implementation process. It is better to have informal conversations rather than to use intuition or to surmise, infer, guess, and/or "mind read" to understand what may or may not be going on related to the program, policy, or practice. It is also possible to address these questions in more formal interviews, although the items would likely need rewording for this purpose.

Review Implementation Cases: When Things Don't Go as Planned

Implementation of programs, policies, or practices in real-world settings often does not go as planned. After implementation monitoring has been conducted, an understanding of these challenges can be gleaned, which may aid others in planning and implementing future programs. Three published cases are presented in this section; each reflects challenges experienced, lessons learned, and recommendations.

Worksheet 9.1   Understanding the Innovation and Its Implementation From the Perspective of Setting Stakeholders

Question	Stakeholder Response (specify leader, implementer, participant, and/or other key people)
How do implementers, participants, leaders, or other key people describe the program, policy, or practice?	
In what ways do the different stakeholder perspectives vary?	
How do implementers, participants, leaders, or others describe the ways in which this program, policy, or practice differs from other innovations or from current practice?	
What do implementers, participants, leaders, or others say is the purpose of the program, policy, or practice?	
What are the perceived benefits of the program, policy, or practice to implementers, participants, leaders, or others? What are the perceived costs?	
To what extent do implementers, participants, leaders, or others value the benefits? In what specific ways do they show that they value the benefits?	
How do implementers, participants, leaders, or others describe the "fit" of the intervention goals with the organization's goals?	
How do implementers, participants, leaders, or others describe the fit of the intervention activities with the organization's activities?	
To what extent do implementers, participants, leaders, or other key stakeholders think the program, policy, or practice, or parts of it, is a good idea for their setting?	
To what extent did implementers demonstrate an understanding of the principles behind the program, policy, or practice during the planned training or orientation and follow-up sessions?	
To what extent do implementers and leaders say they are committed to invest the time, energy, and work needed to carry out the program, policy, or practice?	
To what extent do implementers' and leaders' actions show that they are committed to invest the time, energy, and work needed to carry out the program, policy, or practice?	
How does the program, policy, or practice affect the implementers' work? Does it promote or interfere with getting their work done?	

(Continued)

(Continued)

Question	Stakeholder Response (specify leader, implementer, participant, and/or other key people)
How do implementers, participants, leaders, or others describe the fit of intervention activities with existing work practices and schedules? To what extent is it possible to stay with the intervention timeline in this setting?	
What impact does the program, policy, or practice have on division of labor, resources, power, and responsibility among different groups in the setting?	
What are the positive and negative effects of the innovation on participants as described by implementers, participants, leaders, and others?	
What changes have implementers or others made to the program, policy, or practice? How did these changes originate (e.g., were they decided collaboratively)? How have these changes helped them?	

Source: Adapted from Table 1 in Murray et al. (2010).

Active Winners

An example of an intervention with no intervention effects is Active Winners, a physical activity promotion change effort in an afterschool setting that did not go as planned (Pate et al., 2003). The goals of this program for fifth-grade students were to provide a fun physical activity program for boys and girls in which participants were physically active and their physical activity self-efficacy and skills increased; to create supportive social and physical environments; and to create cues to action for physical activity. Process evaluation showed good fidelity and completeness of implementation for the afterschool program components. These components included Fit for Fun, which involved noncompetitive, inclusive, participatory, and fun physical activities designed to build endurance and strength; Be a Sport, which involved noncompetitive games and modified sports; Social Rap, which involved noncompetitive activities that emphasized learning and using social skills including communication and conflict resolution; and Brain Games, which is supervised study or homework. However, the remaining components pertaining to family, school, and community involvement were incompletely implemented, and reach for all components was very poor, with 5 percent of participants attending half of the total possible sessions due to social factors such as friends not attending the program and the presence of "problem" students.

Active Winners illustrates several of the recurring themes throughout this textbook including a Type III error, the importance of considering the context; having sufficient implementation resources including time; and addressing fidelity, completeness, and reach. Active Winners was a program implemented by a research team using a newly hired interventionist to carry out the program. Much of the needed program infrastructure for recruitment, transportation, staff hiring and training, and scheduling had to be created from scratch, which took considerable time. There were also some initial challenges in the afterschool program related to discipline problems among groups of participants who historically did not get along. It took a great deal of staff time and energy to get the afterschool program running and to overcome the initial implementation problems, leaving little time and energy to implement all components of Active Winners. The research team recommended that future projects ensure sufficient resources for the scope of work, consider the social and cultural context, plan for sufficient time to work with stakeholders, and attend to program infrastructure issues early in the process (Pate et al., 2003).

Workplace Intervention

Aust, Rugulies, Finken, and Jensen (2010) described a workplace innovation, designed to improve psychosocial working conditions, that lead to negative effects. The primary target audience and setting were employees in seven units within a hospital; 128 in the intervention group completed baseline and follow-up surveys. The purpose of the study was to investigate if workplace interventions to improve psychosocial working conditions resulted in changes in the psychosocial work environment; process evaluation was conducted to understand the study results.

The goal of the intervention was to improve the psychosocial working environment and to reduce employee sickness leave. For the intervention, the baseline assessment was used as a starting point for discussion about the psychosocial work environment. Consultants worked with hospital unit leaders to discuss the results of the survey, find out what unit leaders thought was important, and provide coaching sessions. Employees were invited to a kickoff day in which the units established working groups to address the priority areas for improving the environment under the guidance of the consultants. There was no explicit conceptual model identified at the beginning of the project. External consultants facilitated intervention activities.

A two-group evaluation design with nonrandom assignment was used. Baseline and follow-up (at 16 months) assessments were conducted on working conditions and health using the Copenhagen psychosocial questionnaire.

This questionnaire has 13 scales in three domains: demands at work, work organization and job content, and interpersonal relations and leadership. Implementation monitoring methods consisted of a research assistant using qualitative methods to monitor and document implementation, primarily through meeting notes and a log for documenting activities and contextual factors. Meeting notes documented attendance, roles, proceedings, and decisions made. Consultants kept their own notes on meetings with unit leaders, as well.

There were several implementation strengths. All seven units participated in the kick-off event and identified topics for discussion; most employees participated and seemed motivated. All unit leaders participated in the coaching sessions, ranging from two to eight sessions. There were also some implementation challenges. The working groups only met initially or did not meet at all, as they lacked structure and direction and thus became frustrated. The consultants explicitly focused on the unit leaders and leadership over the working groups; in contrast, the hospital administrators wanted more focus on the employee working groups. This revealed that the consultants and the hospital administration were operating on different implicit conceptual models, in other words, a top-down versus bottom-up emphasis, respectively.

In terms of intervention effects, there was a statistically significant worsening of the psychosocial working environment on six scales after adjusting for covariates; authors interpreted reduced scores in one scale, "increased emotional demands," as likely reflecting burnout.

This intervention that was designed to improve the psychosocial working environment not only failed to improve the environment, but resulted in making it worse. The innovation was not fully implemented, particularly with regard to the employee working groups. The working groups needed additional structure and support for this component to succeed, but did not receive it from the consultants, who focused on the leadership versus employee aspects of the project. This reflected a lack of agreement about what the innovation was and how it was supposed to produce its effects among key stakeholder groups: the consultants who were facilitating implementation and the hospital that was the implementing setting. This case illustrates the importance of clarity about the innovation and its conceptual basis among stakeholders.

Quit Together

Zapka, Goins, Pbert, and Ockene (2004) described challenges experienced with an intervention aimed at promoting smoking cessation in community health centers. The primary target audience and settings were low-income pregnant and postpartum women who received care at three community health centers that offer prenatal and pediatric services and a supplemental food program for women, infants, and children (WIC). The purpose of the study was to report on process monitoring methods and to outline lessons learned as well as the challenges of research carried out in community health clinics.

The study design was an effectiveness randomized trial with three intervention and three usual care organizations; one usual care organization subsequently dropped out. The primary outcome was self-reported 7-day smoking status of each assessment point via survey; biochemical validation was performed via cotinine assay of saliva samples. For women who did not quit, the number of cigarettes smoked per day was also collected.

The study was a systems intervention to train existing health care providers to deliver tobacco treatment (smoking cessation) that could potentially improve patient compliance, minimize costs, and be institutionalized by the end of the research study. Quit Together (QT) was a theory- and evidence-based innovation with three key components: (1) a provider-delivered smoking intervention with three provider channels (clinicians and staff from obstetrics/women's health clinics [OB], WIC, and pediatrics [PED]); (2) office practice management system to prompt providers and facilitate follow up; and (3) processes to facilitate communication and linkages between clinics via a program board. Diffusions theory guided QT and was used to identify concepts within key dimensions including the QT concept, organizational context, planning and implementation process, provider participation, patients, interactions, and patient impact and outcomes.

Providers in the clinics implemented QT after receiving a group training session consisting of didactic presentations and practice using the innovation algorithm, held separately for obstetric, pediatric, and WIC providers. They also received support materials including practice guidelines and patient materials. Two months following the training, providers received individual coaching and feedback on the intervention protocol (Pbert et al., 2004).

Multiple data sources included organizational assessment reports to assess program/clinic flow, structure, and process linkages among the clinics and key players via key informant interviews; intervention coordinator's contact logs documenting meetings with key personnel; meeting notes documenting the type of meeting, attendance, agenda, issues discussed, and decisions made for meetings of program boards, clinic work groups, and individual personnel key to the project; training records for all training and booster training provided; follow-up key informant interviews (conducted midway and at the end of the trial) with medical directors and directors of the WIC, OB, and PED programs to assess current smoking cessation activities, perceived changes, and contextual influences; patient exit interviews concerning dose received; patient report of exposure in surveys; and chart reviews in randomly sampled charts to assess presence of cue and algorithm in the record and completeness of documentation. Data triangulation among multiple data sources was used to make observations and identify themes related to critical domains of diffusion theory.

There were a variety of implementation challenges related to the organizational context including major structural changes to five of the six participating health centers; insufficient buy-in from key players; lack of infrastructure such as working groups or committees in some areas; lack of strong leadership in some clinics; unclear decision-making authority regarding the intervention; high staff turnover; high level of patient scheduling and rescheduling; organizational chaos affecting staff morale; lack of essential cooperation within and across the clinics; and external factors, including other tobacco cessation initiatives that influenced activity in the usual care, comparison sites.

Challenges to the planning and implementation process included variable buy-in from advisory boards across the sites; a much lengthier time than anticipated for each step to be completed; a lack of enthusiasm and resources at every level, which created challenges in a hectic environment that could not be overcome; and some operational details that were not considered in the initial planning such as clinic clients' tendency to reschedule or fail to appear.

There were also challenges related to provider participation resulting in less than expected implementation in all three components: There was limited implementation of the systems cue; clinicians delivered QT only if they were personally committed to smoking cessation, and delivery was inconsistent across individual providers; and cross-clinic communication was limited. Providers experienced difficulty integrating QT and often expressed cynicism and lack of optimism about potential effectiveness. Furthermore, pediatric physicians did not view the mothers as their patients, resulting in low implementation in pediatric clinics. Finally, implementation decreased over time.

Little effect was found for smoking cessation or maintenance of abstinence among women in the study. In summary, there were a number of implementation challenges with the QT intervention. According to the authors, the most important contextual factor was the organizational chaos in which the health centers operated; they all experienced some type of significant upheaval during the study, which included fiscal hardship, leadership changes, physical environment changes, and turnover of intervention-trained personnel. Many of the clinics lacked infrastructure including formal communication, existing workgroups or committees, and clear decision-making authority. Low morale made generating enthusiasm for QT challenging as did the hectic pace and high level of client no-shows and rescheduling. Furthermore, provider participation was not at the level anticipated, reflecting difficulty integrating QT into their roles and concerns about the efficacy of the intervention. The concept of QT, to integrate provider provision of smoking cessation services within the clinic, was well received initially; however, in practice this was very difficult to do because of organizational, provider, and contextual factors.

The authors (Zapka et al., 2004) provided the following reminders for future work based on their experience with QT:

- It is important to consider the daily operations of complex organizations, including the lack of communication among parts of an organization; seek natural communication channels.

- Sign-on of clinical directors is necessary but may not be sufficient; involve staff responsible for implementation very early in the process.

- Plan enough time for relationship development and buy-in for leadership and middle management; research timelines can make this challenging.

- Anticipate organizational turmoil, and plan to adapt to constant or frequent change.

- Emphasize research staff visibility and accountability.

- Be flexible; it may be necessary to adjust training mode and/ or materials.

Be able to discuss practical issues for using implementation data in a formative manner.

Formative uses of implementation data are designed to keep a program "on track" as it is being carried out. It is important to distinguish formative use for keeping a planned project on course from formative evaluation that is used to shape the nature of the innovation itself. In this textbook the focus is on formative use of implementation monitoring data for a program that has been developed and is not actively evolving, in other words, a program that is more mature than developing.

There are a number of practical issues to consider for using implementation monitoring data in a formative manner. To be beneficial, formative use of implementation monitoring data must have a high priority within the project; this requires that up-front planning takes place and that it receives sufficient resources including trained personnel. The most immediate practical problem is typically the challenge of turning the information around quickly enough to be used in a meaningful way within the project. Another important issue to consider is the level of objectivity desired.

Implementation monitoring data are more objective if evaluators, or personnel not involved in the intervention, are collecting the data. If only one set of implementation monitoring data can be collected for formative as well as summative purposes, it is better to have evaluators not involved with the intervention to carry out these tasks as the data will likely be more valid (Lillehoj, Griffin, & Spoth, 2004; Resnicow et al., 1998). This requires dedication of project resources to ensure that sufficient implementation monitoring data collection staff are trained and available.

The primary challenge with using objectively collected data for formative purposes is the time it takes to get from field data collection, data entry, and data summary to providing useful feedback to the interventionists or implementers. This challenge can be overcome by effective, up-front planning. Planning should ensure that data are summarized in a form that is meaningful and useful to interventionists or implementers, and that the time frame for turnaround enables interventionists or implementers to make the needed changes.

It is possible to turn data around in near real time; however, this does require that timely use of formative information is a project priority. In general, it is less difficult to turn formative feedback around in 6 or 12 months. This time frame may be sufficient for year-to-year planning, but it may not be frequent enough to address many immediate problems that can occur during implementation. For example, if transportation is not available for participants or the space for an activity is not appropriate, these issues need to be addressed immediately and not down the road.

The Study of Health and Activity in Preschool Environments (SHAPES) will be used to illustrate one approach to using implementation monitoring information in a formative manner. An overview of SHAPES is provided in Table 9.1. SHAPES was a physical activity innovation in preschool settings that aimed to increase physical activity in preschoolers by having interventionists work with preschool teachers to increase physical activity opportunities and to create an encouraging social environment for physical activity (Pfeiffer et al., 2013). A sample of a report to provide formative feedback in SHAPES is provided in Table 9.2. Data collected by the process evaluation staff originally were in a complex form that was not useful to interventionists. Measurement staff worked with the interventionists to create a more user-friendly form for formative feedback (shown in Table 9.2). This information was turned around to interventionists within one week of data collection. Interventionists used this information to tailor training and consultation with teachers. The feedback provided pertained to observations related to the essential or core elements for SHAPES, information for which the interventionists were looking. Specifically, it provided feedback on minutes of opportunity of physical activity and how these were provided in terms of fidelity.

The form in Table 9.2 is structured to capture the opportunities for physical activity provided by the teachers via Move Inside, Move Outside, and Move to Learn throughout the entire preschool day for up to three occasions per observation. Each time a physical activity opportunity was observed, process evaluators also assessed fidelity that included the social environment, enjoyment, and level of physical activity. The form was designed to focus on the essential elements of SHAPES and to provide interventionists weekly feedback at the classroom level.

Another approach is to have a "dual system" in which interventionists, objective evaluators, and/or implementers collect implementation monitoring data. Interventionist- and implementer-collected data are optimally used as formative information, thereby reducing turnaround time considerably. These data may be used in addition to objective evaluated data as part of the data source to triangulate level of implementation for summative purposes.

LEAP provides an illustration of the dual system in which the independent evaluator and the interventionists used the same form to collect data. The interventionists made frequent site visits to the intervention schools, and during part of these visits they observed the PE class; on different days scheduled in advance, the independent process evaluator used the same form to do observations. The interventionists' data were used entirely for formative purposes, whereas the process evaluator's data were used entirely for summative purposes. Classroom teachers became quite accustomed to observation because of the frequency with which it was happening, which reduced the effects that being observed had on their students' classroom behavior over time. The form was also provided to the teachers to do their own observations. See Worksheet 9.2 for a modified copy of the LEAP observation form.

There are several important issues to consider if you plan to provide implementers or other stakeholders with observation tools to use for formative data collection.

Table 9.1 Overview of the SHAPES Intervention

	SHAPES Case Study
Citation	Pfeiffer et al. (2013)
Primary target audience and setting	Preschool children in four public and four private preschools in the Midlands of South Carolina.
Purposes of the study	To examine the effects of a multicomponent intervention on physical activity, sedentary behavior, and physical activity energy expenditure in 3- to 5-year-old children; identify factors associated with change in those variables; and evaluate the intervention implementation process.
Study design and outcome measures	SHAPES was a 2-year randomized trial (nested cohort design), with two conditions (eight intervention and eight control), two measurement occasions, with preschool serving as the unit of analysis. Primary outcomes included accelerometer assessment of physical activity, sedentary behavior, and physical activity energy expenditure.
Goal of the intervention	To work with preschool teachers to integrate physical activity opportunities in the context of a socially supportive environment into the preschool day.
Description of innovation	The innovation had four main components: a) indoor physical activity ("move inside"); b) recess ("move outside"); c) daily lessons ("move to learn"); and d) social environment, which was characterized by adult encouragement and modeling, physically active children, and child enjoyment. Components a–c constituted completeness, and component d constituted fidelity for SHAPES.
Conceptual basis	The social ecological model provided the framework for SHAPES.
Implementation approach and stakeholder involvement	SHAPES was considered a partnership between the SHAPES staff and preschool teachers; SHAPES staff provided teacher and administrator trainings and workshops, site support visits, and newsletters, and facilitated the use of teacher self-monitoring methods. SHAPES was also flexible, adaptive in that it encouraged appropriate teacher adaptation of the SHAPES components to better fit preschool practices, resources, and space. For example, SHAPES components could be integrated throughout the school day; there was no SHAPES curriculum.
Implementation monitoring methods	Comprehensive implementation monitoring of SHAPES completeness and fidelity, using multiple data sources and methods, was carried out. Data collection forms included a process evaluation observation form (focused on observing opportunity for physical activity and social environment enjoyment) and the Observation System for Recording Physical Activity in Children–Preschool version (OSRAC-P), both administered by independent process evaluators.

Source: Content from Pfeiffer et al. (2013).

Table 9.2 LEAP Classroom and Environment Observation Form

(partial, modified version for illustration; note that the time scale for optimal observation varies for classroom versus environmental observation)

Physical Education	Yes	Partial	No
1. Is physical education gender separate to provide a safe and supportive environment for girls?			
2. Are cooperative activities included?			
3. Are a variety and choice of lifetime activities popular among girls provided?			
4. Are girls provided with fun, enjoyable, and successful experiences?			
5. Do instruction and management techniques include the use of small, enduring groups?			
6. Overall, are students physically active for at least 50% of class time?			
7. Are students frequently linked to out-of-school physical activity opportunities?			
School Environment			
1. Does the school have a team that regularly plans, implements, and evaluates student and faculty physical activity programs?			
2. Does the school provide opportunities for students to engage in physical activity outside of physical education?			
3. Does the school regularly promote physical activity through school media (e.g., use letter, loudspeaker, television, stall-talker, video)?			
4. Does the school principal provide support and assistance for physical activity programs?			
Faculty/Staff Wellness Program			
1. Does the school have an active wellness program in place?			
2. Does the program sponsor physical activity programs based on staff interests?			
3. Does the program recognize staff who are active and serve as the physical activity role models?			

Coding: yes = 2; partial = 1; no = 0

First, it is necessary to provide training to ensure effective data collection. It is risky to have implementers or other setting stakeholders serving as the sole data collectors, as they tend to have other priorities; if at all possible, it is preferable

Worksheet 9.2   Providing Formative Process Evaluation Feedback in SHAPES

School _____ Classroom/teacher _____ Date of observation _____

Process Form: Providing physical PA opportunities per day and week for each classroom/teacher

Write in day of week:	Opportunity teacher provides by day of week (one day/observation per week) ✓ = yes	Frequency of opportunities by day of week, duration in minutes, and time of day of each observed on the day of observation				Number of children present
Component		1st occurrence		2nd occurrence		
		Min	Time	Min	Time	
Move In						
Move to Learn						
Move Out (recess)						

Fidelity of PA opportunities provided: Skill shapers/PE

Write in day of week:	PA Fidelity Rating for up to three occasions per day of observation			Notes
Component: _____	1st	2nd	3rd	
(R1) 50% MVPA				
(R2) Opportunity				
(R3) Enjoy				
(R4) Engage				
(R5) Adult encourage				
(R6) Adult active				

OSRAC-P fidelity of PA opportunities provided: Activity level of children during observed intervention components (sedentary, light, or moderate-to-vigorous physical activity)

Write in day of week:	PA level for up to three occasions per day of observation			Notes
Component	1st	2nd	3rd	
_____				

for implementer-collected data to be one of several data sources. Also be aware that collecting data can be disruptive and burdensome; this can potentially have a negative influence on crucial working relationships with stakeholders. Stated more positively, stakeholders are more likely to be amenable to participating in self-monitoring and data collection after solid and effective working relationships have been established. Finally, many stakeholders are averse to checking a box that says *no*, suggesting little or no progress. Instead, response options such as *yes, completely; yes, partially;* and *yes, additional work needed* are likely to yield more accurate results.

Develop a plan for using implementation monitoring data in a formative manner to keep a project on track.

You previously conducted some preliminary planning related to formative and summative uses of implementation monitoring data in Step 7. An adapted version of this worksheet is reproduced in Worksheet 9.3, with an emphasis on using implementation monitoring data for formative purposes.

In summary, consider the following questions:

- What information about program, policy, or practice elements or components is important to know as implementation is taking place?

- Who needs the information, and when do they need it?

- In what form is the information needed to be most useful?

- Who collects this information, and when is it collected?

- When is the information summarized and fed back to those who need it? Is this sufficient for formative purposes?

- What is needed to make this information available in a timely manner? Do any of the following need revision: data collection forms, data collection procedures, and/or reporting frequency?

The wording of the formative questions may be very similar to the wording of the summative implementation monitoring questions. The primary difference is in how the data are being used rather than methodology per se.

Worksheet 9.3   Planning for Formative Uses of Implementation Monitoring Data

Formative Purpose	Who Collects	Data Collection Tools and Procedures	When Collected	Reporting Format	Who Receives Information	Turnaround Time
Fidelity questions:						
Completeness questions:						
Reach questions:						
Context questions:						
Other questions:						

Your Turn: Formative Use of Implementation Monitoring Data

Your task is to make a case for using implementation monitoring data in a formative manner. You need to persuade several members of your research team who are not comfortable with using implementation monitoring data in a formative manner, as they believe it may result in changing the program, policy, or practice and therefore threatening the validity of the outcome/impact evaluation design. What arguments or issues can you bring to your team to convince them of the importance and validity of using implementation monitoring data in a formative manner?

KEY POINTS FOR IMPLEMENTATION
AND USING DATA FOR FORMATIVE PURPOSES

- Be prepared but expect the unexpected during the implementation process.

- Work to understand implementation from the perspective of implementers and stakeholders.

- Incorporate "lessons learned" from others' mistakes into research and practice.

- Formative uses of implementation monitoring data must have a high priority within the project.

- Have a plan for collecting and using implementation monitoring data in a formative manner.

- Consider having a "dual" system for collecting implementation monitoring data.

Information is the oil of
the 21st century, and analytics is the
combustion engine.

-Peter Sondergaard

Collect and Manage Implementation Data

The purpose of this chapter is to convey important principles and practices of sound data management to enable you to develop an implementation monitoring **data management plan** for a specific project. Data management is a process that includes the "development, execution, and supervision of plans, policies, programs, and practices that control, protect, deliver, and enhance the value of data and information assets" (ICF International, n.d.). A data management plan is "a formal document that outlines what you will do with your data during and after you complete your research" (University of Virginia Library Data Management Consulting Group, n.d.).

The principles and practices presented in this chapter are based on those for sound data management in general, with needed adaptations and emphases for implementation monitoring data. See Resource Box 10.1 for additional data management resources. Compared to outcome data, implementation monitoring data have had a lower priority; this often results in less planning, delayed data entry, and increased analysis/synthesis challenges, particularly since implementation data are often voluminous as when multiple data sources are tapped at multiple time points to address multiple evaluation questions. Advance planning and effective data management can prevent implementation monitoring "nightmares" down the road.

Learning Objectives

By the end of this chapter you will be able to

1. List and define important steps and principles of data management

2. Develop a data management plan that identifies tasks for managing implementation monitoring data

3. Review examples of selected data management plans

Resource Box 10.1
Data Management Resources

- http://ori.dhhs.gov/education/products/n_illinois_u/datamanagement/dmotopic.html

This is the Responsible Conduct of Research (RCR) website at Northern Illinois University. It contains online modules on Data Management topics, including overview, data selection, data collection, data handling, data analysis, publication and reporting, and data ownership. This module was developed with the support of RCR Education Grants awarded by the Office of Research Integrity to the Faculty Development and Instructional Design Center at Northern Illinois University.

- http://ori.dhhs.gov/data-management-0

This is the U.S. Department of Health and Human Services Office of Research Integrity website. The "Data Management" section is under the "RCR Resources" tab. Several resources for responsible data management are listed.

List and define important steps and principles of data management.

Below are the important steps and principles that pertain to implementation monitoring data management. Data management involves developing, executing, and supervising plans, policies, programs, and practices that control, protect, deliver, and enhance the value of data and information. In other words, data management describes how data are handled, protected, processed, analyzed, and stored after being collected to ensure that data quality is maintained, identities protected, duplicative efforts are reduced, and analysis and reporting are streamlined (ICF International, n.d.). Throughout the data collection, management, and analysis/synthesis processes it is imperative to maintain protection of human subjects by following Internal Review Board procedures and to maintain data privacy and security by following Health Insurance Portability and Accountability Act of 1996 (HIPAA) and Family Educational Rights and Privacy Act (FERPA) procedures, as applicable. The steps in the data management process include the following: (1) develop data management plan; (2) collect data in the field; (3) transfer data from field to data entry; (4) conduct data entry; (5) clean data; (6) conduct preliminary data processing; (7) ensure secure data storage; (8) develop procedures for access to data; and (9) conduct data analysis/synthesis and reporting.

1. Develop data management plan.

The process ideally begins with the development of a data management plan, which contains the **data dictionary,** or code book. The data dictionary lists variable/field name, values and/or valid ranges, variable type (numeric or character), variable label, variable description, variable source/location (e.g., baseline, follow up, etc., as applicable), and variable derivations for computed or transformed variables (ICF International, n.d.). The data management plan also contains the procedures to carry out the steps in the data management process, presented below. All staff roles, including those of the project coordinator, data manager, statistician, data entry staff, and data collection staff, should be clearly defined with specific responsibilities. There should be written procedures and documentation for all steps. Data collection and data entry staff should be provided training, and an optimal level of proficiency should be attained and maintained throughout the project.

Develop a data management plan from the beginning with end use of data in mind; ensure that all personnel follow the plan. Keeping the use of the data in mind will prevent you from collecting data that are not needed, neglecting to collect data that are needed, and collecting and/or entering data in a form that makes the data very difficult to use. Use approaches that minimize the number of steps and number of people handling data. This simplifies the process, reduces stress and burden among staff, and reduces the chances of losing data or making errors. When scheduling data collection in field-based settings, do your homework ahead of time to find out the schedule of the setting and what days are likely to be problematic for data collection. For example, holidays, teacher workdays, and testing days are days to avoid in school settings. Considering schedules facilitates the scheduling process and the working relationship with setting-based stakeholders. Finally, it is important to document actions and decisions throughout the process and to keep copies of analysis programs and output. Keep detailed and accurate records!

2. Collect data in the field.

After developing a data management plan, the next step in the data management process is data collection in the field. Data collection, in terms of instruments, methods, and procedures, should proceed as described in the implementation monitoring methods in Step 8. Specific planning tasks with the step of data collection include the following:

- Develop written protocols, follow the protocols for data collection, and strive to minimize the number of people and the number of steps involved. For example, use direct electronic entry rather than paper or TeleForm (TeleForm, 2013) data collection to bypass the physical data transfer step.

- Train and "certify" data collectors in the protocol and skills required for data collection to ensure systematic and high-quality data collection.

  o In some ongoing studies, data collectors may need to be recertified periodically to ensure quality data collection.

  o For observational data, plan to conduct interrater and intercoder reliability assessments and, for survey data, to conduct test-retest reliability assessments.

- Minimize reliance on "volunteer" data collectors, such as setting implementers who are asked to complete and return implementation forms with little support or incentives; response rates are typically low for this approach. It can also have an adverse effect on working relationships with stakeholders, who may not see their role as collecting data.

- Coordinate data collection with organizational and intervention schedules to minimize disruption to ongoing activities and to ensure data collectors will have access to participants, documents to be reviewed, and/or environments to be observed.

- Ensure Institutional Review Board (IRB) processes for informed consent and data security procedures are strictly followed.

- Develop and use checklists for steps to be followed during the data collection process, including bringing needed supplies.

- Conduct data quality and completeness checks in the field as data are collected/returned so that corrections can be made immediately, if needed.

- Track the data collection process (e.g., dates that surveys were sent, followed up, and returned) in a database such as Access.

- Data collection planning should include time and resources to conduct follow up, obtain informed consent, and conduct makeup data collection. Do gentle follow up; be willing to go out of your way to make it easier for participants and setting stakeholders.

3. Transfer data from field to data entry.

If data have been collected in the field on paper forms or TeleForms (TeleForm, 2013), they must be physically transferred from the field and entered into the selected software (i.e., data entry). Spell out the detailed procedures, including time frame, for getting the data from the field to the specific person(s) who will conduct the data entry. Note that electronic data entry in the field bypasses the need for physical data transfer, whereas respondent self-administered and TeleForm (TeleForm, 2013) data collection require physical transfer. Direct electronic data entry in the field is preferable because it reduces the steps and number of people handling the data. In both data transfer and entry, define and follow procedures including those for data security. If there are multiple steps in data transfer, create and use a checklist to ensure protocols are followed. Document, document, document!

4. Ensure secure data storage.

Files should be named, organized, and stored in a systematic manner (file storage). Data should be stored in a form that minimizes inadvertent changes. The project should ideally adopt folder and file naming conventions that are consistently used by everyone. In general, avoid using special characters, periods, and spaces in names. File names should be unique and should include a version number and dates with a consistent format. Regularly create backups and secure copies of all files.

5. Develop procedures for access to data.

It is important to establish version control, or the management of changes to computer programs, data sets, and other documents, early in the project

(ICF International, n.d.). Develop procedures to ensure timely data access for appropriate persons while also maintaining file and data security by following written procedures and protocols. Ensure that security policies are followed.

6. Conduct data entry.

Ensure that the data dictionary, or code book, is finalized and that the data entry process has been pilot tested prior to entering data. As previously defined, the data dictionary lists variable/field name, values and/or valid ranges, variable type (numeric or character), variable label, variable description, variable source/location (e.g., baseline, follow up, etc., as applicable), and variable derivations for computed or transformed variables (ICF International, n.d.). This will ensure consistency of use over time. Strive to have the minimum number of data enterers possible. Conduct data entry as the data come in, rather than allowing the data to "pile up."

If there are qualitative fields embedded in a quantitative survey, develop codes and code these open-ended items to facilitate data entry. It is preferable to avoid open-ended response items by doing the formative work needed to develop close-ended response options prior to data collection. If open-ended fields were included in initial data collection, consider revising these items to close-ended response options for future data collection.

Enter all data in the most granular form possible; it can be combined or collapsed into categories later in the analysis process. Enter data into selected software with end uses in mind; examples of end uses include variable formation, data merging, data analysis, and reporting requirements. Run periodic, independent checks on data entered. As previously indicated, minimize the number of steps taken as well as the number of people handling the data. All processes should be documented.

7. Clean data.

The next step is data cleaning, which includes checking for out-of-range values and identifying clerical errors or other anomalies. Some software packages facilitate this step by precluding entering out-of-range data, but clerical errors are still possible if data are entered by hand. Run preliminary descriptive analysis such as frequencies and means to check for anomalous results. Adjust protocols for data collection, field data check, and data entry as needed to ensure data quality. Document all changes.

8. Conduct preliminary data processing.

After the data set is cleaned, data processing follows. Data processing includes variable recoding, transforming raw variables, and making other required data transformations and merges as needed. It is important to select the appropriate tools (software) and to use a format of data entry that facilitates data analysis, merging with other evaluation data sets, and developing interim and final reports. Document all data transformations. Create a permanent implementation monitoring data set. Develop a system for naming and storing files. Ensure that all final documents are clearly indicated and accessible to the appropriate persons.

9. Conduct data analysis/synthesis and reporting.

The final steps in the process are analysis/synthesis and reporting, which were discussed in detail in Step 9 in relation to formative use of implementation monitoring data and will be discussed in Steps 11 and 12 in relation to summative use of implementation monitoring data. It is essential to keep careful records of all analyses including copies of programs, output, and other documentation related to analysis procedures. Create tables for results and develop reporting formats appropriate for internal and external audiences.

Considerations for each step in the data management process are summarized in Table 10.1.

Important key points that apply to the entire process include the following:

- Be very organized and systematic.

- Plan and carry out tasks with the end uses of data in mind.

- Take the fewest steps and involve a minimal number of people to reduce the possibility of errors or misplaced data.

- Use trained and qualified personnel, with clear guidance in the form of written protocols, in all phases of data management.

- Document all steps including procedures, variable definitions and transformation, analyses, and adjustments.

- Protect human subjects and ensure data are secure throughout the process.

Table 10.1 Data Management Steps, Tasks, and Considerations

Step in Data Management	Data Management Tasks and Considerations
Data management plan	• Develop data dictionary (or code book). • Develop a data management plan defining roles and responsibilities for personnel and procedures for all steps below. • Define roles and specific tasks related to data management (e.g., project coordinator, data manager, statistician, data entry staff, and data collection staff). • Plan strategies for remedying breaches of protocol and other problems. • Develop standardized approaches for naming variables, files and versions of files, programs, data sets and other documents, and for coding data. • Collect all relevant documentation including the original proposal, instruments, code book, and other documents that are created. • Develop a detailed schedule for data collection; politely request the optimal schedule but be willing to negotiate with stakeholders to ensure scheduling works for them. • Do upfront work to minimize burden on setting stakeholders.
Data collection in the field	• Develop and follow protocols for data collection. • Be early and be prepared. • Train and "certify" data collectors. • Coordinate data collection with organizational and intervention schedules to minimize disruption. • *Ensure Institutional Review Board processes for informed consent are followed.* • Conduct data quality and completeness check as data are collected/returned. • Track data collection process (e.g., surveys sent, followed up, and returned) in database such as Access (Microsoft Access, 2013).
Data storage	• *Ensure data are stored securely.* • Organize files systematically. • Ensure people will be able to find and access these files in the future.
Data access	• Develop procedures for access to data. • Monitor access to data.
Data transfer	• Define and follow procedures for getting data from field to data entry process. • *Develop and follow data security procedures.*

Step in Data Management	Data Management Tasks and Considerations
Data entry	• Ensure data dictionary, or code book, is finalized. • Pilot test data entry format and procedures. • Train data entry staff on standardized approach. • *Enter data into selected software with end uses in mind (e.g., variable formation, data merging, data analysis, and reporting requirements).*
Data cleaning	• Use built-in features of software to check data for out-of-range values and other anomalies. • Run preliminary descriptive analysis (e.g., frequencies and means) to check for anomalous results.
Data processing	• Based on project requirements, recode raw variables, create new variables, and make other variable transformations as needed. • Merge data sets as needed. • Create permanent implementation monitoring data set.
Data analysis/synthesis and reporting (see Steps 8, 10, and 11)	• Conduct analyses. • *Keep copies of programs, output, and other documentation related to analysis procedures.* • Create tables for results. • Develop reporting format appropriate for the audience.

Note: Key points are set in italics.

Develop a data management plan that identifies tasks for managing implementation monitoring data.

It is important to develop an implementation data management plan that identifies tasks for managing implementation monitoring data. As previously defined, the data management plan is "a formal document that outlines what you will do with your data during and after you complete your research" (University of Virginia Library Data Management Consulting Group, n.d.). Steps involved in data management are presented in Table 10.1. The plan identifies common implementation tasks and the person(s) responsible for each. A plan for data management, beginning with data collection in the field, is essential because process evaluation can generate voluminous amounts of information, much of which may become inaccessible if this phase of the process is neglected. Worksheet 10.1 provides a template for developing a project data management plan.

Worksheet 10.1 Data Management Plan Template

Step in Data Management	Data Management Tasks	Person Responsible
Data Management Plan	• Develop data dictionary (or code book). • Develop a data management plan defining roles and responsibilities for personnel and procedures for all steps below. • Develop standardized approaches for naming variables, files and versions of files, programs, data sets and other documents, and for coding data. • Collect all relevant documentation including the original proposal, instruments, code book, and other documents that are created.	
Data collection in the field	• Develop and follow protocols for data collection. • Train and "certify" data collectors. • Coordinate data collection with organizational and intervention schedules to minimize disruption. • Ensure Institutional Review Board processes for informed consent are followed. • Conduct data quality and completeness check as data are collected/returned. • Track data collection process (e.g., surveys sent, followed up, and returned) in database such as Access.	
Data transfer	• Define and follow procedures for getting data from field to data entry process. • Develop and follow data security procedures.	
Data entry	• Ensure data dictionary, or code book, is finalized. • Pilot test data entry format and procedures. • Train data entry staff on standardized approach. • Enter data into selected software with end uses in mind (e.g., variable formation, data merging, data analysis, and reporting requirements).	
Data cleaning	• Use built-in features of software to check data for out-of-range values and other anomalies. • Run preliminary descriptive analysis (e.g., frequencies and means) to check for anomalous results.	
Data processing	• Based on project requirements, recode raw variables, create new variables and make other variable transformations as needed.	

Step in Data Management	Data Management Tasks	Person Responsible
	• Merge data sets as needed. • Create permanent implementation monitoring data set.	
Data storage	• Ensure data are stored securely. • Organize files systematically.	
Data access	• Develop procedures for access to data. • Monitor access to data.	
Data analysis/ synthesis and reporting (see Steps 8, 11, and 12)	• Keep copies of programs and output (and/or other documentation related to analysis procedures). • Create tables for results. • Develop reporting format appropriate for the audience.	

LEAP Case Illustration

An example worksheet from LEAP is provided in Table 10.2. LEAP had a relatively small implementation monitoring budget and, therefore, staff; nevertheless, it was still important to use a systematic approach to implementation monitoring data collection. Table 10.2 indicates that the implementation monitoring team from LEAP for summative purposes consisted of the process evaluation investigator and a part-time independent process evaluator.

A description of LEAP follow-up data collection, designed to assess implementation 3 years after the formal LEAP intervention was over, illustrates the data collection process (Saunders et al., 2012). A single, trained process evaluator made 32 observations total; each school was observed a minimum of two times. The process evaluator also conducted 14 PE teacher interviews to assess instructional practice elements, 18 (former) LEAP Team member interviews to assess environmental elements, and 13 focus groups with current ninth-grade girls (total $n = 89$) to assess instructional practices. Data analysis for LEAP implementation at follow-up is described in Step 11.

Note that LEAP was implemented in the late 1990s and early 2000s; therefore, LEAP did not have access to some electronic resources that are readily available now. To illustrate use of some of these resources, additional projects are described in Table 10.3, including SHAPES; Faith, Activity, and Nutrition (FAN); and Out-of-School Time (OST) programs.

Table 10.2 LEAP Example Data Management Plan

Step	Data Management Tasks	Data Management Plan for LEAP
Data management plan	• Develop data dictionary (or code book). • Develop a data management plan defining roles and responsibilities for personnel and procedures for all steps below. • Develop standardized approaches for naming variables, files and versions of files, programs, data sets and other documents, and for coding data. • Collect all relevant documentation including the original proposal, instruments, code book, and other documents that are created.	**Personnel** *Independent process evaluator:* Responsible for observing physical education and behavioral skill development classes, conducting focus groups with girls who participated in LEAP PE, conducting LEAP record review, and analyzing LEAP PE end of year survey given to girls by teachers. *LEAP intervention staff:* Responsible for documenting baseline information on each intervention school, collecting descriptive school information, documenting all communications with the school/LEAP team, writing field notes from site visits and phone consultations, documenting progress toward achieving the essential elements with summaries of schools' accomplishments, and documenting all LEAP training sessions including agenda and attendance. *Process evaluation investigator:* Responsible for entering data into SAS (SAS Data Management, n.d.), conducting analysis using SAS software, and developing data dictionary. *Statistician:* Responsible for analyses involving implementation and outcome data together. **Procedures** Process evaluator and LEAP intervention staff collect data on paper and pencil forms according to procedures and data collection schedule. Copies of completed forms are given to process evaluation investigator who enters data; investigator also develops and keeps code book.

Step	Data Management Tasks	Data Management Plan for LEAP
Data collection in the field	• Develop and follow protocols for data collection. • Train and "certify" data collectors. • Coordinate data collection with organizational and intervention schedules to minimize disruption. • Ensure Institutional Review Board processes for informed consent are followed. • Conduct data quality and completeness check as data are collected/returned.	• Process evaluator will be trained and certified in data collection for all instruments. • Process evaluator will be responsible for coordinating schedule for observation with intervention coordinator. • Interventionists and process evaluator will have separate, complete schedules for formative and summative data collection, respectively. • Process evaluator will be responsible for data quality.
Data transfer	• Define and follow procedures for getting data from field to data entry process. • Develop and follow data security procedures.	• Process evaluator will hand deliver hard copies of completed instruments to process evaluation investigator. • Original copies will be kept in secure project files.
Data entry	• Ensure data dictionary, or code book, is finalized. • Pilot test data entry format and procedures. • Train data entry staff on standardized approach. • Enter data into selected software with end uses in mind (e.g., variable formation, data merging, data analysis requirements).	• Process evaluation investigator will hand code and enter quantitative data into SAS. • Process evaluator will code and analyze qualitative data using tables to identify themes.
Data cleaning	• Use built-in features of software to check data for out-of-range values and other anomalies. • Run preliminary descriptive analysis (e.g., frequencies and means) to check for anomalous results.	• Process evaluation investigator will compare entered data to raw data. • Process evaluation investigator will run means and frequencies.*
Data processing	• Based on project requirements, recode raw variables, create new variables, and do other variable transformations as needed.	• Process evaluator will create mean scores for essential element items for each data source (Saunders, Ward, Felton, Dowda, & Pate, 2006).

(Continued)

Table 10.2 (Continued)

Step	Data Management Tasks	Data Management Plan for LEAP
	• Merge data sets as needed. • Create permanent data set.	• Schools will be grouped into high- and low-implementing groups based on scores and on criteria for implementation. • Classification of schools into high and low groups will be provided to statistician for use in outcome analysis.
Data storage	• Ensure data are stored securely. • Organize files systematically.	• Process evaluation investigator will create project system for data storage and organization.
Data access	• Develop procedures for access to data. • Monitor access to data.	• Process evaluator and process evaluation investigator will have access to data as needed.
Data analysis/ synthesis and reporting	• Keep copies of programs and output (and/or other documentation related to analysis procedures). • Create tables for results. • Develop reporting format appropriate for the audience.	• Process evaluation investigator will be responsible for implementation monitoring analysis, documentation, and reporting. • Statistician will be responsible for outcome analysis, documentation, and reporting for process data to be used in outcome analysis.

*This is a very low-tech approach that was appropriate at the time (late 1990s) and given the level of resources available.

Table 10.3 Overview of Data Management in SHAPES (Preschool), FAN (Faith-Based), and Out-of-School Time (OST) Programs

Step of Data Management	Project		
	Study of Health and Activity in Preschool Environments (SHAPES)	Faith, Activity, and Nutrition (FAN)	Out-of-School Time (OST)
Project description	Physical activity intervention in preschool children; work with preschool teachers to change instructional environment to promote physical activity	Community-based participatory research intervention to promote physical activity and healthy eating among adults in faith-based settings by enhancing/ creating health-promoting church environments	Work with adult staff who provide OST programs to facilitate staff behavior consistent with health-promoting physical activity and nutrition policies

Step of Data Management	Project		
	Study of Health and Activity in Preschool Environments (SHAPES)	Faith, Activity, and Nutrition (FAN)	Out-of-School Time (OST)
Project reference	Pfeiffer et al. (2013)	Wilcox et al. (2010, 2013); Saunders, Wilcox, Baruth, and Dowda (2014)	Weaver, Beets, Saunders, and Beighle (2014); Weaver, Beets, Saunders, Beighle, and Webster (2014); Weaver, Beets, Webster, and Huberty (2014)
Implementation monitoring	Observation used to monitor extent to which teachers provided physical activity opportunities (completeness—process form) that were active (fidelity—Observation System for Recording Physical Activity in Children—Preschool version—OSRAC-P—instrument)	Surveyed congregants and interviewed key informants to assess extent to which FAN health-promoting elements were in place	Observation of staff behavior for consistency with healthy eating and physical activity standards—System for Observing Staff Promotion of Activity and Nutrition (SOSPAN) instrument
Data collection and transfer	Observational data collected on paper forms and carried to data entry point	Most data collected on paper forms or TeleForms (TeleForm, 2013) and carried to data entry point; staff directly entered data into electronic form; process monitored in Access database	Data entered by staff onto tablets in the field using Pendragon, (Pendragon Forms, n.d.) which are synced into a database, removing the need for separate data transfer and entry steps; interrater reliability routinely performed
Data entry, cleaning, and processing	Data hand-entered by staff into Excel spreadsheets for use in SAS for cleaning and processing	Survey data (which is where much of process evaluation data came from) was scanned from TeleForm (TeleForm, 2013) forms directly into an Access database. Much of the staff process data (i.e., staff ratings, technical assistance calls, etc.) was directly entered into Access forms.	
Example provided	Data collection instructions and checklists	Sample Access database forms for tracking data collection process	Data collection checklists and screen shots of electronic data collection "forms"

Examples from each of these projects, illustrating elements of the data management plan, are provided below.

Review examples of selected data management plans.

Faith, Activity, and Nutrition (FAN)

Sara Wilcox, Ph.D., Principal Investigator for Faith, Activity, and Nutrition (FAN) (Wilcox et al., 2010, 2013), illustrates the utility of a relational database such as Microsoft Access in data management for process as well as outcome evaluation using FAN.

Resource Box 10.2
Relational Databases

Informative video on relational databases: www.youtube.com/watch?v=ivlwXYfN0Dc

---

Microsoft Access software is an example of a useful database for managing data from a research project. It is especially beneficial when you are managing data from various sources, as is often the case when process evaluation data are collected, when your study is relatively large, and/or when you want real time access to the data in an efficient and user-friendly manner. Access is a relational database management system (DBMS). Data are stored in tables and related to data in other tables. Tables from other programs (e.g., Microsoft Excel) can also be linked to Microsoft Access databases. Queries and reports can be drawn from multiple tables to answer questions about the data. The use of Access forms allows for simple data entry from project staff and is particularly applicable when staff have little data entry experience.

Microsoft Access can be used for collecting, sorting, and reporting data, and is useful in research for several reasons. It is relatively easy to use. There are multiple tutorials available for creating Microsoft Access databases for research. Microsoft Access simplifies the management of large amounts of information and makes it easy to filter, sort, and update data. This feature is especially useful when your data must be available and used in real time. For example, simple queries and reports can be created (and saved for future use) to answer the following types of questions: How many (and which) organizations completed the survey? How many worksites exist in our project with more than 250 employees in a given city? What are the names, phone numbers, and email addresses for all participants due for their 6-month assessment? Who is missing data on X variable(s), or who scored above or below a certain value? The fact that these queries and reports can be saved and run by simply pressing a button allows the research team to routinely run reports that might be used for quality assurance or other purposes, and this feature becomes particularly useful as the size of the database and the complexity of the data collected increases.

The use of Microsoft Access forms facilitates data entry in a user-friendly format. The research staff can enter data in a form that appears more like a questionnaire than a data table, which increases quality, accuracy, and ease. Data entry masks (e.g., requiring that a date is entered as mm/dd/yyyy or not allowing values above or below a value) can also be used to help promote accurate data entry. In addition, multiple users can use Microsoft Access simultaneously, increasing efficiency in research settings.

Examples of a Microsoft Access table, query creation, switchboard of reports and queries, and report are included below (Figures 10.1–10.4).

Study of Health and Physical Activity in Preschool Environments (SHAPES)

Kerry McIver, Ph.D., Measurement Coordinator for Study of Health and Physical Activity in Preschool Environments (SHAPES) (Pfeiffer et al., 2013), uses SHAPES to illustrate the use of data collection protocols specifying detailed instructions pertaining to data collection staff (Figure 10.5) and data collection checklists (Figure 10.6). Note that the terminology in Figure 10.5 is project specific. SHAPES was described in Table 9.3 (details provided in Pfeiffer et al., 2013).

Out-of-School Programs (OST)

Finally, Michael Beets, Ph.D., Principal Investigator, and Glenn Weaver, Ph.D., Project Coordinator, use youth physical activity interventions in out-of-school settings to illustrate the use of data collection checklists (Figures 10.7 and 10.8) as well as the use of a tablet for field data collection to eliminate the data entry and transfer steps from the process (Figure 10.9) (Weaver, Beets, Saunders, & Beighle, 2014; Weaver, Beets, Saunders, Beighle, & Webster, 2014; Weaver, Beets, Webster, & Huberty, 2014).

Figure 10.1 Example of a Portion of a Microsoft Access Table

ID	Time	Staff_ID_sca	CH01A	CH01B	CH01C	CH02A	CH02B
1001	0		1	1	1.75	0	
1001	1	33	1	2	1.75	0	
1001	2	08	1	1	1.75	0	
1002	0		0			0	
1002	1	01	1	2	1.75	0	
1002	2	08	1	1	5.75	0	
1003	0	03	1	3	9.75	0	
1003	1	01	1	4	1.75	0	
1003	2	08	1	4	9.75	0	
1004	0		1	3	5.75	0	
1004	1	33	1	3	1.75	0	
1005	0		1	5	9.75	0	
1005	1	33	1	3	3.75	0	
1005	2	08	1	2	3.75	1	1
1007	0		0			0	
1008	0		1	2	1.75	0	
1008	1	33	1	1	1.75	0	
1009	0		1	2	5.75	0	
1009	1	33	1	2	1.75	0	
1009	2	08	1	2	9.75	0	0
1010	0		1	4	5.75	0	
1010	1	33	1	2	5.75	0	
1010	2	08	1	2	3.75	0	
1011	0		1	6	5.75	0	0
1011	1	33	1	6	5.75	0	0
1011	2	08	1	6	5.75	0	
1012	0		1	2	3.75	0	
1012	1	33	1	1	3.75	0	
1012	2	08	1	1	1.75	0	
1013	0		1	3	3.75	0	
1013	1	33	1	2	9.75	0	

Figure 10.2 Example of Creating a Microsoft Access Query

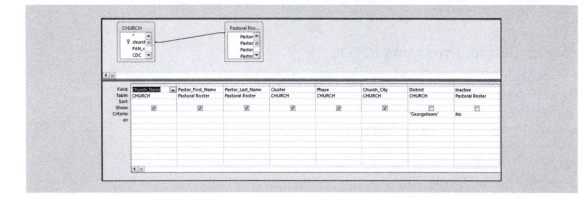

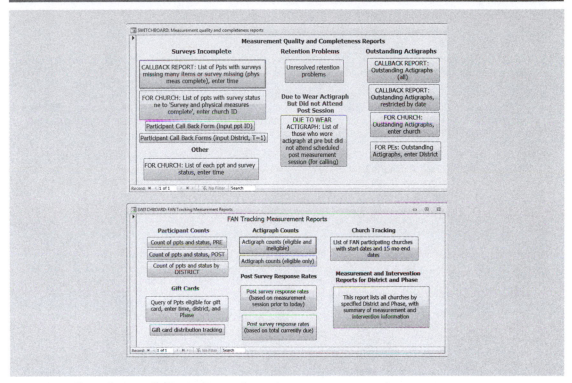

Note: The staff member just clicks on a box, and a report or query is generated.

Figure 10.4   Example of a Report to Monitor Response Rate

	Number	%
Total Due for 12-month visit:	165	
Completed Visit	87	52.73
Visit Scheduled: Future Date	2	1.21
Visit Scheduled: Past Date	28	16.97
Visit Not Scheduled	48	29.09

12/19/2013
8:58 AM

Twelve Month Visit Response Rate

**This reports returns all participants, regardless of status, who are past their 12 month target date (enrollment date + 365 days).

Figure 10.5 SHAPES Data Collection Instructions

SHAPES INSTRUCTIONS—EVENING TASKS

Paper Organization

1. Collect OSRAC correction sheets and place them in the manila file folder located in the black rack on top of the desk in the office. This folder is named "OSRAC Corrections."

2. Collect any notes regarding observation schedule changes, Computer Science and Applications (CSA) Actigraph issues (lost CSAs, downloading problems, etc.). Record information about any missing CSAs on a "Missing Body Boxes" form and place this form in a visible location in the office. (Note: Returned parent surveys should be filed in the corresponding child's folder in the filing cabinet)

3. Make a copy of the daily schedule (where observation completion stickers are placed) and file it in the "Daily Schedule" folder for that school so that the office staff has an up-to-date copy.

Transfer of Files—OSRAC

1. Synchronize HP iPAQ and open the corresponding desktop folder. Move observation files into the folder created for that day.

2. From each desktop folder, copy all files taken from the iPAQ on that day and copy them to the corresponding folder on the V-drive. (Location of the folder is as follows: V-drive → LEAPTAAG → SHAPES – TO STAY → Data Collection → [School Name] → [Wave] → Observation → [Time Period (Baseline, Intervention, or Follow-up)] → [corresponding day])

***NOTE: Files must NOT be opened before they are copied to the V-drive

3. Copy all observation files to the C-drive (C-drive → [School Name] → [Wave] → Observation → [Time Period (Baseline, Intervention, or Follow-up)] → [corresponding day])

4. Qualitative OSRAC notes should be in a Word document compiled throughout the week that is copied to the V-drive and C-drive on the last day of that week. They should go in the "OSRAC Notes" file (…[School Name] → [Wave] → OSRAC Notes)

Transfer of Files—Process

1. From each desktop iPAQ folder copy the process evaluation file for that day into the correct school's Process folder on both the V-drive and C-drive. (Location of the folder in the V-drive is as follows: V-drive → LEAPTAGG → SHAPES – TO STAY → Data Collection → [School Name] → [Wave] → Process → [Time Period (Baseline, Intervention, or Follow-up)]

2. Qualitative Process notes should be in a Word document compiled throughout the week that is copied to the V-drive and C-drive on the last day of that week. They should go in the "Process Notes" file (…[School Name] → [Wave] → Process Notes)

Verifying Files and Recording Times

*Careful attention MUST be given to the naming of files at all times.

1. Verify correct OSRAC file names between the paper daily schedule and the files downloaded from the iPAQs by clicking on the desktop folders corresponding to the iPAQs and comparing the file names under the specific day with the day on the schedule.

2. Compare files between the final paper daily schedule (where completion stickers are placed) and the final electronic daily schedule saved on the computer. If file names need to be updated do so by completing all cells for the day before entering time. Enter observer's initials for each observation session in the electronic daily schedule in the cell marked "Who."

In the event that an observation session was not completed, enter "no session" in the cell corresponding to Time and indicate the reason in the cell corresponding to Probs (field trip, naptime, snacks, etc.).

Open observation files from C-drive (***important not to open V-drive copy***). Copy and paste times from each individual file to their corresponding time cells on the electronic daily schedule. The time can be found in cell Y4 in each observation file. Again, make sure the observation file name corresponds to the paper schedule as times are being pasted.

3. While the observation file is open, verify that the file contains a complete set of 60 intervals. A complete file will extend down to row 63 of the worksheet and should be complete over to column Y.

4. Save the updated schedule to the V-drive and to the C-drive of the SHAPES laptop.

SHAPES Laptop

1. On days where CSAs were downloaded, copy and paste these files from the C-drive of the laptop to the corresponding day's folder on the V-drive. (Location of the folder is as follows: V-drive → LEAPTAGG → SHAPES – TO STAY → Data Collection → [School Name] → [Wave] → Actigraph Data → [Time Period (Baseline, or Follow-up)] → [corresponding day])

2. Make sure the updated daily schedule is on the C-drive of the CHAMPS laptop.

Pack-Up

1. Make sure the SHAPES bag is refilled if needed. Check if extra forms (parent surveys, consent forms) are packed. Check if reminder sheets (CSA instructions, parent survey return reminders, CSA return reminders, etc.) are packed. Check if extra data collection forms are needed (CSA tracking sheets, height/weight/waist circumference sheets, etc.).

2. Make sure equipment is packed. This includes iPAQs (and back-up), clipboards, extra CSAs, USB cord for CSAs, laptop, laptop power cord, etc.

Figure 10.6 SHAPES Data Collection Checklist

SCHOOL: _____   Week 1

Daily Tasks	Day 1	Day 2	Day 3	Day 4	Day 5
Dates					
Sync all units used.					
Copy observation files to the V drive.					
Collect correction sheets and place in folder.					
Collect any notes and place in folder.					
Check for pending issues.					
Copy daily observation schedule and place in folder.					
Download accelerometers.					
Transfer Accelerometer Files To V-drive.					
Fill out CSA—missing in action (MIA) for missing CSAs.					
Place completed forms in proper basket.					
Check files for completeness.					
Person completing task					

IMPORTANT: If several people complete the tasks in a given day, they should put their initials in front of the task they have completed.

Notes:

Figure 10.7   Out-of-School Time Data Collection Checklists

Site:_____   Date:_____   Observer:_____

Items to complete prior to leaving the site	Check if completed
Collected a snack menu for the week	☐
Collected a program schedule for the day/week (what activities are scheduled for the day/week)	☐
Completed snack observation form	☐
Complete "ASP data collection exit form" on tablet	☐
Complete 2 Afterschool "HEPA Standards Checklist" (1 for you 1 given to site leader)	☐
Complete 2 "Afterschool Booster Topics Sheet" (1 for you 1 given to site leader)	☐
Ask site leader how many children attended today	☐
Thank the site leader and staff	☐
Items to be completed upon returning to USC	**Check if completed**
File "Booster Topics Sheet" and "HEPA Standards Checklist" in the R01 Fall 2013 file cabinet (located in 127) in the corresponding site's "Booster Materials" folder	☐
Return the state vehicle keys and sign them back in	☐
Return completed snack observation form to snack observation box	☐
Return snack menu to snack menu box	☐
Return "Eating Snack 2013" form to Falon's box	☐
Place bag back on the wall on the proper hook	☐
Place tablet/s in "Tablets" box and plug into the charger	☐
Return this form to Glenn's Inbox	☐

Field notes

Figure 10.8 Data Collection Exit Checklist Booster and Process

Site:_____   Date:_____   Observer:_____

Items to complete prior to leaving the site	Check if completed
Collected a snack menu for the week	☐
Collected a program schedule for the day/week (what activities are scheduled for the day/week)	☐
Completed snack observation form	☐
Complete "ASP data collection exit form" on tablet	☐
Ask site leader how many children attended today	☐
Thank the site leader and staff	☐
Items to be completed upon returning to USC	**Check if completed**
Return the state vehicle keys and sign them back in	☐
Return completed snack observation form to snack observation box	☐
Return snack menu to snack menu box	☐
Place bag back on the wall on the proper hook	☐
Place tablet/s in "Tablets" box and plug into the charger	☐
Return this form to Glenn's Inbox	☐

Field notes

Figure 10.9 OST Screen Shots of Electronic Data Collection Tablet "Forms": Screen Shot of the Custom User Interface in Pendragon Forms VII© on the Samsung Galaxy Tablets© 158x270mm (96 x 96 DPI)

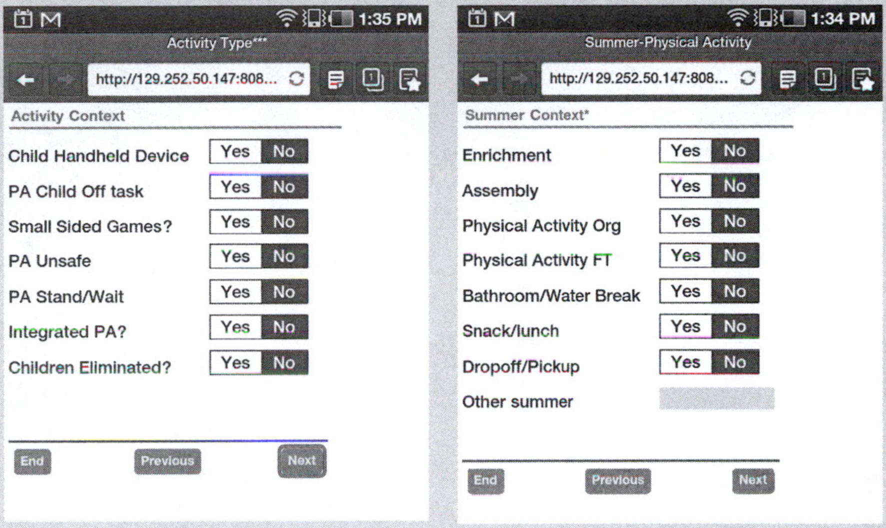

Your Turn: Resource Priorities

You are the evaluator on your planning team; your group is short on resources and is therefore hesitant to provide support for managing the implementation monitoring data, even though they have approved a comprehensive implementation monitoring data collection plan. Using information in Resource Box 10.1 and the American Evaluation Association's Guiding Principles for Evaluators (available at www.eval.org/p/cm/ld/fid=51) diplomatically explain to your team the ethical issues pertaining to poor data management.

KEY POINTS ON COLLECTING AND MANAGING IMPLEMENTATION DATA

- It is important to develop a data management plan prior to beginning data collection.

- The data management plan should define in writing the roles and responsibilities for personnel, procedures for all steps, and standardized approaches for documentation.

- Components of the data management plan include procedures for data collection in the field, data transfer, data entry, data cleaning, data processing, data storage, data access, and data analysis/synthesis and reporting.

Analysis/Synthesis, Reporting, and Use

The final phase, which consists of two steps, involves analyzing/synthesizing the data collected through implementation monitoring and reporting and using the results. Common goals are to describe the extent to which the program, policy, or practice components were put into place (completeness), were put into place as intended (fidelity), and reached the intended audience (reach). Quantitative and/or qualitative data may also be used to describe the recruitment processes as well as to describe, assess, and/or analyze the influence of contextual factors. Also important in this phase of the process is reporting results to stakeholders and using implementation monitoring information as appropriate for different stakeholder audiences.

Figure V.1   The Implementation Planning and Monitoring Process, With Phase V, Analysis/Synthesis, Reporting, and Use, Highlighted

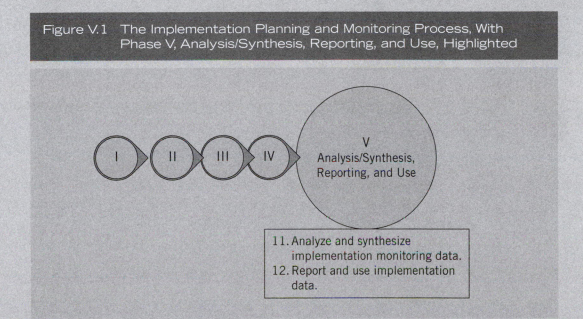

True genius resides in the capacity for evaluation of uncertain, hazardous, and conflicting information.

—Winston Churchill

Analyze and Synthesize Implementation Monitoring Data

This step presents options for analyzing or synthesizing quantitative implementation monitoring data, illustrates **data analysis and synthesis** using specific project examples, and guides you to conduct analysis/synthesis of quantitative implementation monitoring data using an analysis worksheet. Data analysis and synthesis is the process of systematically applying statistical and/or logical techniques to describe and illustrate, condense and recap, and evaluate data (Responsible Conduct in Data Management, n.d.). As in previous steps, the LEAP case study as well as other examples will be used to illustrate these steps.

Conduct analysis/synthesis of implementation data.

In this step, you conduct analysis/synthesis of implementation data to address implementation monitoring questions. The specific approach taken for data analysis/synthesis should be guided by the implementation monitoring questions included in the implementation monitoring plan. Most implementation monitoring plans will have questions or objectives that address the extent to which the program, policy, or practice was put into place (completeness), was put into place consistently with the conceptual model (fidelity), and reached the intended audience (reach). In fact, the implementation monitoring plan developed previously identified the analysis and/or synthesis approach to be used to address each implementation monitoring question (or objective).

Learning Objectives

By the end of this chapter you will be able to

1. Conduct analysis/synthesis of implementation data

2. Understand the Lifestyle Education for Activity Program (LEAP) implementation analysis

3. Understand the Environmental Interventions in Children's Homes (ENRICH) implementation analysis

The complexity and analytic sophistication of the analysis depend on stakeholder needs and expectations as reflected in the implementation monitoring plan. Other considerations that influence the sequence of steps in the analysis process include the size and complexity of the project; resources such as sufficient personnel with expertise; amount and type of information collected (e.g., nominal, ordinal, or numerical data); extent to which multi-item indicators are used; and extent to which multiple data sources will be triangulated. Allow sufficient time for data analysis; the analysis process can sometimes take longer than initially anticipated, but the time-consuming element is "digesting" the information after analysis so that the results, as well as the implications of the results, are fully understood.

In the simplest scenario, one data source and instrument with a single yes-no item is used to address one implementation monitoring question. Little analysis is involved as there is only a single item, and it has a dichotomous response option. To illustrate the point, suppose the completeness evaluation question is, "Did implementers carry out all components of the program?" This is not a particularly good question because it provides very little information about what is or is not happening, especially if the answer is no, and it is used here only to illustrate a very simple approach to analysis. If the question is answered for each site, a site-level answer to the question is thereby obtained for each organization. The frequency and percentage of sites that answered yes would provide an overall answer to the question of what proportion of sites implemented the program.

This approach provides a simple "answer" to the implementation monitoring question, but a single indicator at one point in time is not the optimal approach to portray implementation of programs, policies, or practices in a complex setting, even if the data source is an "objective" one. It is best to use multiple data sources as indicators at appropriate points in time (Bouffard, Taxman, & Silverman, 2003; Helitzer, Yoon, Wallerstein, & Dow y Garcia-Velarde, 2000; Resnicow et al., 1998) in which multiple data sources are considered together, or triangulated, to examine evidence for implementation of one or more particular program, policy, or practice elements. An analogy is the proverbial elephant being examined by six blindfolded individuals. One individual is examining an ear, one is examining the tail, one is examining a leg, one is examining a tusk, one is examining the side, and a sixth individual is examining the trunk (Figure 11.1). All six individuals will have very different, and conflicting, views of the elephant, unless they share information to create an overall picture of the elephant.

The following sections provide examples illustrating the steps in the analysis process: applying criteria for evidence of implementation, triangulating multiple data sources to examine patterns, and using this information to answer the implementation monitoring questions.

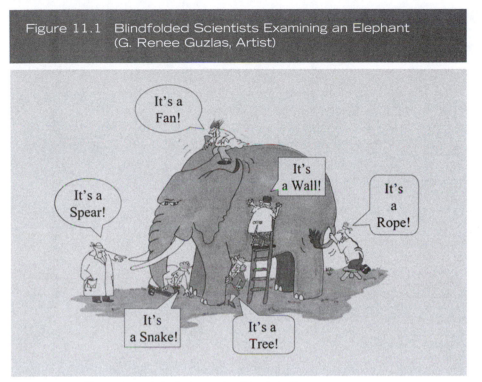

Source: Himmelfarb, Stenvinkel, Ikizler, and Hakim (2002).

To review briefly, the data collection plan should include criteria for evidence of essential/core element implementation for (1) each data collection tool, (2) multiple data collection tools/data sources, and (3) all program, policy, or practice elements (see Step 8). The steps for data analysis/synthesis, portrayed in Figure 11.2 (labeled A–G), are described below and illustrated with LEAP and ENRICH.

Understand LEAP implementation analysis.

1. Tool/Instrument/Data Source Level

A. Average or summarize multiple items from a single data collection tool/data source that were used to assess implementation at one point in time, as applicable.

If multiple items from a single data collection tool and data source were used to assess implementation, the first step in analysis is to average or summarize these. For example, three scaled items reflecting essential elements were averaged to

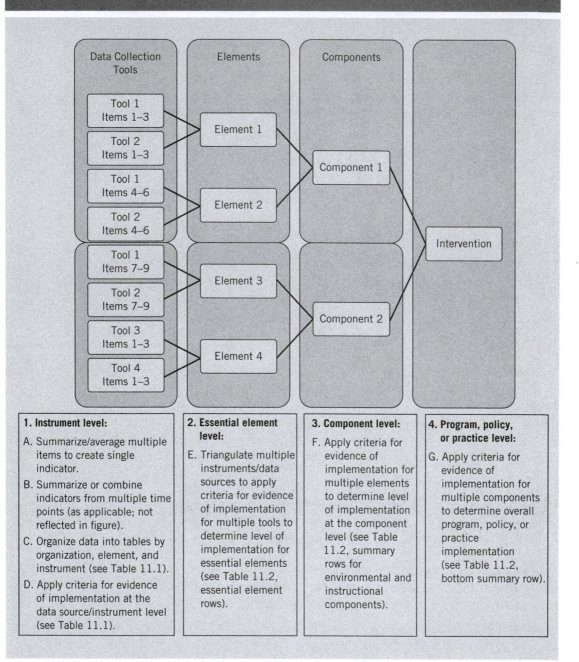

Figure 11.2 Steps in Analysis/Synthesis of Implementation Monitoring Data From Multiple Data Sources

Data Collection Tools

Tool 1 Items 1–3
Tool 2 Items 1–3
Tool 1 Items 4–6
Tool 2 Items 4–6
Tool 1 Items 7–9
Tool 2 Items 7–9
Tool 3 Items 1–3
Tool 4 Items 1–3

Elements

Element 1
Element 2
Element 3
Element 4

Components

Component 1
Component 2

Intervention

1. Instrument level:

A. Summarize/average multiple items to create single indicator.

B. Summarize or combine indicators from multiple time points (as applicable; not reflected in figure).

C. Organize data into tables by organization, element, and instrument (see Table 11.1).

D. Apply criteria for evidence of implementation at the data source/instrument level (see Table 11.1).

2. Essential element level:

E. Triangulate multiple instruments/data sources to apply criteria for evidence of implementation for multiple tools to determine level of implementation for essential elements (see Table 11.2, essential element rows).

3. Component level:

F. Apply criteria for evidence of implementation for multiple elements to determine level of implementation at the component level (see Table 11.2, summary rows for environmental and instructional components).

4. Program, policy, or practice level:

G. Apply criteria for evidence of implementation for multiple components to determine overall program, policy, or practice implementation (see Table 11.2, bottom summary row).

assess implementation for the LEAP environmental component, and 10 scaled items reflecting essential elements were averaged to assess implementation for instructional practices at the end of the LEAP intervention (Saunders, Ward, Felton, Dowda, & Pate, 2006). In the LEAP follow-up study, some methods were qualitative in nature (Saunders et al., 2012). For qualitative data sources used in LEAP, themes were identified and rated as providing or not providing evidence for the presence of a particular essential element. To illustrate, if a theme identified in the focus groups with girls attending PE classes was consistent with one of the essential elements such as the use of small-group methods in PE class, this provided evidence for sustained implementation of this essential element.

B. Average or summarize multiple items, means, or sums from a single data collection tool/data source that were used at multiple points in time, as applicable.

If single or multiple items are used to assess implementation over time, the planning team will need to determine how best to summarize the data to reflect evidence for implementation over the duration of the project. In many cases, data collected at baseline, prior to program, policy, or practice implementation, would not be used, as implementation is not expected at that point. However, it may be possible to use baseline data to control for baseline levels if the data are numeric, as was done in Faith, Activity, and Nutrition (FAN) (Wilcox et al., 2010, 2013).

Data collected at multiple points in time after implementation was initiated could be averaged or summed, depending on the nature of the data (e.g., dichotomous or scaled). For example, in the Active by Choice Today (ACT) afterschool program, observations were made for 6 program days at the beginning, middle, and end of the program (for a total of 18 days); the 6 days were averaged to reflect early, middle, and late levels of implementation, and full implementation was denoted by the mean for all three time periods (Wilson et al., 2009). In LEAP, observations and ratings were made each semester and averaged to obtain a mean for the year.

C. Organize information into tables by organization, essential or core element, and data sources/collection tools.

Table 11.1 is an example from the LEAP follow-up study (Saunders et al., 2006) that illustrates data display using three data sources (numbered 1, 2, and 3), by school (lettered A through K) and by essential element (left-hand column). This example addresses the implementation monitoring question concerning the extent to which the LEAP intervention was being implemented completely and with fidelity 3 years after the formal study concluded.

Table 11.1 Using Multiple Data Sources to Establish Evidence of Implementation for Instructional Component of LEAP by School at Follow-Up

Environment Essential Element	Schools (A–K) and Data Sources (1–3)																																
	A			B			C			D			E			F			G			H			I			J			K		
	1	2	3	1	2	3	1	2	3	1	2	3	1	2	3	1	2	3	1	2	3	1	2	3	1	2	3	1	2	3	1	2	3
1. Support from administrator for physical activity	✓	✓		✓	✓														✓	✓					✓			✓			✓		
2. Active school physical activity team																✓			✓						✓								
3. Faculty/ staff health promotion			✓			✓													✓	✓					✓			✓			✓		
4. Messages promoting physical activity			✓		✓	✓									✓	✓	✓	✓	✓	✓	✓	✓				✓		✓			✓	✓	

Instruction Essential Element	A			B			C			D			E			F			G			H			I			J			K		
	4	5	6	4	5	6	4	5	6	4	5	6	4	5	6	4	5	6	4	5	6	4	5	6	4	5	6	4	5	6	4	5	6
5. Gender-separated PE classes	✓	✓	✓		✓						✓									✓												✓	✓
6. Cooperative activities are included	✓	✓			✓	✓					✓						✓	✓					✓		✓	✓					✓	✓	
7. Lifelong physical activity is emphasized	✓	✓	✓		✓					✓	✓	✓			✓			✓		✓			✓			✓				✓	✓	✓	✓
8. Classes are fun and enjoyable	✓	✓	✓			✓				✓	✓	✓	✓				✓	✓	✓			✓			✓	✓		✓		✓		✓	
9. Teaching methods are appropriate	✓	✓	✓	✓	✓				✓	✓	✓		✓					✓				✓				✓		✓				✓	
10. Behavioral skills are taught	✓	✓		✓					✓		✓					✓								✓			✓			✓			✓
11. At least 50% of class is active	✓	✓		✓	✓	✓			✓	✓	✓	✓	✓	✓		✓	✓								✓	✓		✓	✓		✓		

Source: From Saunders et al. (2012).

1 = PE teacher interview; 2 = LEAP team players interview; 3 = 9th grade PE observation;

4 = 9th grade PE observation; 5 = PE teacher interview; 6 = 9th grade focus groups;

✓ = evidence for presence of the indicated element for a given data source

D. Apply criteria for evidence of implementation at the data source/data collection tool level.

The checkmarks in Table 11.1 indicate that the criteria for evidence of implementation at the instrument level were met. These criteria, described in Step 8, were a rating of 2 or 3 on the observational checklist (observed "most" or "all" of the time) and a theme consistent with an essential element identified in focus groups or interviews by two independent coders. For example, School A met criteria for implementation for Item 6 ("Cooperative activities are included") in the PE teacher interview and the LEAP team players interview, but not in the ninth-grade PE observation.

2. Essential Element Level

E. Apply criteria considering multiple data sources to determine implementation at the essential element level (i.e., triangulate multiple instruments/data sources).

The criteria for element implementation are having evidence for one environmental data source (Elements 1–4) and for two instructional data sources (Elements 5–11), as depicted in Table 11.1. Table 11.2 summarizes LEAP implementation for each essential element by school from Table 11.1. Note that the Essential Element summary is provided by the row total, showing evidence of support from the school administrator in six schools, whereas the organizational (School) view is presented in the columns, showing evidence for implementation of nine of 11 elements in School A.

3. Component Level

F. Apply criteria considering multiple elements of the program, policy, or practice to determine implementation at the component level.

Table 11.3 summarizes implementation for the instructional and environmental components by school at follow-up, shown in the summary rows "Total for Environmental Elements and Rating per School" (evidence for at least two of four elements being implemented) and "Total for Instructional Practices and Rating per School" (evidence for at least four of seven elements being implemented), respectively. Results revealed that five of 11 schools were implementing the environmental component and six of 11 schools were implementing the instructional component 3 years after the formal study concluded.

Table 11.2　Intervention Essential Element Implementation by School at Follow-Up

Essential Element (EE)	School A	B	C	D	E	F	G	H	I	J	K	Tot. EE
1. Support for physical activity promotion from the school administrator	✓	✓					✓		✓	✓	✓	6
2. Active school physical activity team									✓		✓	2
3. Faculty health promotion provides adult modeling of PA						✓	✓		✓		✓	4
4. Messages promoting physical activity are prominent in the school	✓	✓			✓	✓	✓		✓	✓		7
5. Gender-separated PE classes	✓	✓					✓				✓	4
6. Cooperative activities are included	✓	✓		✓			✓		✓		✓	6
7. Lifelong physical activity is emphasized	✓			✓	✓	✓	✓	✓	✓			7
8. Classes are fun and enjoyable	✓	✓		✓	✓	✓	✓	✓	✓		✓	8
9. Teaching methods are appropriate (e.g., small groups)	✓	✓		✓			✓	✓	✓		✓	7
10. Behavioral skills are taught	✓			✓			✓					3
11. At least 50% of class is active	✓	✓		✓		✓						4
Total EE per school	9	7	0	6	3	4	10	3	8	3	8	

Source: Adapted from Saunders et al. (2012).

✓ = evidence for presence of the indicated element for a given school

Table 11.3 Intervention Component (Instruction and Environment) Implementation by School at Follow-Up

Essential Element (EE)	School											Tot EE
	A	B	C	D	E	F	G	H	I	J	K	
1. Support for physical activity promotion from the school administrator	✓	✓					✓		✓	✓	✓	6
2. Active school physical activity team							✓		✓			2
3. Faculty health promotion provides adult modeling of PA							✓		✓	✓	✓	4
4. Messages promoting physical activity are prominent in the school	✓	✓			✓	✓	✓		✓		✓	7
Total number of environmental elements and rating per school*	2/4 I	2/4 I	0/4 N	0/4 N	1/4 N	1/4 N	4/4 I	0/4 N	4/4 I	2/4 I	3/4 I	
5. Gender-separated PE classes	✓	✓					✓				✓	4
6. Cooperative activities are included	✓	✓		✓			✓		✓		✓	6
7. Lifelong physical activity is emphasized	✓	✓		✓	✓	✓	✓		✓			7
8. Classes are fun and enjoyable	✓	✓		✓	✓	✓	✓	✓	✓	✓		8
9. Teaching methods are appropriate (e.g., small groups)	✓	✓		✓			✓	✓	✓		✓	7
10. Behavioral skills are taught	✓			✓			✓					3
11. At least 50% of class is active	✓			✓		✓		✓				4
Total for instructional practice elements and per school **	7/7 I	5/7 I	0 N	6/7 I	2/7 N	3/7 N	6/7 I	3/7 N	4/7 I	1/7 N	5/7 I	

Source: Adapted from Saunders et al. (2012).

✓ = evidence for presence of the indicated element for a given school

* I = environment element implementation (evidence for at least 2/4 elements being implemented); N = not implementing (< 2/4 being implemented)

** I = instructional element implementation (evidence for at least 4/7 elements being implemented); N = not implementing (< 4/7 being implemented)

Shaded = classified as "implementing" at follow-up

250

4. Program, Policy, or Practice Level

G. Apply criteria considering multiple components of the program, policy, or practice to determine overall implementation.
The definition of overall implementation at follow up in LEAP required evidence in at least six of 11 elements and implementation in both instructional and environmental components. As shown in the bottom row in Table 11.4, five schools were considered to be implementing LEAP at follow up. Note that School D met the total number of elements for criteria (evidence for six elements) but did not have at least one environmental element and, therefore, did not meet the criteria for overall implementation.

Understand ENRICH implementation analysis.

Below, the steps in the analysis/synthesis process are illustrated with another project in a different organizational setting—ENRICH (Saunders et al., 2013). ENRICH aimed to promote physical activity and healthful nutrition among children living in residential homes by creating or enhancing health-promoting environments in those settings. This example addresses the implementation monitoring question concerning the extent to which the ENRICH intervention was implemented completely and with fidelity.

1. Tool/Instrument/Data Source Level

A. Average or summarize multiple items from a single data collection tool/data source that were used to assess implementation at one point in time, as applicable.

In the ENRICH project, three yes-no items from the dinner observation (0 = no and 1 = yes) were summed as an indicator of the social environment (e.g., encouraging children to eat fruits and vegetables). Similarly, seven items rated on a 3-point scale (1 = needs improvement; 2 = average; 3 = excellent) were averaged for the evaluator's post-visit rating (see Table 11.5) (Saunders et al., 2013).

B. Average or summarize multiple items, means, or sums from a single data collection tool/data source that were used at multiple points in time, as applicable.

ENRICH had a 2-year intervention; process observations and data were collected once per year for most indicators and averaged or summed for the 2-year intervention period (data not shown).

Table 11.4 Overall LEAP Intervention Implementation by School at Follow-Up

Essential Element (EE)	A	B	C	D	E	F	G	H	I	J	K	Tot EE
1. Support for physical activity promotion from the school administrator	✓	✓					✓		✓	✓	✓	6
2. Active school physical activity team							✓		✓			2
3. Faculty health promotion provides adult modeling of PA							✓		✓	✓	✓	4
4. Messages promoting physical activity are prominent in the school	✓	✓			✓	✓	✓		✓		✓	7
5. Gender-separated PE classes	✓	✓					✓		✓		✓	4
6. Cooperative activities are included	✓	✓		✓			✓		✓		✓	6
7. Lifelong physical activity is emphasized	✓			✓	✓	✓	✓	✓	✓		✓	7
8. Classes are fun and enjoyable	✓	✓		✓	✓	✓	✓	✓	✓	✓	✓	8
9. Teaching methods are appropriate (e.g., small groups)	✓	✓		✓			✓	✓	✓		✓	7
10. Behavioral skills are taught	✓	✓		✓			✓					3
11. At least 50% of class is active	✓	✓		✓		✓						4
Total elements for each school and final rating	9/11	7/11	0/11	6/11	3/11	4/11	10/11	3/11	8/11	3/11	8/11	
	I	I	N	N	N	N	I	N	I	N	I	

Source: Adapted from Saunders et al. (2012).

✓ = evidence for presence of the indicated element for a given school

Shaded = classified as "implementing" at follow-up

C. Organize information into tables by organization, essential or core element, and data sources/collection tools.

An example of data display from ENRICH (Saunders et al., 2013) is provided in Table 11.5, which shows means for each data source/data collection tool arranged into a table by organization. Data from 17 organizations (children's homes) are depicted, designated by the letters A–Q in the left-hand column. The six remaining columns reflect the mean values for nutrition implementation from one of six data sources for each organization. Without knowing what these numbers mean, it is very difficult to interpret this table. In the next step, the criteria for evidence of implementation will be applied to help interpret the data.

Table 11.5   Mean Scores by Data Collection Tool for Each ENRICH Organization

| Home | Nutrition Implementation Data Sources | | | | | |
	End-of-Year	Post-Visit	End-of-Intervention	Media Observation	Dinner Observation Social Environment	Dinner Observation Fruits/Vegetables
A	2	2.6	2	1	2.5	1
B	2	2.1	2	0	2.8	2
C	1	2.9	3	1	2	2
D	2	2.0	1	1	2.5	1
E	2	1.0	1	1	2.5	1
F	2	2.9	3	1	2.3	2
G	1	1.9	2	1	1.8	1
H	1	2.3	2	1	2.5	0
I	1.5	2.6	2	1	3	2
J	1.5	2.1	1	1	2.5	0
K	1.5	2.0	3	1	2	1
L	1	1.1	1	0	2.3	0
M	1	1.0	2	1	1	0
N	2	1.9	2	0	2.5	2
O	1	.9	2	1	2	2
P	1.5	2.0	2	1	3	1
Q	2	2.9	3	0	2.3	1

Source: Adapted from Saunders et al. (2013).

D. Apply criteria for evidence of implementation at the data source/data collection tool level.

Table 11.6 duplicates ENRICH Table 11.5 with the addition of the criteria for evidence of implementation in the bottom row and applied to each organization. A highlighted cell indicates that the criterion for evidence of implementation has been met. The picture is still incomplete, however, until all data sources have

Table 11.6 ENRICH Organizations Meeting Criteria for Evidence of Implementation for Six Data Collection Tools

| Home | Nutrition Implementation Data Sources | | | | | | |
	End-of-Year	Post-Visit	End-of-Intervention	Media Observation	Dinner Observation Social Environment	Dinner Observation Fruits/Vegetables	Sum*
A	2	2.6	2	1	2.5	1	5/6
B	2	2.1	2	0	2.8	2	5/6
C	1	2.9	3	1	2	2	4/6
D	2	2.0	1	1	2.5	1	4/6
E	2	1.0	1	1	2.5	1	3/6
F	2	2.9	3	1	2.3	2	5/6
G	1	1.9	2	1	1.8	1	3/5
H	1	2.3	2	1	2.5	0	4/6
I	1.5	2.6	2	1	3	2	6/6
J	1.5	2.1	1	1	2.5	0	4/6
K	1.5	2.0	3	1	2	1	4/6
L	1	1.1	1	0	2.3	0	0/6
M	1	1.0	2	1	1	0	2/6
N	2	1.9	2	0	2.5	2	5/6
O	1	.9	2	1	2	2	3/6
P	1.5	2.0	2	1	3	1	5/6
Q	2	2.9	3	0	2.3	1	3/6
Criteria	Rated ≥ 1.5	Top ~2/3 score	Top ~2/3 score	Rated 1	Rated ≥ 2.5	Rated 2	4 or 6/6

Source: Adapted from Saunders et al. (2013).

*Sum = number of data sources out of six possible that meet implementation criteria.

Shaded = met criteria.

been considered together; triangulating multiple data sources is the focus of the next step in implementation analysis (Step F).

2. Essential Element Level

E. Apply criteria considering multiple data sources to determine implementation at the essential element level (i.e., triangulate multiple instruments/data sources).

For some program, policy, or practice interventions the "essential element" and "component" levels are synonymous and, therefore, are not separate levels. In some cases the data collection tools assess implementation of essential elements, which are considered components. It is also possible that multiple data sources are considered in aggregate to assess the component level; this is the case for ENRICH.

3. Component Level

F. Apply criteria considering multiple elements of the program, policy, or practice to determine overall implementation.

In the ENRICH case, triangulation consisted of tallying the number of data sources providing evidence for implementation with the criteria for strong evidence (four or more out of the six data sources). The level of criteria was set at approximately 66% or higher, based on a review that indicated a relationship between implementation and outcomes at this level (Durlak & DuPre, 2008; Saunders et al., 2013). In the right-hand column of Table 11.6 is a summary of the number of data sources meeting the criteria out of six possible. A total of 11 of 17 organizations met the criteria for "complete and acceptable" (i.e., complete implementation with fidelity) nutrition implementation in ENRICH, based on this criteria. A similar analysis for the physical activity component of ENRICH (not shown) revealed that nine organizations met the criteria for physical activity implementation.

4. Program, Policy, or Practice Level

G. Apply criteria considering multiple components of the program, policy, or practice to determine overall implementation.

Table 11.7 shows overall implementation for ENRICH organizations, based on implementation of physical activity and nutrition components. A total of five of 17 organizations (29%) met the criteria for implementation in both nutrition and physical activity (high or complete implementation); 10 of 17 (59%) met the criteria in one component or the other (medium or partial implementation); and two of 17 (12%) did not meet the criteria in any component (low implementation).

Table 11.7 Summary of Implementation at the Organizational Level Based on Both Nutrition and Physical Activity Implementation in ENRICH

Home	Nutrition Implementation	Physical Activity Implementation	Implementation Summary
A	High	High	High/complete
B	High		Medium/partial
C	High		Medium/partial
D	High	High	High/complete
E		High	Medium/partial
F	High	High	High/complete
G		High	Medium/partial
H	High	High	High/complete
I	High	High	High/complete
J	High		Medium/partial
K	High		Medium/partial
L			Low
M			Low
N	High		Medium/partial
O		High	Medium/partial
P	High		Medium/partial
Q		High	Medium/partial
Summary	11/17 = 65%	9/17 = 53%	High/complete: 5/17 = 29% Medium/partial: 10/17 = 59% Low: 2/17 = 12%

Source: Adapted from Saunders et al. (2013).

Shaded = met criteria for high/complete implementation.

Worksheet 11.1 Template for Conducting Analysis and Triangulation of Multiple Implementation Data Sources (based on ENRICH and LEAP)

Organization	Data Sources				Summary
	Data Source 1—Mean, sum, or score	Data Source 2—Mean, sum, or score	Data Source 3—Mean, sum, or score	Data Source 4—Mean, sum, or score	
A					
B					
C					
D					
E					
F					
G					
H					
I					
J					
Criteria					

Worksheet 11.1 provides a template for synthesizing data from multiple data sources. The next step is reporting and using implementation monitoring data and is presented in Step 12.

Your Turn: Are All Data Sources Created Equal?

You are charged with synthesizing information from multiple data sources including observation of activities, implementer report, and participant report. The analytic approaches presented in this step assume that all data sources and all elements are equally important. To what extent do you agree or disagree with this assumption for your data sources? Describe a possible scenario in which it may not be appropriate to assume that all data sources (or all elements of the program, policy, or practice) should receive equal weighting when triangulating multiple data sources to determine the overall level of implementation.

KEY POINTS FOR ANALYZING AND SYNTHESIZING IMPLEMENTATION MONITORING DATA

- Analysis or synthesis of implementation monitoring data should follow the implementation monitoring plan to answer implementation monitoring questions.

- The complexity and analytic sophistication of the analysis depend on stakeholder needs and expectations as reflected in the implementation monitoring plan.

- Analysis or synthesis takes place sequentially, beginning at the data collection tool level, progressing through program, policy, or practice elements and components, and ending with the overall implementation of the full program, policy, or practice.

- Criteria for evidence of implementation are applied at each level.

- Triangulating data from multiple data sources and data collection tools enables the planning team to approximate a more complete understanding of level of implementation in the setting.

Facts do not cease to exist because they
are ignored.

-Aldous Huxley

STEP

12

Report and Use Implementation Data

In this chapter, you will review a stakeholder perspective on reporting and using implementation data, review summative uses of implementation monitoring information, and develop a plan for reporting and using implementation data. As in previous chapters, the Lifestyle Education for Activity Program (LEAP) case study as well as other examples will be used to illustrate how you can carry out these steps.

Understand reporting from a stakeholder perspective.

It is essential to understand reporting from a stakeholder perspective to ensure that the information is meaningful and useful. There are five principles to guide the reporting of summative implementation monitoring results for stakeholders (Patton, 2008; Stetson, 2008; Torres, Preskill, & Piontek, 2005).

1. Identify the audience(s) to whom you are reporting.

It is important to understand the perspective of the audience(s) to whom you are reporting and to use language that is appropriate for each audience. In Step 1, you identified potential audiences or key stakeholders using Worksheet 1.1; refer back to this list to identify your potential audiences. There may be audiences beyond this initial list of stakeholders, as well, such as the general public (Torres et al., 2005).

Learning Objectives

By the end of this chapter you will be able to

1. Understand reporting from a stakeholder perspective

2. List and describe summative uses of implementation data

3. Develop a plan for reporting and using implementation data for the project and for stakeholders

Most program, policy, or practice change initiatives have multiple stakeholder groups such as the planning team, implementers, those affected by the program, and funders; multiple audiences may require multiple formats for reporting. For example, the planning team may want to see multiple and detailed tables of numbers that convey the entire process for generating the implementation monitoring results to show all steps in the analysis process. However, many setting stakeholders will not find this level of detail informative; in fact, it will likely be confusing to them. Some stakeholders may not want to see tables or numbers at all but would prefer to have the information conveyed in graphs or figures, or perhaps in a narrative story form. It is important to discuss with stakeholders the format that is most meaningful and informative for them.

2. Define the purpose of the communication.

In addition to identifying the audience receiving the report or communication, it is critical to define the purpose of the communication. What is the report or other form of communication intended to accomplish? Torres and colleagues (2005) described three general purposes for the evaluation communication and reporting: to convey information, to facilitate understanding and create meaning, and to support decision making. They also described specific reasons for communicating and reporting, which include building awareness and/or support, facilitating growth and improvement, and demonstrating results and being accountable. Examples include providing information about evaluation activities and results, reviewing or offering input into findings, and providing results that will be used. The depth of the information provided, as well as the format, may vary based on the purpose of the communication. More detailed information will likely be needed for stakeholders with greater involvement such as those using the results in their work or persuading their organization to make policy changes based on the results.

3. Determine how the information will be communicated.

There are many possible communication and report formats from which to choose, depending on the audience and purposes of the communication. Torres and colleagues listed the following: short communications such as memos, emails, and postcards; interim and final reports; executive summaries; newsletters, bulletins, briefs, and brochures; news media communications; website communications; verbal and video presentations; posters and poster sessions; working sessions; synchronous electronic communications such as chat rooms, teleconferencing, web- and videoconferencing; personal discussions; and creative formats such as photography, cartoons, poetry, and drama (Torres et al., 2005). These formats may also be used in combination.

Writing an effective report that communicates key messages in an appropriate manner to stakeholders takes time and effort. Consider the needs and perspectives of the specific audience (e.g., community agency heads, parents, academics, legislators) in selecting the format and detail. For example, community agency heads likely prefer an executive summary that emphasizes findings, whereas an academic researcher likely prefers more detail including the methodology (ACET, Inc., 2013). Each possible format has strengths and weaknesses (see Table 2.4 in Torres et al., 2005); five of these are described below (taken from ACET, Inc., 2013):

- The *traditional evaluation report* is typically comprehensive and detailed and includes background information about the project, evaluation design, a description of measures and methodology for administration, results, conclusions, and recommendations.

  o Advantages include its orientation to detail and rigor, making this type of report useful to justify or promote funding, advocate for change, or make other improvements.

  o Disadvantages include the investment of time required to produce and to read the report; some stakeholders may also find the amount of information overwhelming.

- The *executive summary* is a brief and concentrated presentation of results, often written in paragraph or bulleted form in less than a page.

  o Advantages include its brevity and focus; as a result it is typically cost-effective to reproduce and disseminate.

  o Disadvantages include loss of detail including contextual information that may enhance interpretation of the findings; it is also time-consuming to write.

- *Newsletters* are visually appealing text- and graphic-based summaries of results.

  o Advantages include flexibility in length, organization, and content, and ability to be distributed in many ways including by mail, pick up, or electronic means.

  o Disadvantages include perception as marketing or fundraising materials, or in electronic format as spam or junk, which results in the information not being read by the intended audience; mailed newsletters can also be expensive to produce and send.

- *Multimedia presentations* such as PowerPoint or Prezi are typically presented orally, can be interactive, and produce visually appealing displays and evaluation findings.

  o Advantages include fidelity to incorporate a range of content such as text, visual movement, and links to external pages, videos, spreadsheets, and/or other files.

  o Disadvantages include space limitations for presenting, costly investment in software, and/or time needed to create appealing presentations.

- A *dashboard* is a visual summary of results for multiple, repeated variables that are typically numerical and may also be interactive in nature; the audience interprets the data themselves as there is typically no accompanying narrative.

  o Advantages include efficiency in sharing results.

  o Disadvantages include the need for specialized software, lack of comfort with data among some users, and limited use of quantitative information (ACET, Inc., 2013).

4. Clearly articulate the results and recommendations in language that is appropriate to the audience.

Present the results fully and ethically. Recommendations should be based on findings of the evaluation. If the recommendations have a political nature, as is often the case with program and/or policy improvement, involve key stakeholders prior to developing and releasing "final" recommendations.

If the audience is the project team, the report can reflect more technical language because team members are familiar with the terminology. If the audience consists of program participants or setting stakeholders, the language needs to communicate the information without relying on technical terminology and jargon, as these will likely not be meaningful to these stakeholders. It should go without saying that the language should also treat participants, change agents, and all stakeholders with respect, regardless of the audience receiving the report.

Torres and colleagues provided the following tips for writing in a clear, jargon-free style (Torres et al., 2005, pp. 68–72):

- Avoid jargon and technical terms that your audience may not understand.

- Adopt a conversational style.

- Use shorter sentences.

- Limit use of passive voice.

- Use word processing tools for spelling, grammar, and writing style.

- Develop a logical structure for long communications and reports.

- Write, rewrite, and rewrite.

- Write within a collaborative team.

- Allow plenty of time to write several drafts, get feedback, and proofread.

5. Make the report, handout, presentation, or other form of communicated material visually appealing and appropriate to the audience.

See Torres and colleagues (2005) for detailed guidelines for constructing tables and figures (including pie charts, bar charts, line graphs, and illustrations) to make information more understandable. Torres and colleagues provided the following tips for using tables and figures (pp. 56–68):

- Use a visual presentation that will convey the essence of the message most accurately.

- Keep figures and tables simple.

- Consider if more than one table or figure is needed to present the information.

- Include headings and titles for all tables and figures.

- Make each table and figure self-explanatory by including keys, labels, and footnotes.

- Interpret each table and figure in the narrative of the report.

- Construct the visuals first, then write the text.

- Make the tables and figures easily accessible within a report.

- Do not overuse color.

- Allow sufficient time for developing tables and figures.

In summary, each stakeholder group and audience has a different perspective and different needs concerning the information and format for summative implementation data. The material in the section below is based largely on Joly (2003), who provided an overview titled "Writing Community-Centered Evaluation Reports." Prerequisites to writing an effective evaluation report, including one for implementation monitoring, are to have a solid evaluation plan and to involve stakeholders in the project. These issues have been discussed in previous sections of this textbook. Joly (2003) integrated many of the principles presented above into her recommendations regarding evaluation report writing for community audiences:

Visual Appearance

It is important to make the report aesthetically pleasing by focusing on the layout or the combination of text and graphics. The optimal layout is the one that *works for the specific audience* and organizes information so that the reader will use it. Other tips include the following:

- Consider using headers and subheaders to indicate the major components for layout, to assist the reader in scanning through the document.

- Balance text and white space to make the document easier to read.

- Single space evaluation reports.

- Include figures, charts, tables, and other diagrams within the text.

- Use at least a 12-point font size. If the community audience is older, add a point for every decade after age 40; larger font sizes may also be used for headings or titles and to highlight main ideas.

- Use color in tables and figures if printing resources allow.

Organization of the Report

A community-centered report should have *helpful and descriptive* information. Following is a list of helpful information to include:

- A title page (title and location of the program, date of submission for the report, and names and affiliations of both the program evaluators and agency representatives)

- Table of contents with page numbers

- Executive summary

- Appendices

- Labels for all charts and tables found within the text

Descriptive information is provided as the primary narrative of the report; below is a list of typical content in a traditional evaluation report:

- Executive summary

- Project background

- Project purpose and goals

- Timeline

- Stakeholders

- Evaluation methods including data collection and analysis techniques

- Findings and results

- Discussion

- Recommendations

- Next steps

Language

A community-centered report is characterized by concrete language, short sentences, and use of active voice. Effective community reports tend to score between the seventh- and ninth-grade reading level on a readability

Worksheet 12.1 Template for Planning How to Communicate Implementation Monitoring Results to Stakeholders

Audience/Stakeholder group	
Purpose of the communication	
Format and modality of communication	
Outline of content	
Key findings to be communicated	
Key visual elements of the communication	

test; therefore, the language should be simple and avoid jargon. If technical terminology is used, it should be defined or explained.

Worksheet 12.1 provides a template for planning how to communicate implementation monitoring results to a specific stakeholder group. See Resource Box 12.1 for resources on communicating evaluation results effectively.

Resource Box 12.1
Communicating Evaluation Results

http://comm.eval.org/resources/searchlibrary. Search for resources and tips on the American Evaluation Association website ("Search Library—American Evaluation Association," n.d.).

Evergreen, Stephanie D. H. (2013). *Presenting data effectively: Communicating your findings for maximum impact.* Thousand Oaks, CA: Sage.

Patton, M. Q. (2008). *Utilization-focused evaluation* (4th ed.). Thousand Oaks, CA: Sage.

Stetson V. (2008). *Communicating and reporting on an evaluation: Guidelines and tools.* American Red Cross/CRS M&E Module Series. Washington, DC, and Baltimore, MD: American Red Cross and Catholic Relief Services (CRS).

Torres, R. T., Preskill, H., & Piontek, M. E. (2005). *Evaluation strategies for communicating and reporting: Enhancing learning in organizations* (2nd ed.). Thousand Oaks, CA: Sage.

List and describe the summative uses of implementation data.

Summative uses of implementation monitoring data include describing (1) the extent to which the program, policy, or practice components were put into place (completeness); were put into place consistently with the conceptual model (fidelity); and reached the intended audience (reach); (2) variations in implementation based on setting, organizational characteristics, or other preplanned comparisons; and (3) the relationship between implementation and study outcomes. Items 1 and 2 above are descriptive uses of implementation data, whereas Item 3 refers to the use of implementation data in outcome analyses to understand the influence of implementation on outcomes.

Examples of descriptive uses of implementation monitoring data, reported in academic journals, include:

- Ward, D. S., Saunders, R. P., Felton, G. M., Williams, E., Epping, J. N., & Pate, R. R. (2006). Implementation of a school environment intervention to increase physical activity in high school girls. *Health Education Research, 21*(6), 896–910.

  o This article reports a detailed description of the LEAP intervention and stakeholder reactions to the intervention.

- Felton, G., Saunders, R. P., Ward, D. S., Dishman, R. K., Dowda, M., & Pate, R. R. (2005). Promoting physical activity in girls: A case study of one school's success. *The Journal of School Health, 75*(2), 57–62.

  o This article reports a case study of one school's implementation of the LEAP intervention. Because it is a case study, it goes into considerable depth on how one school adapted LEAP for its setting.

- Saunders, R. P., Evans, A. E., Kenison, K., Workman, L., Dowda, M., & Chu, Y. H. (2013). Conceptualizing, implementing, and monitoring a structural health promotion intervention in an organizational setting. *Health Promotion Practice, 14*(3), 343–353.

  o This article presents the methods and analyses details for assessing implementation of Environmental Interventions in Children's Homes (ENRICH) in residential group home settings.

Examples of using implementation monitoring data in outcome analyses include:

- Saunders, R. P., Ward, D., Felton, G. M., Dowda, M., & Pate, R. R. (2006). Examining the link between program implementation and behavior outcomes in the Lifestyle Education for Activity Program (LEAP). *Evaluation and Program Planning, 29*(4), 352–364.

  - This article presents analysis details for LEAP and shows how the level of implementation in LEAP was related to vigorous physical activity in high school girls at the end of the LEAP intervention. Implementation monitoring data were used to classify schools into "higher" and "lower" implementing categories to assess effects of level of implementation on study outcomes. "Higher" implementing schools had a significantly greater proportion of girls engaging in vigorous physical activity.

- Pate, R. R., Saunders, R., Dishman, R. K., Addy, C., Dowda, M., & Ward, D. S. (2007). Long-term effects of a physical activity intervention in high school girls. *American Journal of Preventive Medicine, 33*(4), 276–280.

  - This article uses the implementation monitoring results in the LEAP sustainability study to relate long-term implementation to increased vigorous physical activity in high school girls 3 years after the end of the LEAP intervention. Implementation monitoring data were used to classify schools into "higher" and "lower" implementing categories at the 3-year follow-up. This information was used along with level of implementation at the end of the study to assess effects of level of sustained implementation on study outcomes. The four high schools that sustained implementation had a significantly greater proportion of girls engaging in vigorous physical activity.

- Saunders, R. P., Wilcox, S., Baruth, M., & Dowda, M. (2014). Process evaluation methods, implementation fidelity results and relationship to physical activity and healthy eating in the Faith, Activity, and Nutrition (FAN) study. *Evaluation and Program Planning, 43*, 93–102.

o   This article presents sequential mediation analysis for FAN and shows how the FAN intervention resulted in increased implementation for all physical activity and most healthy eating components. Implementation data were collected pre- and posttest and analyzed as continuous variables (versus categorical level of implementation as in LEAP) at the church level. Mediation analyses revealed no direct association between implementation and increased physical activity; rather, sequential mediation analysis showed that implementation of physical activity messages was associated with improved self-efficacy at the church level, which was associated with increased physical activity.

Develop a plan for reporting and using implementation data for the project and for stakeholders.

It is now time to develop a plan for reporting implementation data to stakeholders.

Worksheet 12.2 provides a template for developing a traditional implementation monitoring report for stakeholders. This type of report is formatted similarly to an academic report. Worksheet 12.3 provides a template for a stakeholder-centered implementation report and is followed by a LEAP example of a stakeholder-centered implementation report (Figure 12.1 LEAP Model Evaluation Report).

Worksheet 12.2 Template for Developing an Implementation Monitoring Report

Stakeholder Report for: _____

Title page	
Table of contents	
Executive summary	
Project background	
Project purpose and goals	
Timeline	
Stakeholders	
Evaluation methods including data collection and analysis techniques	
Findings and results	
Discussion	
Recommendations	
Next steps	
Appendices	

Worksheet 12.3   Template for Stakeholder-Focused Implementation Monitoring Report

---

[Logo, illustration, or other picture here]

Note: The report will be more visually appealing if you coordinate the colors used with the organization's logo; use these same colors in charts.

Implementation Monitoring Evaluation Report [Template*]

[Date]

[Name of writers or compilers]

*Template developed by

Kelli Kenison, Ph.D.
Carley Prynn, MPH
Lauren Workman Ph.D.

Center for Health Services and Policy Research
Arnold School of Public Health
University of South Carolina

Sarah Griffin, Ph.D.

Public Health Sciences Department
Clemson University

TABLE OF CONTENTS

Executive Summary

Introduction

Findings

Lessons Learned/Recommendations

Summary

Evaluation Measures and Methods

Appendices

EXECUTIVE SUMMARY

The executive summary contains a complete overview of the program and the major findings in the order that they will be presented throughout the document. The idea is to define the problem and provide a potential solution to the identified problem.

The idea is to say as much as possible in the fewest amount of words. The executive summary is not meant to be comprehensive and should be the length of about 5–10% of the whole report. It is designed to help with decision making for people who will not have time to read the whole report or are deciding if it is necessary. This should be useful for people, including funders, politicians, and policy makers.

INTRODUCTION

The introduction will provide an overview of the program being implemented. This will likely include location, audience, key components, and funding. This section will also briefly describe the geographical, socioeconomic, political, environmental, and historical context and setting, as relevant to the initiative. Understanding context is critical to understanding the evaluation.

A full description of the initiative allows an external person to have a better understanding of what was done.

Consider including the following:

- The issue and how it was addressed

- Overall goal, purpose, and specific objectives of the initiative

- Who the initiative was aimed at

- Setting and context for services and activities

- What services and activities took place

- Who was involved in providing the services/activities

- Involvement of other organizations, sectors, and community people (as applicable)

The introduction should also include an overview of the evaluation purpose and evaluation questions.

FINDINGS

The findings section presents the results. A summary of the data is presented and explained in this portion of the document. Usually, an evaluation will contain a mix of qualitative data and quantitative data.

Identifying performance indicators for the program. Identify implementation monitoring indicators (i.e., fidelity, completeness, reach, contextual factors, and recruitment as applicable to the implementation monitoring plan).

Presentation of quantitative results with data tables, pie charts, and or graphs where appropriate. Presentation of qualitative data as descriptive themes and allow the voices of the people who were a part of the evaluation to be heard while considering the confidentiality of the informants.

If relevant, report on any unexpected outcomes.

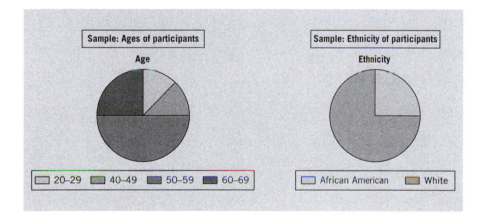

Key Findings

Summarize the most important findings in two or three phrases and insert here.

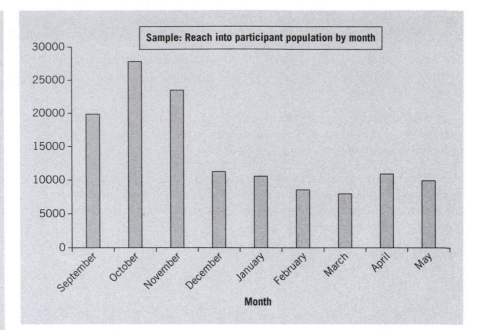

LESSONS LEARNED AND RECOMMENDATIONS

This section of the report is a compilation of lessons learned throughout the program evaluation. Through a collaborative discussion with the program leaders, staff, and evaluators the evaluation results are reviewed and lessons learned/recommendations developed. Ideally this occurs throughout the life of the project and evaluation with a summary included in this final report.

Documenting lessons learned provides information for ongoing improvement of the program as it is being implemented.

Lessons-learned questions:

What worked well—or didn't work well—either for this project or for the project team?

What needs to be repeated or done differently?

What surprises did the team have to deal with?

What project circumstances were not anticipated?

Were the project goals attained? If not, what changes need to be made to meet goals in the future?

Should this project in total or specific elements be implemented in the future?

Lessons Learned and Recommendations

• • •

Key points presented in bulleted form

SUMMARY

The summary portion of the report is intended to report the main information in a condensed form. This portion will be written with the perspective that the project is complete and will include the purpose of the project and report and why it was performed.

It will include a brief description of the problem and how it was solved, along with the research methods used throughout the program and an explanation of how the information was gathered and analyzed. This portion will also answer the question, "What did you find out?" Key results and findings will be reported.

EVALUATION MEASURES AND METHODS

The following section describes each evaluation measure, procedures for administering them, and corresponding analytical approaches to address evaluation questions or objectives. For each tool, describe when it was completed, how it administered, who completed it, and how it was summarized. Measures and tools could include mailed or online surveys, in-person or online interviews, and focus group guides.

Evaluation Measures

List evaluation measures here

APPENDIX

Include copies of the logic model, data collection tools, detailed data tables, results of statistical analyses, and other items, as appropriate, that would interrupt the flow of the main report.

Figure 12.1 LEAP Model Evaluation Report

LEAP Implementation Monitoring Report[*]

January 28, 2014

Ruth P. Saunders

Dianne S. Ward

Gwen M. Felton

Marsha Dowda

Russell R. Pate

* Saunders, R. P., Ward, D., Felton, G. M., Dowda, M., & Pate, R. R. (2006). Examining the link between program implementation and behavior outcomes in the Lifestyle Education for Activity Program (LEAP). *Evaluation and Program Planning, 29*(4), 352–364. doi:10.1016/j.evalprogplan.2006.08.006

Ward, D. S., Saunders, R., Felton, G. M., Williams, E., Epping, J. N., & Pate, R. R. (2006). Implementation of a school environment intervention to increase physical activity in high school girls. *Health Education Research, 21*(6), 896–910. doi:10.1093/her/cyl134

TABLE OF CONTENTS

Executive Summary

Introduction

Findings

Lessons Learning and Recommendations

Evaluation Measures and Methods

Appendices

EXECUTIVE SUMMARY

Lifestyle Education for Activity Program (LEAP) was a multicomponent intervention that emphasized developing physical activity self-efficacy and self-management skills in a school environment that promoted and supported physical activity for young women. LEAP was flexible-adaptable and process oriented, allowing each school to adapt the intervention, guided by seven core instructional elements and four core environmental elements for a better fit with local contexts. LEAP was implemented by teachers and staff with training, guidance, and support from the LEAP intervention staff.

The core instructional and environmental elements guided data collection through record reviews, observation, and LEAP staff rating of school progress. Examination of this information revealed seven high- and five low-implementing schools at the end of the intervention. Higher implementing schools are more likely to have an active physical activity team, health promotion for faculty staff, and an emphasis on lifelong physical activity in physical education at the organizational level. Higher implementing schools, compared to lower implementing and control schools, also had significantly higher proportion of girls who engaged in vigorous physical activity. Overall, instructional elements were implemented more frequently than environmental elements.

The LEAP essential elements provided an effective framework for a comprehensive assessment of LEAP implementation and enabled us to organize, synthesize, and use an extensive amount of information for summative process evaluation purposes. The flexible, adaptive approach to implementation was beneficial in LEAP and may be beneficial in other real world contexts. Triangulating multiple data sources by rank ordering schools based on level of implementation is an effective approach to summarizing different points of view.

INTRODUCTION

Program description. LEAP was a group randomized evaluation of a multicomponent intervention funded by NIH to promote physical activity in 24 high schools in South Carolina (12 intervention and 12 control). LEAP included a gender-sensitive physical education (PE) program with activities designed to be fun and age appropriate for high school girls. LEAP also emphasized developing physical activity self-efficacy and self-management skills in a school environment that promoted and supported physical activity for young women.

LEAP instructional Practices included LEAP PE and health education. The goal of LEAP PE was to provide girls with the physical and behavioral skills needed to adopt a physically active lifestyle during their teenage years and to maintain that active lifestyle into adulthood. The goal of health education was to reinforce messages delivered in PE on the benefits of physical activity and to teach behavioral skills that will enable students to initiate and maintain a physically active lifestyle.

The LEAP school environment included policies and practices related to physical activity, school health services, faculty staff health promotion, and family and community involvement. The goal of Healthy school environment was to institute schoolwide policies and practices that promote the physical activity within and outside of the school by increasing the involvement of school health services (i.e., the school nurse) and the family and community organizations in the creation of a school and community environment that supports and reinforces physical activity among students. The goal of faculty and staff health promotion was to create a supportive school environment with physically active adult role models (Ward et al., 2006).

Implementation approach. LEAP was a flexible, adaptive intervention that was implemented by school teachers and staff with training, guidance, and support from LEAP staff. LEAP instructional practices were integrated into ninth grade PE and health education according to the individual school's approach to offering health education. The school environment components were implemented via the LEAP Team, which met and planned based on schedules of LEAP Team members within each school. LEAP Team membership and size varied by school but often included some combination of PE teacher, health (or other classroom) teacher, school nurse, wellness coordinator, and media specialist (Ward et al., 2006).

Evaluation purposes. LEAP implementation monitoring was designed to address the following evaluation questions (Saunders et al., 2006):

1. To what extent did LEAP team members install all seven instructional and four environmental essential elements?

2. To what extent was implementation associated with physical activity-promoting organizational policies and practices?

3. To what extent was implementation associated with physical activity in high school girls?

FINDINGS

To what extent did LEAP team members install all seven instructional (I) and four environmental (E) essential elements?

Instructional elements were implemented by more schools than environmental elements, with the exception of teaching behavioral skills for physical activity. All schools emphasized lifelong physical activity in physical education and most schools emphasized fun and active physical activity classes as well as gender separation. Three-quarters of the schools included cooperative activities in physical education and had an active LEAP team for working on the school environment. Half of the schools had an active faculty/ staff health promotion program, used appropriate methods in physical education, offered administrative support, and taught behavioral skills for physical activity.

Intervention Component	Number of Schools Implementing
Emphasizes lifelong physical activity in PE (I)	12
Physical education classes are fun and enjoyable (I)	10
Girls are physically active in physical education (I)	10
Messages about physical activity are prominent in the school (E)	10
There is gender separation in physical education classes (I)	9
Physical education includes cooperative activities (I)	8
There is an active LEAP team (E)	8
There is faculty/staff health promotion (E)	6
Teachers use appropriate methods in physical education (I)	6
There is administrative support (E)	6
Behavioral skills for physical activity are taught (I)	6

I = Instructional E = Environmental

Based on information from multiple sources, several schools were consistently high implementers across all essential elements, as five schools were consistently lower.

Key Findings

• • •

More schools implemented instructional components than environmental elements.

Seven schools were considered higher and five were lower implementers.

Higher implementers were more likely to have PA-promoting policies and more girls engaging in vigorous physical activity.

To what extent was implementation associated with physical activity-promoting organizational policies and practices?

Based on assistant principal report, higher implementing schools reported significantly higher organizational policies and practices related to lifelong physical activity in physical education, administrator support, and faculty staff wellness. (See Appendix D.)

To what extent was implementation associated with physical activity in high school girls?

More girls in the higher implementing schools, compared to lower implementing and control schools, reported engaging in vigorous physical activity at the end of the intervention. (See Appendix E.)

LESSONS LEARNED AND RECOMMENDATIONS

The LEAP essential elements framework, implementation approach, and use of multiple data sources to examine implementation was an effective strategy. However, this approach does require advanced planning and commitment of project resources.

- The LEAP essential elements provided an effective framework for a comprehensive assessment of LEAP implementation

  o Guided the selection of data sources and development of data collection instruments

  o Provided an effective structure for prioritizing, collecting, and summarizing implementation data from multiple data sources

  o Enabled us to organize, synthesize, and use an extensive amount of information for summative process evaluation purposes

- A flexible, adaptive approach to implementation was beneficial in LEAP and may be beneficial in other real-world contexts.

- Record review, using staff records as a data source, is an effective approach to the extent records are kept consistently.

- Use of multiple data sources enabled us to tap into differing perspectives and multiple elements of the intervention.

- These multiple perspectives are valid individually and not directly comparable.

- Triangulating multiple data sources by rank ordering schools based on level of implementation is an effective approach to summarizing different points of view.

EVALUATION MEASURES AND METHODS

Evaluation Measures and Methods

• • •

Record Review

Physical Education Observational Checklist

LEAP Criteria

Organizational Assessment

3DPAR

There were three primary data sources to assess implementation and to rank order schools from highest to lowest level of implementation:

- Record review—an independent process evaluator reviewed systematically kept school documentation and rated progress relative to the essential elements using a four point scale; mean scores were calculated.

- Physical education observational checklist—an independent process evaluator systematically observed physical education classes and the school environment once per semester and rated progress relative to essential elements using a four point scale; mean scores were calculated.

- LEAP intervention staff: LEAP criteria—the two interventionists rated progress on leap essential elements once per year based on observations and impressions using a three point rating scale; mean scores were calculated.

Two additional measures were used to assess school policies and practices and physical activity in high school girls:

- Organizational assessment—an independent process evaluator interviewed the assistant principal once per year to assess school policies and practices relative to physical activity instructional practices and environment within the school; items were rated on a four point scale and means were calculated.

- 3-Day Physical Activity Recall (3DPAR)—the 3-DPAR is a self-reported activity questionnaire that was administered by trained research staff and established validity and reliability; activity is summarized into 30-minute blocks based on intensity (i.e., vigorous, moderate).

See also Appendix B for more information on measures and Appendices D–F for details of implementation monitoring and statistical analyses.

Appendix A LEAP Logic Model to Organize the Implementation Monitoring Plan

	Inputs	Outputs			Outcomes–Impacts		
	What We Invest	What We Do	Who Is Reached and Expected Effects	Changes Made by "Change Agent"	Short-Term Changes, Impact on Influence Variables	Medium-Term Change on Individual Behavior Outcome	Long-Term Change on Health Outcomes
Logic Model	Resources provided enable us to. . .	conduct training and other activities that will. . .	reach the change agents and provide them tools and skills needed to. . .	carry out the intervention which will result in. . .	change in influence variables, which will influence the. . .	behavior of individuals reached by intervention that, if sustained, will. . .	have positive effects on health outcomes. . .
					Impact/outcome: Influence variables or determinants	Impact/outcome: Individual behavior	Outcome: Health issue or problem
Evaluation Elements and Sample Questions	Dose delivered		Reach and dose received	Fidelity and completeness			
	To what extent did LEAP staff provide all intervention components, materials, and equipment through training, technical assistance, and ongoing support?		To what extent did LEAP team members attend training?	To what extent did LEAP team members install all seven instructional and four environmental essential elements?			
			To what extent did LEAP team members have the confidence and skills needed to carry out LEAP in their school?				
	ACTION MODEL—Implementation monitoring				CHANGE MODEL—Outcome evaluation		

Appendix B LEAP Action Model

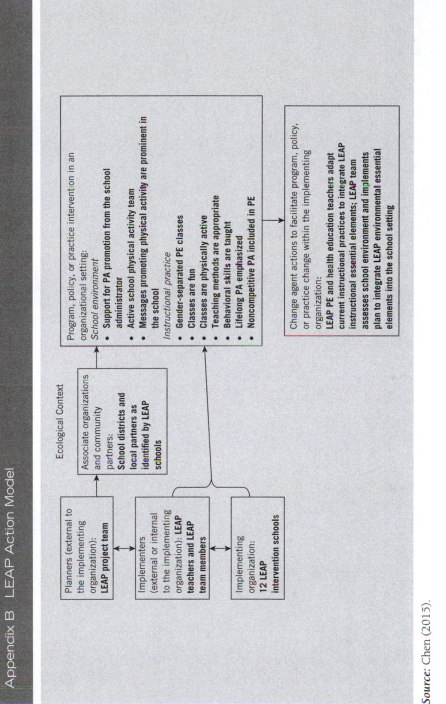

Ecological Context

Planners (external to the implementing organization): **LEAP project team**

Implementers (external or internal to the implementing organization): **LEAP teachers and LEAP team members**

Implementing organization: **12 LEAP intervention schools**

Associate organizations and community partners: **School districts and local partners as identified by LEAP schools**

Program, policy, or practice intervention in an organizational setting:
School environment
- **Support for PA promotion from the school administrator**
- **Active school physical activity team**
- **Messages promoting physical activity are prominent in the school**

Instructional practice
- **Gender-separated PE classes**
- **Classes are fun**
- **Classes are physically active**
- **Teaching methods are appropriate**
- **Behavioral skills are taught**
- **Lifelong PA emphasized**
- **Noncompetitive PA included in PE**

Change agent actions to facilitate program, policy, or practice change within the implementing organization:
LEAP PE and health education teachers adapt current instructional practices to integrate LEAP instructional essential elements; LEAP team assesses school environment and implements plan to integrate LEAP environmental essential elements into the school setting

Source: Chen (2015).

Appendix C   LEAP Data Sources and Tools Based on the Definitions of Complete and Acceptable Delivery/Installation of the Intervention

Element and Definition of Complete and Acceptable Delivery/Installation	Data Sources	Tools and Rating Scale	Sample Items
LEAP PE—Characterized by -Gender separation -Fun classes -Physically active classes -Appropriate teaching methods -Teaching behavioral skills -Lifelong physical activity (PA) emphasized -Noncompetitive PA included	Written records maintained by LEAP staff including training activities, training attendance, field notes, school files, and communication.	*Record review* (35 item rating scale) 0 = not found in records 1 = documents indicate some activity 2 = documents indicate organized activity 3 = document indicated organized activity that is highly consistent with LEAP theory	Rate evidence for: *Instruction* -Lifelong PA emphasized -Teaching behavioral skills *Environment* -School physical activity team -Administrative support for PA
Healthy School Environment— Characterized by -School administrator support for PA promotion -Active school physical activity team	Observation of physical education class and school environment	*Observational checklist* (25 items) 0 = no or none 1 = sometimes 2 = most of the time 3 = all of the time	*Instruction* -Students are organized into small, enduring groups *Environment* -Girls are linked to out-of-class physical activity opportunities via school media messages.
-PA-promoting messages in the school	LEAP staff made systematic assessments based on observation and results documented in written records.	*LEAP Criteria* (36-item rating scale) 0 = no 1 = partially 2 = yes, completely	*Instruction* Are noncompetitive activities included in physical education? *Environment* Does school have an active wellness team?

Appendix D LEAP Intervention Schools (*n* = 12) Ranked From Highest to Lowest Index Score for Level of Implementation of Essential Elements (Year 2) Using Multiple Data Sources

Rank	Record review	PE Observations	LEAP Criteria	LEAP Criteria PE
1	G	G	I	C, G, L
2	C	L	G	B, J
3	A, B	F	C, J	A, F
4	F	A	B, L	H
5	D*	B	F	K*
6	J, L	D*	A	I*
7	H*	J	D*	E*
8	K*, E*	C	K*	D*
9	I*	I*	H*	
10		H*	E*	
11		K*		
12		E*		

Source: Saunders et al. (2006).

Note: Schools ranked in the lower third are shaded; Schools with an asterisk are assigned to low implementation group.

Appendix E   Comparing High Implementing Intervention Schools, Low Implementing Intervention Schools, and Control Schools on Organizational Assessment Using Wilcoxon Scores (Rank Sums)

| Essential Element | Rank Sum Score | | | Chi Square | P |
| | Intervention | | Control (n = 12) | | |
	High (n = 7)	Low (n = 5)			
Active physical activity team	**18.0**	**11.6**	**9.7**	**7.34**	**.03**
Administrative support	13.9	9.5	13.2	2.44	.29
Emphasizing lifelong PE	15.5	8.6	12.4	4.84	.09
Cooperative options in PE	15.4	10.9	11.4	3.13	.21
Provide health services	14.7	14.4	10.4	2.86	.24
Health promotion for staff	**19.0**	**10.6**	**9.5**	**9.59**	**.01**
Provide health education	12.8	12.1	12.5	.07	.35
Coordinate physical activity events with community	15.4	12.7	15.6	2.09	.39
Family involvement	12.0	10.0	13.8	1.46	.48

Source: Saunders et al. (2006).

Appendix F Comparison of Physical Activity Variables in Girls Attending High- and Low-Implementing Intervention Schools and Control Schools

Variable	Unadjusted Means (±SD)						Adjusted Means at Follow-Up (±SD)				
	Control (n = 740)		Low (n = 336)		High (n = 527		Control	Low	High	P Group	P Trend
	Pre	Post	Pre	Post	Pre	Post					
One block VPA/day (%)	45.6 (3.4)	39.1 (2.9)	41.7 (5.2)	37.1 (4.4)	39.1 (4.3)	47.0 (3.7)	36.4 (2.8)	39.8 (3.9)	47.6 (3.2)	.05	.02

Source: Saunders et al. (2006).

Note: Controlling for wave, wave x group interaction, baseline BMI, race, and school.

KEY POINTS FOR REPORTING AND USING IMPLEMENTATION MONITORING DATA

- It is essential to identify the audience, purpose, format and modality, content, and key visual elements for each communication.

- The specific format and length of communication of implementation monitoring results will vary according to the purpose of the communication or report and the audience receiving it.

- Results should be presented clearly, accurately, and in a manner appropriate to the audience.

"Would you tell me, please, which way I ought to go from here?"

"That depends a good deal on where you want to get to," said the Cat.

"I don't much care where-" said Alice.

"Then it doesn't matter which way you go," said the Cat.

–Lewis Carroll, Alice's Adventures in Wonderland

Future Directions

In this section, you will review the current state of implementation monitoring, future directions for research and practice in implementation monitoring, and options for moving forward.

Current State of Implementation Monitoring

Current issues discussed below include progress in the priority placed on implementation monitoring, advances in implementation monitoring methods, continuing challenges in key term definitions and measurement, challenges related to the predominant focus on individual behavior change versus on populations and settings, and defining organizational and environmental change.

Due to progress across multiple disciplines including program evaluation and translational research, practitioners and researchers place a higher priority on program, policy, and practice implementation and on the importance of conducting implementation monitoring, which has been contributing to progress in implementation monitoring methodology over the past 10 years. As evidenced in this textbook, there has been a substantial increase in published implementation monitoring reports, review articles, and conceptual articles. There is also increasing acceptance of the importance of quantitative in addition to qualitative methods, of including multiple data sources, and of using process evaluation to understand null or negative findings.

Nevertheless, relative to outcome/impact assessment, there is a greater tendency to conduct implementation monitoring more or less informally and as an afterthought (e.g., "Shouldn't we collect some process data?"). The approach endorsed in this textbook favors upfront implementation monitoring planning that enables the team to conduct real-time implementation monitoring as the project unfolds, assessing both expected and unexpected effects and contextual influences.

Comprehensive assessment of implementation monitoring using multiple data sources and both qualitative and quantitative methodology requires resources and project commitment upfront. There is increasing recognition of this reality; however, implementation monitoring evaluation often has a lower priority compared to outcome/impact evaluation. This is unfortunate given that it may not make sense to invest resources in outcome/impact evaluation for a project that has not been implemented or that has not reached the identified audience.

Many researchers lament the lack of standard definitions for terminology within literature pertaining to implementation monitoring, which is a source of confusion. The profusion of terminology is likely due to the independent development of implementation monitoring approaches from the perspectives of diverse professional fields. Ultimately, development of common terminology will be essential to progressing on monitoring the implementation of innovations in organizational settings. At the very least, it is important to recognize differing definitions for common terms across various fields. For example, *fidelity* has many definitions depending on the field and the specific publication. Even so, there is increasing acceptance for the elements that need to be addressed when performing implementation monitoring. In this textbook, these include fidelity, completeness, reach, and context, although additional elements including dose delivered and dose received may also be appropriate in many projects.

Another common lament is the lack of valid and reliable measures for constructs used in implementation monitoring. Given that most of the measures are project and setting specific, however, it may not be realistic to strive for a set of measures that can be used to assess level of implementation across diverse settings. Greater attention to conceptualizing the change process and how it can be operationalized and assessed within a given setting may be a more appropriate goal than creating an idealized set of measures. It may be that for measures, as with innovations themselves, "one-size-does-not-fit-all" settings. It is essential, however, that appropriate measurement work is done on the instruments and tools used in implementation monitoring including addressing measurement validity and reliability.

In the majority of published articles to date that pertain to implementation monitoring, the researchers conceptualize change at the individual level and often do not conceptualize or address innovations that target the organizational level or program, policy, practice, and environmental change, although there has been some recent improvement. The challenge is due in part to the common practice of designing implementation monitoring based on previous studies, which conceptualize and target change at the individual level, and in part on the relative scarcity of frameworks for conceptualizing organizational and environmental change and the mechanisms through which these approaches influence population behavior.

There are a number of important future directions to consider for practice and research in implementation monitoring of programs, policies, and practices within organizational settings. These are organized into five categories and discussed in the next section.

Future Directions for Research and Practice in Implementation Monitoring

Areas that require future work in implementation monitoring research and practice include innovation conceptualization and planning, intervention in complex settings, integration of work with change agents and stakeholders, use and integration of quantitative and qualitative methods, and moving beyond assessing level of implementation. Many of these issues have been addressed previously in this textbook and will therefore be summarized below.

Expand innovation conceptualization and planning.

Conceptualizing the change process and how it can be operationalized in a given setting by developing the change or conceptual model is the essential first step in implementation monitoring planning. That is, it is important to develop an understanding of *how* the program, policy, or practice change will work to produce desired outcomes. Ideally, the program, policy, or practice and the implementation plan, along with the implementation monitoring plan, are fully conceptualized prior to implementation. In many cases, however, the experience of implementation will facilitate increased understanding of *how* the program, policy, or practice works within the setting.

Approaches to conceptualizing individual level change are more common than those aiming to change environments, policies, and practices by focusing on organizational change. Environmental and organizational interventions take place in phases over time in complex settings and may therefore require new ways of conceptualizing innovations, particularly for sustainable change in organizations.

Logic models are widely used for planning interventions and working with stakeholders, but less so for organizing a comprehensive evaluation plan. Implementation and implementation monitoring can also be enhanced through the use of tools such as action and change models as well as integrated evaluation plans. These provide a framework to organize the volumes of data often collected in implementation monitoring. Used flexibly, these tools can also serve as useful guides for discussions among team members and with stakeholders to fully incorporate contextual information and to avoid overly simplistic planning.

Areas for future work include the following:

- Reexamine the conceptualization of programs and approaches to implementation in organizational settings.

    o Continue to develop conceptual and practical application of flexible, adaptive innovation based on standardized processes rather than a standardized form; Examples include the Lifestyle Education for Activity; the Faith, Activity, and Nutrition study; and the Environmental Interventions in Children's Homes examples in this textbook.

- Increase the use of logic models for testing of integrated action and change models and as organizing frameworks for a comprehensive evaluation plan.

    o Comprehensive and integrated logic models are useful tools that should be understood by all stakeholders.

- Further define and test change or conceptual models for understanding mechanisms involved with program, policy, and practice change.

    o Operationalize, measure, and assess the relationships among constructs in the action model, change or conceptual model, and desired outcomes.

- Incorporate concepts from the program life cycle into program planning, implementation planning, and implementation monitoring planning.

    o Develop specific plans to facilitate adoption, implementation, and sustainability from the outset (see Steps 2 and 4).

    o Conduct implementation monitoring during continued implementation or sustainability phases, as well as during formative evaluation and implementation phases.

Apply broader conceptualization of intervention in complex settings.

It is important to focus on the complexity of settings into which innovations are introduced as much as the complexity of innovations. This will require new ways of thinking about settings and how to manage their inherent "messiness," including conceptualizing and assessing contexts. For example, the traditional approach to translational research involves initial testing in ideal, controlled settings as in efficacy studies, but it is often difficult to implement these evidence-based innovations in real-world settings to achieve similar outcomes. The result is a long and uncertain path from discovery to practice. Perhaps it is time to reconsider this paradigm for approaches designed for organizational, as well as community settings.

One useful approach would be to measure and control for contextual factors in outcome assessments; another would aim to better understand in what contexts particular intervention approaches are likely to be successful. Meaningful engagement of stakeholders from early in the process can facilitate this and is discussed in the section following this one. Below are some specific areas in which to concentrate work efforts:

- Integrate systems thinking into implementation planning.

  o Accept complexity as part of reality, not as a "nuisance" to be overcome.

  o Consider the setting as an active "participant" that responds to change efforts, often in unexpected ways.

- Strive to learn as much as possible about the setting and how it operates.

- Improve the conceptualizing and measuring of contexts and contextual factors that influence implementation and project outcomes.

- Reconsider the traditional translational research paradigm that progresses through basic, efficacy, and effectiveness to dissemination research.

  o Develop and test programs, policies, and practices that can be implemented at scale in real-world settings from the outset.

Fully integrate work with change agents and stakeholders in innovation planning, implementation planning, and implementation.

It may not be appropriate for all projects to be full-scale, formal "community-based participatory research," but most, if not all, projects could benefit from some level of stakeholder, change agent, and participant engagement. As a researcher or expert from outside of the implementing setting, you may feel that you have knowledge and expertise that will be beneficial. Keep in mind, however, that the people within the implementing setting are the experts in their setting, population, and profession. Therefore, it will take both of you working in partnership to create change that benefits the setting and the people within that setting. Some considerations for the future are as follows:

- Monitor yourself for "expertitis," or thinking you know the setting, the people, and what is best for them.

- Recognize that project and stakeholder priorities may not align initially, and work to establish a common goal and common ground.

- Appreciate that all human beings deserve to be treated with respect and dignity and should be accorded autonomy.

  o Always be polite and courteous.

- Allow time to establish working relationships with change agents and stakeholders.

- Work to define meaningful roles for all involved in the project.

- In collaboration with stakeholders, develop ongoing mechanisms for meaningful interaction and communication with all stakeholders.

  o Not everyone will want to be or should be engaged at the same level.

- Become familiar with the literature on participatory approaches and strive to incorporate participatory principles in your research and practice.

Use and integrate quantitative and qualitative methods.

Methods should directly relate to the implementation monitoring questions, which should be based on sound conceptualization of the change process and best approaches to operationalize it within a given setting. Quantitative methods produce data that may be used in outcome analysis; however, qualitative methods are needed to examine unexpected results and adaptations. Using multiple methods and data sources is optimal in complex settings, but strategies are needed for integrating and synthesizing multiple sources of information. Following are some specific areas that need additional work:

- Further define and test components of an implementation monitoring plan for the program, policy, and practice change, such as defining fidelity in environmental versus individual behavior change.

- Increase the use of proactive, quantitative methods in addition to qualitative methods.

- Conceptualize and test approaches to establish levels for evidence of implementation.

- Define and test approaches to analyze and synthesize quantitative implementation monitoring data.

- Define and test approaches to triangulate information from multiple data sources.

Move beyond assessing level of implementation.

This textbook has focused on conceptualizing and monitoring implementation of program, policy, and practice change in organizational settings. Influences on this process have been addressed in the context of facilitating innovation implementation. However, an important area for research is the systematic study of factors that influence the implementation process. There are many promising frameworks addressing influences on the implementation process. This is a growth area for research. Also, this book has focused on organizational settings, though many of the concepts and principles may be applicable to community and other settings. Below are some specific considerations regarding future areas of study:

- Use and test comprehensive conceptual and analytic models to understand factors that influence the implementation process and how this relates to study outcomes/impacts.

- Apply the principles, strategies, and methods described in this textbook to other settings including communities.

- Devote increased attention to publishing "failures" in the literature to enable researchers and practitioners to learn from others' mistakes. For example, focus less on "what works" and more on "under what conditions does this work."

Options for Moving Forward

Start from wherever you are and start now! You may wish to practice the planning, implementation, analysis, and reporting methods described in this textbook first. Or you may be in a position to advance the field by addressing suggestions for future actions. Either way, progress can be achieved by students, practitioners, planning and evaluation teams, stakeholders in implementing settings, and organizations engaging in thoughtful and intentional actions and activities. Suggestions for the reader include but are not limited to the following:

- Make it a personal and professional priority for action.

- Seek out opportunities to try your own new ideas, and practice taking small steps, including volunteer work if you are a student.

- Invest time and effort; that is, you must *do* it.

- Embrace learning from experience, especially when it doesn't go as planned.

- Understand *your* context; that is, the evaluation culture of your team or organization and receptivity to an expanded or new approach.

- Get support as an individual. For example, read the literature and find like-minded colleagues.

- Get support as a professional; join professional organizations such as the American Evaluation Association (http://www.eval.org/).

- Advocate for a supportive team and/or organizational culture.

GLOSSARY

An **action model** (Step 6) is "a systematic plan for arranging staff, resources, settings and support organizations in order to reach a target population and deliver intervention services" (Chen, 2015, p. 23).

An **action plan** (Step 6) describes actions needed to deliver and/or install the program, policy, or practice; it identifies all key stakeholders and summarizes the strategies used to facilitate adoption, implementation, and sustainability.

Adaptation or **reinvention** (Step 2) is the degree to which the innovation is changed or modified by a user in the process of adoption (Rogers, 2003, p. 476).

Adoption (Introduction, Overview, and Perspectives) of a program, policy, or practice is a decision to use an innovation, usually made by an administrator, board of directors, or other organizational decision maker.

A **champion** (Step 5) is a "charismatic individual who throws his or her weight behind an innovation, thus overcoming indifference or resistance that any new idea might provoke an organization" (Rogers, 2003, p. 473).

A **change agent** (Step 1) is an individual, group of individuals, or group who work as a catalyst for change within an organization or "an individual who influences clients' innovation-decisions in a direction deemed desirable by a change agency" (Rogers, 2003, p. 473).

A **change** or **conceptual model** (Step 1) shows relationships among key constructs, environmental elements, and behavior. The change model conveys assumptions about the causal processes through which an intervention is supposed to work (Chen, 2015).

Completeness or **dose delivered** (Step 4) is defined as the amount, number, and/or duration of intended components, content, activities, media messages, and/or other elements delivered, provided, or installed.

Context (Step 7) includes the organizational, community, or greater environment that may

influence program, policy, or practice implementation or study outcomes.

Criteria for evidence of implementation (Step 8) are standards for complete and acceptable delivery; they may include values on rating scale, percentages, or indices that indicate acceptable level of implementation.

Data analysis/synthesis (Steps 8 and 11) is the process of systematically applying statistical and/or logical techniques to describe and illustrate, condense and recap, and evaluate data (Responsible Conduct in Data Management, n.d.). Statistical tests and/or qualitative approaches are used to analyze, synthesize, and/or summarize information gathered.

Data collection procedures (Step 8) are detailed protocols for the administration of data collection tools in quantitative data collection and procedures for qualitative methods.

Data collection tools (Step 8) are instruments, tools, and guides used for gathering data (e.g., surveys, checklists, observation forms, interview guides, focus group guides).

A **data dictionary** (Step 10) provides a complete description of all variables in the data set including created variables, the variable and field name, values and/or valid ranges, variable type (numeric or character), variable label, variable description, variable source/location (e.g., baseline, follow-up, etc., as applicable), and variable derivations for computed or transformed variables (ICF International, n.d.).

Data management (Step 8) is a process that includes the "development, execution, and supervision of plans, policies, programs, and practices that control, protect, deliver, and enhance the value of data and information assets" (ICF International, n.d.).

A **data management plan** (Step 10) is "a formal document that outlines what you will do with your data during and after you complete your research"

(University of Virginia Library Data Management Consulting Group, n.d.).

Data sources (Step 8) are sources or origins of information (e.g., who and/or what will be surveyed, observed, interviewed, etc.).

Design or **evaluation design** (Step 8) refers to when and from what groups (i.e., study conditions) data are to be collected.

Direct delivery/installation takes place when the planning team (or an agent of the planning team) installs or delivers the program, policy, or practice in the setting.

Dissemination and diffusion (Introduction, Overview, and Perspectives) refers to the planned and unplanned spread, respectively, of the innovation beyond the initial implementing organization.

Dose received (Step 4), at the individual level, is defined as the extent to which participants actively engage with, interact with, are receptive to, and/or use materials or recommended resources. At the organizational level, dose received pertains to change agents' response to intervention training and to their role in planned program, policy, and practice changes, and may also include their follow-up activities after training.

Effectiveness evaluation (Introduction, Overview, and Perspectives) assesses the extent to which an intervention achieved its objectives or attained desired impacts or outcomes. It is also known as summative evaluation.

Fidelity (Step 4) is the extent to which program, policy, or practice implementation is consistent with the conceptual framework and/or underlying philosophy or approach.

Formative evaluation (Step 1, Step 7) involves obtaining data to inform a program that is being developed or refined.

Formative purposes (Step 7) for process evaluation data refer to using implementation monitoring data to keep a defined program on track as it is happening.

Impact evaluation (Step 1) applies evaluation methodology to assess intervention effects or effectiveness.

Implementation (Introduction, Overview, and Perspectives) is the constellation of processes though which a program, policy, or practice is assimilated into an organization (Damschroder et al., 2009); the "active and planned efforts to mainstream an innovation" (Greenhalgh, Robert, Macfarlane, Bate, & Kyriakidou, 2004, p. 582); or "act of converting program objectives into actions, policy changes, regulation, and organization" (Green & Kreuter, 2005, p. G-5). Other terms used interchangeably with implementation in this book are *program delivery* and *policy and/or practice installation*.

Implementation monitoring (Introduction, Overview, and Perspectives) refers to methods used during active program implementation to monitor the ongoing implementation process and context. It is a more specific term than *process evaluation*.

Indirect delivery/installation takes place when setting change agents deliver or install the innovation with or without guidance from the planning team.

Innovation (Introduction, Overview, and Perspectives) is "an idea, practice, or object that is perceived as new by an individual or other unit of adoption" (Rogers, 2003, p. 12).

Innovation development (Introduction, Overview, and Perspectives) refers to the initial phase in the program lifecycle when the new program, policy, or practice is created.

Interorganizational networks (Step 2) are multiple organizations participating in formal (e.g., professional associations) and informal (e.g., loosely organized coalitions) groups of organizations.

Intervention (Introduction, Overview, and Perspectives) refers to the actions being taken to facilitate implementation of a program, policy, or practice.

Logic models (Step 6) provide a graphical portrayal of the framework used throughout program planning, implementation, and evaluation that demonstrates the relationships between the resources and inputs, activities, outputs, and outcomes of a program (Bucher, 2009). They are a graphic way to organize information, display thinking, and describe planned actions with expected results (Knowlton, 2013).

A **multilevel organizational system** (Step 2) is the larger system of which the implementation setting is considered a part (e.g., classrooms within schools, within a school district, and overseen by a state agency).

Mutual adaptation (Step 2) refers to changes in both the innovation and the organization during the innovation process (Rogers, 2003, p. 425).

Organizational settings (Introduction, Overview, and Perspectives) are places where people gather to live, to work, to learn, and/or to play and are directed by rules and norms specific to the place (Green & Kreuter, 2005).

Outcome evaluation (Step 1) applies evaluation methodology to assess intervention effects or effectiveness.

The **planning team** (Introduction, Overview, and Perspectives) is the group of people responsible for conducting program planning and evaluation planning, including implementation planning.

Policies and organizational practices or **policies and practices** (Introduction, Overview, and Perspectives) refer to existing procedures, policies, bylaws, practices, or organizational routines within an organization or "the set of objectives and rules guiding the activities of an organization or an administration, and providing authority for allocation of resources" (Green & Kreuter, 2005, p. G-6).

Priority audience (Step 1) refers to the intended beneficiaries of a program, policy, or practice; it is sometimes known as the "target audience."

Process evaluation (Introduction, Overview, and Perspectives) encompasses methods employed preimplementation (e.g., to assess quality of the program plan and materials, and technical and cultural competence of program providers); methods employed during implementation (e.g., to monitor the ongoing implementation process and context); and methods employed following implementation (e.g., to describe the program, implementation process, and/or context with the methods that conduct assessment *after-the-fact*).

Program life cycle (Introduction, Overview, and Perspectives) includes the overlapping and nonlinear phases through which programs evolve: development, implementation, maintenance, and dissemination (Scheirer, 2005).

Program, policy, and practice interventions or innovation (Introduction, Overview, and Perspectives) refer specifically to intended, introduced, and planned social and/or physical changes in an organizational setting to achieve certain objectives or obtain certain benefits within that setting (Chen, 2015; McDavid, Huse, & Hawthorn, 2013).

Programs (Introduction, Overview, and Perspectives) are usually a set of external activities, curricula, or other stand-alone entities that will be introduced into an organizational setting, or "a set of planned activities over time designed to achieve specified objectives" (Green & Kreuter, 2005, p. G-6) or any intervention that transforms inputs into outputs through the five components of input, transformation, output, feedback, and environment (Chen, 2015).

Qualitative methods (Step 8) involve an inductive approach to gathering information about the *how* and *why* of human behavior through observation, interviews, focus groups, and other means (e.g., storytelling and open-ended interview questions versus surveys with close-ended questions).

Quantitative methods (Step 8) involve collecting data that are in numerical form or can be changed to numerical form for mathematical/statistical analysis.

Reach (Step 4), at the individual level, is the proportion of individuals within the population who attend sessions or events or are exposed to the program, policy, or practice. At the organizational level, it is the proportion of units within the organization (e.g., classrooms in the school) or the proportion of organizations that are exposed to the program, policy, or practice or that participate in change agent training.

Recruitment (Step 7) refers to organized and systematic efforts to obtain participants for an intervention at the organizational and/or individual levels.

Reinvention or **adaptation** (Step 2) is the degree to which the innovation is changed or modified by a user in the process of adoption (Rogers, 2003, p. 476).

Sampling (Step 8) refers to how individuals, organizations, or environments are chosen to be included in a study.

Secular trends (Step 7) refer to widespread media and broader events in the environment unrelated to intervention activities.

Stakeholders (Step 1) are individuals who have an investment or an interest (i.e., a stake) in the outcome of a program (Green & Kreuter, 2005) or who are "involved in or affected by a course of action" ("Stakeholder," 2013).

Summative evaluation (Introduction, Step 1) refers to assessing the overall effectiveness of a program.

Summative purposes (Step 7) refer to using process data to make a judgment about the extent to which the program, policy, or practice was implemented as planned.

Sustainability (Introduction, Overview, and Perspectives) refers to continuation or integration of the program, policy, or practice in the organizational setting in an enduring fashion.

A **systems perspective** (Introduction, Overview, and Perspectives) includes the following premises: A whole is greater than the sum of the parts; parts are interdependent; focus is on interconnected relationships; systems are made up of subsystems that function within larger systems; and systems boundaries are necessary and equitably arbitrary (Patton, 2008, pp. 365–367).

Triangulation or **data triangulation** (Step 8) is using two or more data sources to examine evidence for level of implementation.

Working relationships (Step 1) refer to interpersonal relationships formed around achieving a common goal characterized by positive interactions and harmony.

REFERENCES

ACET, Inc. (2013). *Finding the right report for your needs.* Minneapolis, MN: Author.

AEA—American Evaluation Association: Home. (n.d.). Retrieved December 12, 2013, from http://eval.org/

Alliance for Health Policy and Systems Research, & World Health Organization. (2009). *Systems thinking for health systems strengthening.* Geneva, Switzerland: Author.

Astbury, B., & Leeuw, F. L. (2010). Unpacking black boxes: Mechanisms and theory building in evaluation. *American Journal of Evaluation, 31*(3), 363–381. doi:10.1177/1098214010371972

Aust, B., Rugulies, R., Finken, A., & Jensen, C. (2010). When workplace interventions lead to negative effects: Learning from failures. *Scandinavian Journal of Public Health, 38*(3 Suppl), 106–119. doi:10.1177/1403494809354362

Baranowski, T., & Stables, G. (2000). Process evaluations of the 5-a-day projects. *Health Education & Behavior: The Official Publication of the Society for Public Health Education, 27*(2), 157–166.

Bartholomew, L. K., Parcel, G. S., Kok, G., & Gottlieb, N. H. (2006). *Planning health promotion programs: An intervention mapping approach* (2nd ed.). San Francisco, CA: Jossey-Bass.

Behrens, T. R., & Foster-Fishman, P. G. (2007).

Developing operating principles for systems change. *American Journal of Community Psychology, 39*(3–4), 411–414. doi:10.1007/s10464-007-9106-3

Berman, P., & McLaughlin, M. W. (April 1975). *Federal programs supporting educational change: Vol. IV: The findings in review.* Santa Monica, CA: RAND.

Bopp, M., Saunders, R. P., & Lattimore, D. (2013). The tug-of-war: Fidelity versus adaptation throughout the health promotion program life cycle. *The Journal of Primary Prevention.* doi:10.1007/s10935-013-0299-y

Bouffard, J. A., Taxman, F. S., & Silverman, R. (2003). Improving process evaluations of correctional programs by using a comprehensive evaluation methodology. *Evaluation and Program Planning, 26*(2), 149–161. doi:10.1016/S0149-7189(03)00010-7

Bucher, J. A. (2009). Using the logic model for planning and evaluation: Examples for new users. *Home Health Care Management & Practice, 22*(5), 325–333. doi:10.1177/1084822309353154

Campbell, M., Fitzpatrick, R., Haines, A., Kinmonth, A. L., Sandercock, P., Spiegelhalter, D., & Tyrer, P. (2000). Framework for design and evaluation of complex interventions to improve health. *BMJ (Clinical Research Ed.), 321*(7262), 694–696.

Campbell, N. C., Murray, E., Darbyshire, J., Emery, J., Farmer, A., Griffiths, F., . . . Kinmonth, A. L. (2007). Designing and evaluating complex interventions to improve health care. *BMJ (Clinical Research Ed.), 334*(7591), 455–459. doi:10.1136/bmj.39108.379965.BE

Centers for Disease Control and Prevention. (1999). Framework for program evaluation in public health. *MMWR, 48*(RR-11).

Chen, H. (2015). *Practical program evaluation: Theory-driven evaluation and the integrated evaluation perspective* (2nd ed.). Thousand Oaks, CA: Sage.

Cohen, D. A., Scribner, R. A., & Farley, T. A. (2000). A structural model of health behavior: A pragmatic approach to explain and influence health behaviors at the population level. *Preventive Medicine, 30*(2), 146–154. doi:10.1006/pmed.1999.0609

Commers, M. J., Gottlieb, N., & Kok, G. (2007). How to change environmental conditions for health. *Health Promotion International, 22*(1), 80–87. doi:10.1093/heapro/dal038

Craig, P., Dieppe, P., Macintyre, S., Michie, S., Nazareth, I., Petticrew, M., & Medical Research Council Guidance. (2008). Developing and evaluating complex interventions: The New Medical Research Council guidance. *BMJ (Clinical Research Ed.), 337*, a1655.

Damschroder, L. J., Aron, D. C., Keith, R. E., Kirsh, S. R., Alexander, J. A., & Lowery, J. C. (2009). Fostering implementation of health services research findings into practice: A consolidated framework for advancing implementation science. *Implementation Science: IS*, *4*, 50. doi:10.1186/1748-5908-4-50

Dearing, J. W. (2008). Evolution of diffusion and dissemination theory. *Journal of Public Health Management and Practice: JPHMP*, *14*(2), 99–108. doi:10.1097/01.PHH.0000311886.98627.b7

Devaney, B., & Rossi, P. (1997). Thinking through evaluation design options. *Children and Youth Services Review*, *19*(7), 587–606. doi:10.1016/S0190-7409(97)00047-9

DeVellis, R. F. (2012). *Scale development: Theory and applications*. Thousand Oaks, CA: Sage.

Dishman, R. K., Motl, R. W., Saunders, R., Felton, G., Ward, D. S., Dowda, M., & Pate, R. R. (2004). Self-efficacy partially mediates the effect of a school-based physical-activity intervention among adolescent girls. *Preventive Medicine*, *38*(5), 628–636. doi:10.1016/j.ypmed.2003.12.007

Dishman, R. K., Motl, R. W., Saunders, R., Felton, G., Ward, D. S., Dowda, M., & Pate, R. R. (2005). Enjoyment mediates effects of a school-based physical-activity intervention.

Medicine and Science in Sports and Exercise, *37*(3), 478–487.

Dishman, R. K., Saunders, R. P., Motl, R. W., Dowda, M., & Pate, R. R. (2009). Self-efficacy moderates the relation between declines in physical activity and perceived social support in high school girls. *Journal of Pediatric Psychology*, *34*(4), 441–451. doi:10.1093/jpepsy/jsn100

Dunst, C. J., Trivette, C. M., & Raab, M. (2013). An implementation science framework for conceptualizing and operationalizing fidelity in early childhood intervention studies. *Journal of Early Intervention*, *35*(2), 85–101. doi:10.1177/1053815113502235

Durlak, J. A., & DuPre, E. P. (2008). Implementation matters: A review of research on the influence of implementation on program outcomes and the factors affecting implementation. *American Journal of Community Psychology*, *41*(3–4), 327–350. doi:10.1007/s10464-008-9165-0

Earp, J. A., Viadro, C. I., Vincus, A. A., Altpeter, M., Flax, V., Mayne, L., & Eng, E. (1997). Lay health advisors: A strategy for getting the word out about breast cancer. *Health Education & Behavior: The Official Publication of the Society for Public Health Education*, *24*(4), 432–451.

Elder, J. P., Shuler, L., Moe, S. G., Grieser, M., Pratt, C., Cameron, S., . . . Guth Bothwell, E. K. (2008). Recruiting a diverse

group of middle school girls into the trial of activity for adolescent girls. *Journal of School Health*, *78*(10), 523–531. doi:10.1111/j.1746-1561.2008.00339.x

Evergreen, S. D. H. (2014). *Presenting data effectively: Communicating your findings for maximum impact*. Thousand Oaks, CA: Sage

Felton, G., Saunders, R. P., Ward, D. S., Dishman, R. K., Dowda, M., & Pate, R. R. (2005). Promoting physical activity in girls: A case study of one school's success. *The Journal of School Health*, *75*(2), 57–62.

Fixsen, D. L., Naoom, S. F., Blase, K. A., Friedman, R. M., & Wallace, F. (2005). *Implementation research: A synthesis of the literature*. Tampa, FL: Univerity of South Flordia, Louis de la Parte Flordia Mental Health Institute, The National Implementation Network. Retrieved from http://www.pdfdownload.org/pdf2html/pdf2html.php?url=http%3A%2F%2Fnirn.fpg.unc.edu%2Fsites%2Fnirn.fpg.unc.edu%2Ffiles%2Fresources%2FNIRN-MonographFull-01-2005.pdf&images=yes

Foster-Fishman, P. G., & Behrens, T. R. (2007). Systems change reborn: Rethinking our theories, methods, and efforts in human services reform and community-based change. *American Journal of Community Psychology*, *39*(3–4), 191–196. doi:10.1007/s10464-007-9104-5

Foster-Fishman, P. G., Nowell, B., & Yang, H. (2007). Putting the system back into systems change: A framework for understanding and changing organizational and community systems. *American Journal of Community Psychology*, *39*(3–4), 197–215. doi:10.1007/s10464-007-9109-0

Glasgow, R. E., Lichtenstein, E., & Marcus, A. C. (2003). Why don't we see more translation of health promotion research to practice? Rethinking the efficacy-to-effectiveness transition. *American Journal of Public Health*, *93*(8), 1261–1267.

Greenhalgh, T., Robert, G., Macfarlane, F., Bate, P., & Kyriakidou, O. (2004). Diffusion of innovations in service organizations: Systematic review and recommendations. *The Milbank Quarterly*, *82*(4), 581–629. doi:10.1111/j.0887-378X.2004.00325.x

Green, L., Daniel, M., & Novick, L. (2001). Partnerships and coalitions for community-based research. *Public Health Reports (Washington, D.C.: 1974)*, *116 Suppl 1*, 20–31.

Green, L. W., & Kreuter, M. W. (1999). *Health promotion planning: An educational and ecological approach* (3rd ed.). Mountain View, CA: Mayfield Pub. Co.

Green, L. W., & Kreuter, M. W. (2005). *Health program planning: An educational and ecological approach* (4th ed.). New York, NY: McGraw-Hill.

Hall, G. E., & Hord, S. M. (2015). *Implementing change: Patterns, principles and potholes* (4th ed.). Upper Saddle River, NJ: Pearson Education.

Hawe, P., Shiell, A., & Riley, T. (2009). Theorising interventions as events in systems. *American Journal of Community Psychology*, *43*(3–4), 267–276. doi:10.1007/s10464-009-9229-9

Helitzer, D., Yoon, S. J., Wallerstein, N., & Dow y Garcia-Velarde, L. (2000). The role of process evaluation in the training of facilitators for an adolescent health education program. *The Journal of School Health*, *70*(4), 141–147.

Himmelfarb, J., Stenvinkel, P., Ikizler, T. A., & Hakim, R. M. (2002). The elephant in uremia: Oxidant stress as a unifying concept of cardiovascular disease in uremia. *Kidney International*, *62*(5), 1524–1538. doi:10.1046/j.1523-1755.2002.00600.x

ICF International. (n.d.). *Data management for public health principles and practices*. Retrieved November 26, 2013, from http://www.icfi.com/insights/white-papers/2013/data-management-public-health-principles-practices

Johnson, K., Hays, C., Center, H., & Daley, C. (2004). Building capacity and sustainable prevention innovations: A sustainability planning model. *Evaluation and Program Planning*, *27*(2), 135–149. doi:10.1016/j.evalprogplan.2004.01.002

Joly, B. M. (2003). Writing community-centered evaluation reports. *Health Promotion Practice*, *4*(2), 93–97.

Kealey, K. A., Peterson, A. V., Jr, Gaul, M. A., & Dinh, K. T. (2000). Teacher training as a behavior change process: Principles and results from a longitudinal study. *Health Education & Behavior: The Official Publication of the Society for Public Health Education*, *27*(1), 64–81.

Kilbourne, A. M., Neumann, M. S., Pincus, H. A., Bauer, M. S., & Stall, R. (2007). Implementing evidence-based interventions in health care: Application of the replicating effective programs framework. *Implementation Science*, *2*(1), 42. doi:10.1186/1748-5908-2-42

King, J. A., Morris, L. L., & Fitz-Gibbon, C. T. (1987). *How to assess program implementation*. Newbury Park, CA: Sage.

Knowlton, L. W., & Phillips, C. C. (2013). *The logic model guidebook: Better strategies for great results* (2nd ed.). Thousand Oaks, CA: Sage.

Kremers, S., Reubsaet, A., Martens, M., Gerards, S., Jonkers, R., Candel, M., . . . de Vries, N. (2010). Systematic prevention of overweight and obesity in adults: A qualitative and quantitative literature analysis. *Obesity Reviews: An Official Journal of the International Association for the Study of Obesity*, *11*(5), 371–379. doi:10.1111/j.1467-789X.2009.00598.x

Lang, J., Franks, R., & Bory, C. (2011). *Statewide implementation of best practices: The Connecticut TF-CBT Learning Collaborative*. Child Health and Development Institute of Connecticut. Retrieved from http://www.chdi.org/

Lillehoj, C. J., Griffin, K. W., & Spoth, R. (2004). Program provider and observer ratings of school-based preventive intervention implementation: Agreement and relation to youth outcomes. *Health Education & Behavior, 31*(2), 242–257. doi:10.1177/1090198103260514

MacDonald, M. A., & Green, L. W. (2001). Reconciling concept and context: The dilemma of implementation in school-based health promotion. *Health Education & Behavior: The Official Publication of the Society for Public Health Education, 28*(6), 749–768.

Marks, J., Barnett, L. M., Foulkes, C., Hawe, P., & Allender, S. (2013). Using social network analysis to identify key child care center staff for obesity prevention interventions: A pilot study. *Journal of Obesity, 2013*, 919287. doi:10.1155/2013/919287

McCormick, L. K., Steckler, A. B., & McLeroy, K. R. (1995). Diffusion of innovations in schools: A study of adoption and implementation of school-based tobacco prevention curricula. *American Journal of Health Promotion: AJHP, 9*(3), 210–219.

McDavid, J. C., Huse, I., & Hawthorn, L. R. L. (2013).

Program evaluation and performance measurement: An introduction to practice. Thousand Oaks, CA: Sage.

McDonough, R. P., & Doucette, W. R. (2001). Dynamics of pharmaceutical care: Developing collaborative working relationships between pharmacists and physicians. *J Am Pharm Assoc, 41*(5), 682–692.

McGraw, S. A., Sellers, D., Stone, E., Resnicow, K. A., Kuester, S., Fridinger, F., & Wechsler, H. (2000). Measuring implementation of school programs and policies to promote healthy eating and physical activity among youth. *Preventive Medicine, 31*(2), S86–S97. doi:10.1006/pmed.2000.0648

Mercer, S. L., DeVinney, B. J., Fine, L. J., Green, L. W., & Dougherty, D. (2007). Study designs for effectiveness and translation research: Identifying trade-offs. *American Journal of Preventive Medicine, 33*(2), 139–154. doi:10.1016/j.amepre.2007.04.005

Meyers, D. C., Durlak, J. A., & Wandersman, A. (2012). The quality implementation framework: A synthesis of critical steps in the implementation process. *American Journal of Community Psychology, 50*(3–4), 462–480. doi:10.1007/s10464-012-9522-x

Microsoft Access. (2013). Redmond, Washington: Microsoft. Retrieved from http://office.microsoft.com/en-us/access/

Minkler, M., & Wallerstein, N. (2008). *Community-based participatory research for health: From process to outcomes* (2nd ed.). San Francisco, CA: Jossey-Bass.

Mowbray, C. T. (2003). Fidelity criteria: Development, measurement, and validation. *American Journal of Evaluation, 24*(3), 315–340. doi:10.1177/109821 400302400303

Murray, E., Treweek, S., Pope, C., MacFarlane, A., Ballini, L., Dowrick, C., . . . May, C. (2010). Normalisation process theory: A framework for developing, evaluating and implementing complex interventions. *BMC Medicine, 8*, 63. doi:10.1186/1741-7015-8-63

Pate, R. R., Saunders, R., Dishman, R. K., Addy, C., Dowda, M., & Ward, D. S. (2007). Long-term effects of a physical activity intervention in high school girls. *American Journal of Preventive Medicine, 33*(4), 276–280. doi:10.1016/j.amepre.2007.06.005

Pate, R. R., Saunders, R. P., Ward, D. S., Felton, G., Trost, S. G., & Dowda, M. (2003). Evaluation of a community-based intervention to promote physical activity in youth: Lessons from Active Winners. *American Journal of Health Promotion: AJHP, 17*(3), 171–182.

Pate, R. R., Ward, D. S., Saunders, R. P., Felton, G., Dishman, R. K., & Dowda, M.

(2005). Promotion of physical activity among high-school girls: A randomized controlled trial. *American Journal of Public Health*, 95(9), 1582–1587. doi:10.2105/AJPH.2004.045807

Patton, G., Bond, L., Butler, H., & Glover, S. (2003). Changing schools, changing health? Design and implementation of the Gatehouse Project. *The Journal of Adolescent Health: Official Publication of the Society for Adolescent Medicine*, 33(4), 231–239.

Patton, M. Q. (2008). *Utilization-focused evaluation* (4th ed.). Thousand Oaks, CA: Sage.

Pbert, L., Ockene, J. K., Zapka, J., Ma, Y., Goins, K. V., Oncken, C., & Stoddard, A. M. (2004). A community health center smoking-cessation intervention for pregnant and postpartum women. *American Journal of Preventive Medicine*, 26(5), 377–385. doi:10.1016/j.amepre.2004.02.010

Pender, N. J. (2011). *Health promotion in nursing practice* (6th ed.). Upper Saddle River, NJ: Pearson.

Pender, N. J., Smith, L. C., & Vernof, J. A. (1987). Building better workers. *AAOHN Journal: Official Journal of the American Association of Occupational Health Nurses*, 35(9), 386–390.

Pendragon Forms. (n.d.). (Version 7.2). Chicago, IL: Pendragon Software Corporation. Retrieved from http://www.pendragonsoftware.com/

Peterson, S. (2013). Readiness to change, effective implementation processes for meeting people where they are. In *Applying implementation science in early childhood programs and systems* (Ch. 3). Baltimore, MD: Paul H. Brookes Pub. Co.

Pfeiffer, K. A., Saunders, R. P., Brown, W. H., Dowda, M., Addy, C. L., & Pate, R. R. (2013). Study of Health and Activity in Preschool Environments (SHAPES): Study protocol for a randomized trial evaluating a multi-component physical activity intervention in preschool children. *BMC Public Health*, 13(1), 728. doi:10.1186/1471-2458-13-728

Plsek, P. E., & Greenhalgh, T. (2001). Complexity science: The challenge of complexity in health care. *BMJ (Clinical Research Ed.)*, 323(7313), 625–628.

Pluye, P., Potvin, L., & Denis, J.-L. (2004). Making public health programs last: Conceptualizing sustainability. *Evaluation and Program Planning*, 27(2), 121–133. doi:10.1016/j.evalprogplan.2004.01.001

Pluye, P., Potvin, L., Denis, J.-L., Pelletier, J., & Mannoni, C. (2005). Program sustainability begins with the first events. *Evaluation and Program Planning*, 28(2), 123–137. doi:10.1016/j.evalprogplan.2004.10.003

Poland, B., Krupa, G., & McCall, D. (2009). Settings for health promotion: An analytic framework to guide intervention design and implementation. *Health Promotion Practice*, 10(4), 505–516. doi:10.1177/1524839909341025

Potter, C., & Brough, R. (2004). Systemic capacity building: A hierarchy of needs. *Health Policy and Planning*, 19(5), 336–345.

Resnicow, K., Davis, M., Smith, M., Lazarus-Yaroch, A., Baranowski, T., Baranowski, J., . . . Wang, D. T. (1998). How best to measure implementation of school health curricula: A comparison of three measures. *Health Education Research*, 13(2), 239–250.

Responsible Conduct in Data Management. (n.d.). Data Analysis. Retrieved from http://ori.dhhs.gov/education/products/n_illinois_u/datamanagement/datopic.html#

Rogers, E. M. (2003). *Diffusion of innovations* (5th ed.). New York, NY: Free Press.

Rossi, P. H. (2004). *Evaluation: A systematic approach* (7th ed.). Thousand Oaks, CA: Sage.

SAS Data Management. (n.d.). (Version 9). Cary, NC: Author. Retrieved from http://www.sas.com/en_us/home.html?gclid=CL6T5f2j4cACFQto7AodgXgAcA

Saunders, R. P., Evans, M. H., & Joshi, P. (2005). Developing a process-evaluation plan for assessing health promotion program implementation: A how-to guide. *Health Promotion Practice*, 6(2), 134–147. doi:10.1177/1524839904273387

Saunders, R. P., Evans, A. E., Kenison, K., Workman, L., Dowda, M., & Chu, Y. H. (2013). Conceptualizing, implementing, and monitoring a structural health promotion intervention in an organizational setting. *Health Promotion Practice*, *14*(3), 343–353. doi:10.1177/1524839912454286

Saunders, R. P., Pate, R. R., Dowda, M., Ward, D. S., Epping, J. N., & Dishman, R. K. (2012). Assessing sustainability of Lifestyle Education for Activity Program (LEAP). *Health Education Research*, *27*(2), 319–330. doi:10.1093/her/cyr111

Saunders, R. P., Ward, D., Felton, G. M., Dowda, M., & Pate, R. R. (2006). Examining the link between program implementation and behavior outcomes in the Lifestyle Education for Activity Program (LEAP). *Evaluation and Program Planning*, *29*(4), 352–364. doi:10.1016/j.evalprogplan.2006.08.006

Saunders, R. P., Wilcox, S., Baruth, M., & Dowda, M. (2014). Process evaluation methods, implementation fidelity results and relationship to physical activity and healthy eating in the Faith, Activity, and Nutrition (FAN) study. *Evaluation and Program Planning*, *43*, 93–102. doi:10.1016/j.evalprogplan.2013.11.003

Scheirer, M. A. (2005). Is sustainability possible? A review and commentary on empirical studies of program sustainability. *American Journal of Evaluation*, *26*(3), 320–347. doi:10.1177/1098214005278752

Scheirer, M. A., Shediac, M. C., & Cassady, C. E. (1995). Measuring the implementation of health promotion programs: The case of the Breast and Cervical Cancer Program in Maryland. *Health Education Research*, *10*(1), 11–25.

Scriven, M. (1967). The methodology of evaluation. *AREA Monograph Series on Curriculum Evaluation*, *1*, 39–83.

Search Library—American Evaluation Association. (n.d.). Retrieved February 3, 2014, from http://comm.eval.org/resources/searchlibrary

Shediac-Rizkallah, M. C., & Bone, L. R. (1998). Planning for the sustainability of community-based health programs: Conceptual frameworks and future directions for research, practice and policy. *Health Education Research*, *13*(1), 87–108. doi:10.1093/her/13.1.87

Shiell, A., Hawe, P., & Gold, L. (2008). Complex interventions or complex systems? Implications for health economic evaluation. *BMJ (Clinical Research Ed.)*, *336*(7656), 1281–1283. doi:10.1136/bmj.39569.510521.AD

Stakeholder. (2013). *Merriam-Webster*. Retrieved from http://www.merriam-webster.com/dictionary/stakeholder

Steckler, A. B., & Linnan, L. (2002). *Process evaluation for public health interventions and research* (1st ed.). San Francisco, CA: Jossey-Bass.

Sterman, J. D. (2006). Learning from evidence in a complex world. *American Journal of Public Health*, *96*(3), 505–514. doi:10.2105/AJPH.2005.066043

Stetson, V. (2008). *Communicating and Reporting on an Evaluation: Guidelines and Tools*. Catholic Relief Services, American Red Cross, USAID. Retrieved from http://www.crsprogramquality.org/storage/pubs/me/MEmodule_communicating.pdf

TeleForm. (2013). (Version 10.8). Brookline, MA: Cardiff. Retrieved from http://www.teleform-cardiff.com/?gclid=CLyLyPim4cACFQQSMwodCE0Azw

Torres, R. T., Preskill, H. & Piontek M. E. (2005). *Evaluation strategies for communicating and reporting: Enhancing learning in organizations* (2nd ed.). Thousand Oaks, CA: Sage.

University of Virginia Library Data Management Consulting Group. (n.d.). Data management planning. Retrieved November 26, 2013, from http://dmconsult.library.virginia.edu/plan/

Viadro, C. I., Earp, J. A. L., & Altpeter, M. (1997). Designing a process evaluation for a comprehensive breast cancer screening intervention: Challenges and opportunities. *Evaluation and Program Planning*, *20*(3), 237–249. doi:10.1016/S0149-7189(97)00001-3

Ward, D. S., Saunders, R., Felton, G. M., Williams, E., Epping, J. N., & Pate, R. R. (2006). Implementation of a school environment intervention to increase physical activity in high school girls. *Health Education Research*, *21*(6), 896–910. doi:10.1093/her/cyl134

Ward, D. S., Saunders, R. P., & Pate, R. R. (2007). *Physical activity interventions in children and adolescents*. Champaign, IL: Human Kinetics.

Weaver, R. G., Beets, M. W., Saunders, R. P., & Beighle, A. (2014). A coordinated comprehensive professional development training's effect on summer day camp staff healthy eating and physical activity promoting behaviors. *Journal of Physical Activity & Health*. *11*(6):1170–1178.

Weaver, R. G., Beets, M. W. Saunders, R., Beighle, A. & Webster, C. (2014). A comprehensive professional development training's effect on afterschool program staff behaviors to promote healthy eating and physical activity. *Journal of Public Health Management and Practice, 20*(4), E6–E14.

Weaver, R. G., Beets, M. W., Webster, C., & Huberty, J. (2014). System for Observing Staff Promotion of Activity and Nutrition (SOSPAN). *Journal of Physical Activity & Health, 11*(1), 173–185.

Wholey, J. S., Hatry, H. P., & Newcomer, K. E. (2010). *Handbook of practical program evaluation*. San Francisco, CA: Jossey-Bass.

Wilcox, S., Laken, M., Parrott, A. W., Condrasky, M., Saunders, R., Addy, C. L., . . . Samuel, M. (2010). The Faith, Activity, and Nutrition (FAN) Program: Design of a participatory research intervention to increase physical activity and improve dietary habits in African-American churches. *Contemporary Clinical Trials, 31*(4), 323–335. doi:10.1016/j.cct.2010.03.011

Wilcox, S., Parrott, A., Baruth, M., Laken, M., Condrasky, M., Saunders, R., . . . Zimmerman, L. (2013). The Faith, Activity, and Nutrition Program: A randomized controlled trial in African-American churches. *American Journal of Preventive Medicine, 44*(2), 122–131. doi:10.1016/j.amepre.2012.09.062

Wilson, D. K., Griffin, S., Saunders, R. P., Kitzman-Ulrich, H., Meyers, D. C., & Mansard, L. (2009). Using process evaluation for program improvement in dose, fidelity and reach: The ACT trial experience. *The International Journal of Behavioral Nutrition and Physical Activity, 6*, 79. doi:10.1186/1479-5868-6-79

Zapka, J., Goins, K. V., Pbert, L., & Ockene, J. K. (2004). Translating efficacy research to effectiveness studies in practice: Lessons from research to promote smoking cessation in community health centers. *Health Promotion Practice, 5*(3), 245–255. doi:10.1177/1524839904263713

INDEX

⑤SAGE video

We are delighted to announce the launch of a streaming video program at SAGE!

SAGE Video online collections are developed in partnership with leading academics, societies and practitioners, including many of SAGE's own authors and academic partners, to deliver cutting-edge pedagogical collections mapped to curricular needs.

Available alongside our book and reference collections on the *SAGE Knowledge* platform, content is delivered with critical online functionality designed to support scholarly use.

SAGE Video combines originally commissioned and produced material with licensed videos to provide a complete resource for students, faculty, and researchers.

NEW IN 2015!

- Counseling and Psychotherapy
- Education
- Media and Communication

sagepub.com/video
#sagevideo